BEYOND SYMBOLISM

BEYOND SYMBOLISM

Textual History and the Future of Reading

KEVIN NEWMARK

Cornell University Press

Ithaca and London

Copyright © 1991 by Cornell University

All rights reserved. Except for brief quotations in a review, this book, or parts thereof, must not be reproduced in any form without permission in writing from the publisher. For information, address Cornell University Press, 124 Roberts Place, Ithaca, New York 14850.

First published 1991 by Cornell University Press.

International Standard Book Number 0-8014-2577-8
Library of Congress Catalog Card Number 91-55056
Printed in the United States of America
Librarians: Library of Congress cataloging information appears on the last page of the book.

♾ The paper in this book meets the minimum requirements of the American National Standard for Information Sciences—Permanence of Paper for Printed Library Materials, ANSI Z39.48-1984.

Historia abscondita.— . . . Es ist gar nicht abzusehen, was alles einmal noch Geschichte sein wird. Die Vergangenheit ist vielleicht immer noch wesentlich unentdeckt!
—Nietzsche

Secret history.— . . . There's just no way of telling what still remains to become history. The past may still be essentially undiscovered!
—Nietzsche

Contents

	Preface	ix
1	Toward the Question That Can Still Be Called Historical	1
2	The Forgotten Figures of Symbolism: Nerval's *Sylvie*	34
3	Beneath the Lace: Mallarmé, the State, and the Foundation of Letters	68
4	Ingesting the Mummy: Proust's Allegory of Memory	106
5	The Duplicitous Genre of André Gide	142
6	Resisting, Responding: Maurice Blanchot and the Promise of Writing	168
7	Beyond Movement: Paul de Man's History	195
	Index	231

Preface

This is not a book about French Symbolism properly speaking. But that does not mean the authors, themes, and problems commonly associated with this movement in late nineteenth- and early twentieth-century French literature and thought will be entirely absent from the following pages. Rather, since the difficulty of articulating coherent principles of selection turns out to be one of the major stumbling blocks to writing critically about Symbolism, such principles are taken here only in a very loose and provisional sense. Hence the focus in some of the chapters on the description and analysis of symbolic language in the texts of writers who are, more or less, recognized as legitimate precursors, representatives, or heirs of French Symbolism: Nerval, Baudelaire, Mallarmé, and Proust. On the other hand, including in the book more recent, idiosyncratic investigations into the nature and working of the linguistic symbol by writers and critics like André Gide, Ferdinand de Saussure, Maurice Blanchot, and Paul de Man allows the questions involved in any understanding of Symbolism to be documented and unfolded in even further detail before normative value is accorded to historically or generically precise definitions of the kind of literary language at issue here.

For if it is true, as Paul Valéry argued in a 1936 essay called, suggestively enough, "Existence of Symbolism," that Symbolism cannot be defined in a positive way because it does not have an aesthetic that would be proper to it, then it is also true that *no* book could ever simply be about Symbolism properly speaking—all the useful books that have been written precisely about Symbolism notwithstanding. No book can be about Symbolism properly speaking because, whatever else it is, Symbolism always turns out to refer to the negative thrust that is part and parcel of all language. In other words, Symbolism is another name for that potential in language to go beyond the simple possibility of affirming, defining, or speaking properly, about anything . . . including itself. Symbolism properly speaking will therefore always have to be a literary movement constantly drifting toward becoming symbolism in a slightly different, more allusive, indeterminate, and inclusive sense. This means, among other things, that no description, interpretation, or analysis can really be about Symbolism without itself somehow coming to terms with, and therefore being affected by, the essential indeterminacy of the language it would take as its (proper) object of study. For a method of study that cannot be made to correspond to the specificity of its object—which in this case would be something like the systematic undoing of specificity itself—cannot by the same token be considered to have achieved its own descriptive and cognitive aims. It would be fair to add, though, that even this rather schematic description of a conclusion that could occur in a rigorous sense only in the details of each of the following chapters should not in principle be taken uncritically as a positive cognitive result in its own right.

As Valéry himself well knew, this state of affairs complicates things a great deal for us whenever the historical "existence" of Symbolism is at issue, as it always seems to be. For an "event" that cannot be properly described and understood without producing an "effect" on this very act of description and understanding must affect in its turn our notion of history itself and the way that it happens. If every new attempt to account for what actually occurs in the texts Valéry calls Symbolist is thereby necessarily opened up to being altered by them in new and unexpected ways, then the historical existence of Symbolism—and all that it touches—is no longer something to be construed solely on the basis of the past and its certitudes, but rather must be rethought in terms of an indeterminate future. Contrary to what one might have expected or been led to believe, the figural negativity inherent in Symbolism turns out to have a profoundly historical correlative as well. Valéry himself described this figural negativity that is also historical in terms of a mode of *reading* that is always future-oriented. The radical indeterminacy of the literary movement that has already taken place in Symbolism is such that, again according to Valéry, it must always produce, or bring into being, its very own readers. Unprepared for these texts by anything familiar to them, such readers could exist only in the future and therefore strictly unnameable mode of whatever these peculiar texts of the past would eventually be able to make out of them.

The historical existence of Symbolism, then, is also linked to the future of reading in a very specific, if somewhat surprising, way. The textual history of Symbolism is not just dependent on our continued willingness and ability to read it in the most straightforward sense of the word; the future itself, as a genuinely historical category of openness, can also become accessible as such if we learn to read the heretofore unheard-of events such texts alone have embedded in their writing. Reading, then, is not just something that has a future; it is also what gives a future by means of its specifically textual relation to the past. Thus, and beyond whatever else we already know or thought we knew about the writing of Symbolism, reading such textual events anew always includes the potential to transform for the future the way we now think about ourselves as readers, that is, as those capable of historical thought and knowledge.

It is, of course, not at all clear from these overly summary remarks what further complications might attend a fuller exposition and reading of Valéry's text—not only the one, just mentioned, about Symbolism, but also the ones that, along with his entire signature, actually participate in Symbolism. The virtual absence of these writings from a book purportedly about "symbolism" is already the mark of a certain orientation. For this absence from the book, once it has been disclosed and named as such, becomes a hidden source of attraction that can begin to exert pressure at all points in the book; it therefore constitutes a convenient vector by which to gauge the book's own future.

Earlier versions of several of the chapters of this book have previously appeared in print: "The Forgotten Figures of Symbolism: Nerval's *Sylvie*," in *Yale French Studies* 74 (1988); "Beneath the Lace: Mallarmé, the State, and the Foundation of Letters," in *Yale French Studies* 77 (1990); "Ingesting the Mummy: Proust's Allegory of Memory," in *Yale French Studies* 70 (1991); "Resisting Responding," in *Responses: On Paul de Man's Wartime Journalism,* ed. Werner Hamacher, Neil Hertz, and Thomas Keenan (Lincoln: University of Nebraska Press, 1989); and "Paul de Man's History," in *Reading de Man Reading,* ed. Lindsay Waters and Wlad Godzich (Minneapolis: University of Minnesota Press, 1989). Permission to use this material here is gratefully acknowledged. The writing of this book was also substantially aided by a year's leave from teaching provided through Yale University's Morse Fellowship, as well as by a travel grant from the Griswold Fund at Yale.

The debt this book owes to certain individuals or texts—Paul de Man, Jacques Derrida, Andrzej Warminski, E. S. Burt, Cathy Caruth, H. L. N., among others—lies beyond the reach of each of its pages in the form of an unfinished reading and writing.

Unless otherwise noted, all translations in the book are my own.

KEVIN NEWMARK

North Haven, Connecticut

BEYOND SYMBOLISM

1 Toward the Question That Can Still Be Called Historical

> That is a type of question, let's still call it historical, of which we are today only able to glimpse the *conception,* the *formation,* the *gestation,* the *labor.* And I say these words, granted, with an eye to the process of giving birth; but also with an eye to those who, in a society from which I do not exclude myself, avert their eyes before the still unnameable that announces itself and can only announce itself, as is necessary whenever a birth is in the works, as a species of non-species, in the unformed form, the mute, infans, and terrifying form of monstrosity.
> —Jacques Derrida, "La Structure, le signe et le jeu"

If it were possible to write a coherent history of literature—that is, a history that would be able to describe and account for what actually occurs in literary texts as such—then the literary event commonly known as "Symbolism" would certainly have to constitute a privileged moment within such a history. For the very term *symbol-ism* names the possibility of bringing together into one system of articulation and meaning *historical* actuality and *linguistic* structures: as an *ism,* it points not just to a mere possibility or empty name but to the actual historical existence of a particular doctrine and aesthetic practice; and through its reference to the literary *symbol,* it emphasizes the essentially linguistic nature of such a historical movement as well as of the potential significance it would as a consequence be capable of engendering. So, preeminent among taxonomic categories such as classicism, romanticism, naturalism, realism, surrealism, and so on, only "symbolism" explicitly draws attention to the fact that a history of literature must always also be a history of how the phenomenon of language can be said to happen as a historical event in the first place. But *is* it possible to write a coherent history of literature? More specifically, just what happens when one tries to describe and account for what does in fact occur in the texts of "symbolism"?

That is a question that is still historical, though it does not necessarily take for granted what history already is or what it can still do. Obviously, to ask how literature has occurred (in history) is a historical question, and a rather straightforward, even banal one at that. But, more radically, to ask what happens when we try to write a history of literature is also a historical question in a somewhat different sense. For this question is not just about the simple existence of past events, in this case literary texts, that can be assumed to have occurred once and for all in order to take their place within a completed history whose principles of order and understanding lie far behind us—even if, someday, this same history would be able to reach and go beyond what we ourselves have accomplished in it. The question is also about the possibility of a *future* event. What will happen, what will occur, what will take place, when we bring together for critical analysis in our own writing an understanding of how things exist and can be described in history with the fact of a given literary event? In a certain sense, one could even say that this question of what will happen is *more* historical than the all-too-familiar historical question of what has already happened. Only the first question allows for something to occur not just as a mere *representation* of past historical occurrences but as an actual *event* that could occur historically in its own right. And happening anew in this way, such a historical event could even happen *to* and have an effect *on* what we ordinarily call "history": that is, a systematic model for documenting and understanding the occurrence of any and all events. Only such a future event could sufficiently alter the way we now think about history that we would as a result have to change as well our notion of those events we thought we knew had already taken place *in* history—in literary texts, for instance, and more precisely, in the texts of what we call symbolism.

Taken together, then, the chapters of this book point retrospectively toward a twofold hypothesis about symbolism and history. On the one hand, they suggest that because the term "symbolism" designates the historical existence and development of a given linguistic structure, there can be no study of the literary symbol that does not at the same time start with familiar historical models of organization and understanding for the reading of these texts. On the other hand, they also suggest that "symbolist" texts, in pushing to the limit our understanding of how a literary event occurs, actually help to *produce* history by bringing forth a slightly different model for thinking about historical occurrences. That is, in addition to taking their place within a chronological procession of completed moments and movements, symbolist texts also have the power to disrupt and displace such a sequential model of historical periodization, understanding, and change by putting it into contact with and subjecting it to their own specifically linguistic conditions of possibility.

As a consequence, the possibility of writing a coherent history of literature becomes questionable not because of any merely contingent failings or lapses on the part of those attempting to do so, but rather for fundamental and ineluctable reasons. The possibility of writing a history that would be adequate to describing and accounting for the existence of literature is *always* put into question to the precise extent that the language of a text is not something that could ever simply appear in history as one fact among others. As the very mode of production and reception of meaning, language is itself an *event,* the one and only event that actively conditions the possibility of history's occurring in a historical, that is, meaning-producing way. History is disclosed by these texts as having no meaning, as being incapable of occurring historically, and therefore as achieving no genuine historicity, without first coming to terms with the necessarily linguistic structure of the production of all meaning. The conclusion, which can only be reached pragmatically from an analysis of the way language actually occurs in individual texts rather than from general historical or theoretical presuppositions, is that "history," and a fortiori a history *of* symbolism, remains to be conceived. Because it could occur only by altering the course of the concept of history we now have, such a history always lies ahead of us in the challenge of an indeterminate textual future rather than in the simple certainty of an empirical or an ideal past.

Such a future—which by definition remains strictly unnameable and inaccessible as such—could be approached only by way of examining critically how a textual event occurs historically, that is, by way of *reading,* in the fullest sense of the term, how and to what extent the language of a given text works to achieve its historical existence as reference and meaning. For if, as is self-evident, every history (*historia*) is also always and necessarily the history of the events that comprise it (*historia rerum gestarum*), then it stands to reason that there can be no question of a history *of literature* until the existence of its language is accounted for as an event or an occurrence (*res gestae*) in its own right, and whose specificity is the *production* of future meaning rather than its simple embodiment or fulfillment. When (literary) history asks only about the completed "forms," "intentions," "meanings," or "effects" of texts rather than about their constitution *as* meaningful and formal entities, it bypasses by the same token their most historical dimension. What such pseudohistories forget or willfully ignore is the specific mode according to which a text's language is constituted, that is, actually *happens*. Language, at least historically speaking, is neither a form nor a meaning, but consists rather in the production of a system of formal relationships whose potential for meaning by definition exceeds its phenomenal appearance as a language system. If any history worthy of the name is also always not just a catalog of events but their more or less systematic classification according to some principle of order and intelligibility as well, then it also stands to reason that *every* history is at least implicitly nothing other than a history of texts. To the extent that every historical occurrence, by means of given principles of selection, presentation, and arrangement, is able to acquire a potential for meaning that exceeds its mere appearance as event, it also necessarily turns into a text and becomes thereby, at least in part, dependent for its occurrence as history on *linguistic* rather than on purely empirical or ideal conditions.

Every text is historical, then, to the extent that it actually occurs; but all of history is textual to the extent that in order to allow for intelligibility, a necessary condition of genuine historicity, it must first conform to formal principles of meaning-production that are linguistic through and through. If, as it could now be argued, literature is the possibility of any meaning whatsoever to occur, then history would be the resulting promise that whatever occurs could one day be made meaningful. Such a reversal of attributes between history and the literary text may not turn out to be as reassuringly symmetrical as it might at first appear, however, since one should by no means assume too quickly the possibility of verifying, much less controlling or even understanding, properties, such as the ones under discussion here, that can be determined only by reference to precisely what they are not supposed to be, or, at any rate, not yet capable of becoming fully. For it would only be after the most extensive preliminary considerations and operations that one could call certain historical events mere "texts" or certain texts genuine "events" without undue risk of losing by the same token the irreducible, if problematic, specificity of both history and literature.

If the relation between history and literature can no longer be said to be one of mutual exclusion, that does not mean that it would then become one of simple identification or reflexivity. As one textual event that both describes and enacts the complex relation between historical occurrences and linguistic structures, "symbolism" thus names a mode of literary and historical activity that can provide the basis for some of these preliminary operations. But if it is possible in this way that a literary movement such as symbolism can still occur historically to challenge our very understanding of what constitutes a historical event in the first place, then by the same token there is every reason to believe that we do not yet know for certain what it means for a text to *be* "symbolist" in a historically precise way. The same texts that can work to change our notion of what constitutes history can also work to change our notion of what makes these texts the "same," period.

For this reason, the fact that this study treats two "pre"-symbolist poets, two "post"-symbolist novelists, and two "critico"-symbolist essayists cannot be considered simply as the result of a naive or prejudicial gesture. Rather, it is part of the book's historical hypothesis that remains to be confirmed. The confrontation between history and literary language that occurs in "symbolism" cannot be governed a priori by the very historical or formal determinations that are themselves at stake in these writings, though this does not mean that one would therefore be free simply to discard or ignore such determinations of chronology or genre without further ado. Perhaps more naive still than lending such conventions of literary history and philosophy normative value would be to pretend that such norms do not themselves exist as actual forces, and in such a way as to exert pressures that are every bit as historical as literary in their consequences. Hence the order of the chapters in the book, which, though recognizing the provisional indispensability of chronological and generic principles, in no way restricts what could eventually happen to these principles through the course of reading the texts under discussion. The implicit argument the book develops in a cumulative way, then, is that these particular texts cannot in principle be considered marginal or aberrant examples—or for that matter examples "properly speaking"—of a historically precise and identifiable symbolist writing whose own linguistic tensions and uncertainties could then be left unexplored because they are taken for granted. For it is in large part thanks to what occurs in the "margins" of all such texts that "symbolism" might no longer be understood primarily to refer, more or less, to the determinate period from 1885 to 1916 in France or to the formal predominance in it of any one of the genres of poetry, narrative, or critical prose.

Reading these textual occurrences demonstrates that "symbolism," like language "itself," does in fact partake of both formal and historical elements. Yet it does so in such a way that it cannot simply be reduced to any one or the other of these systems of classification and meaning as they have been conceived traditionally. At least, it cannot be reduced to a universal logic of generic or chronological definitions without thereby losing its textual, that is, its historical, specificity, which is what always makes "symbolist" literature different from, or other than, what it is supposed to be. Contrary to common belief, the writers whose work is examined here are neither "for" literature nor "against" history—nor, of course, could they any more be said to be "against" literature and "for" history. Rather, reading what occurs in these texts points toward the linguistic *and* historical necessity of articulating a different concept of the literary as well as an *other* concept of history. These writers are all "beyond" symbolism in the sense that their texts resist the understanding of that term as it is provided by canonical models of history, language, and literary figuration. Such models still work according to historically outdated and illusionary principles of identity and exclusion, and they are therefore contested and shown to be inadequate to the realities of both language and history that are inscribed in all these texts.

The book therefore proceeds by analyzing how in each writer's work a supposedly formal question leads back inevitably to a historical dimension that has until now been overlooked, dismissed, or misunderstood by literary-historical scholarship. For the most part, this analysis proceeds by following canonical interpretations to the point where they fail to do justice to one or more of the elements operative in a central issue or crux of the text under examination. Thus, each chapter adopts a particular economy or strategy in reading a given author, although in all cases there is a moment when the reading must account for an underlying discrepancy occurring in the text between actual figural discourse and the attempt to describe and understand in adequate fashion the historical activity of which this language would itself have to be a product. In the case of Nerval, for instance, the reading reassesses the historical status of the narrative's own pretension to move beyond the delusions of poetry and its peculiar madness. It focuses, in Mallarmé, on the political institution that founds poetic music and rhythm within the organization of the historical state and the subjects of its power. The analysis of Proust's text discloses how the coordination of memory and self-knowledge required by any personal history can occur only in the privative mode of an impersonal and generalizable allegory. Gide's writing is of interest for the way it reopens and questions the existential possibility of ever progressing entirely beyond the necessarily formal principles of literature's inaugural *mise en abyme*. For Blanchot, the question becomes one of examining the unpredictable force of writing that is implicated in any attempt to account for and adequately understand an irreversible historical event. In de Man's case, it is possible to follow the occurrence and functioning of the term *history* itself as it moves from general theoretical and biographical registers toward a reading of the exemplary "symbolist" poem of French literature, Baudelaire's "Correspondances."

Ultimately, the book documents the necessary but necessarily unresolvable tension that results in the writings of each of these authors whenever an attempt is made to bring together in a coherent fashion the prefigurative structure of historical narrative with the actual production of figural structures in a text. And by revealing in all cases the fundamental coimplication that holds between formal structures of meaning and the actual forces that condition them, the book in its entirety could be said to propose a *textual* model of history. To claim for history a textual model rather than, say, one taken uncritically from a concept of immediate experience or retrospective representation and proleptic understanding is to name the constitutive moment of linguistic inscription and figuration that grounds the occurrence of every event *as* history, that is, in its very historicity. For it is only by achieving the status of a text—that is, through the capacity to refer beyond itself to empirical experiences and/or ideal meanings not purely and simply exhausted in it—that any so-called "event" could ever be prevented from disappearing without a trace *from* history. Thinking history as a text, then, also has the potential to become an occurrence in its own right, because such a thinking would not necessarily leave intact either the so-called formalist or materialist understandings of what constitutes the actuality of historical events, both in their past existence and in their future production. But the fact, which should be obvious in itself, that such a model of "textual history" can make no claim to absolute originality immediately raises the specter of historical patterns of development and influence that are not themselves in principle textual in the sense just alluded to, and so it calls once again for supplementary commentary.[1]

The most straightforward and useful description of what is meant by the emergence of textual history would have to stress the introduction of a specifically linguistic terminology to talk about the way events in the world can be experienced and assigned meaning as actual historical occurrences. It should at some point also account for the implicit presence of writers such as Kierkegaard, Nietzsche, Marx, and Freud within any articulation of textual history, but it could afford to begin in detail with the arrival on the critical scene of the linguistic and philosophical models of more recent thinkers, like Saussure and Heidegger. Why Saussure and Heidegger, for instance? In order not to predetermine the dimensions of the answer by referring it immediately back to precritical notions like historical "importance" or "influence," we should first of all note how in the case of both Heidegger and Saussure an attentiveness to the *form* of the historical occurrence is accompanied and offset by a recognition of its *force,* and vice versa. Textual history can be said to be at issue whenever the model for the historical event or occurrence is able to account for both the force required for an actual happening to take place in history *and* the formal character of the traces such events necessarily leave in their wake.

In Heidegger's case, for example, the critique of metaphysics goes hand in hand with a rethinking of the way history and language are coimplicated in any genuine happening. It would be a relatively

1. The two writers who have recently come closest to naming and elaborating a concept of textual history are Paul de Man and Jacques Derrida. In an oblique but sustained commentary on de Man's affirmation that "textual allegories . . . *generate* history," Derrida remarks: "Such a sentence makes precise a certain strategy of Paul de Man's most recent texts in terms of historicity: it is 'defined' in terms of a new 'definition' of the *text,* and it diverges from the dominant philosophical, that is to say, teleological, concept of history" (*Mémoires,* trans. Cecile Lindsay, Jonathan Culler, Eduardo Cadava [New York: Columbia University Press, 1986], 144). But if it is true that the specificity of textual history resides precisely in the way it would "diverge" from dominant philosophical and historical models and definitions, then it is equally true that such a history could never be adequately "conceived" simply by deriving it genealogically from what we understand to be its textual antecedents.

straightforward task, though it would take an inordinate amount of space to chart the subtle and complex itinerary of individual texts, to show how in Heidegger a receptivity to and thinking of the historical event, or *Ereignis*, is always doubled by a thinking of language as both a structure (or form) and an act (or force). Thus, the oft-repeated but seldom read "die Sprache spricht" is itself a formulation that draws our attention to the fact that language is at one and the same time a structure (*Sprache*) and an act (*sprechen*) that necessarily pushes that structure out beyond the closure of its own limits. Whatever else it does, then, this affirmation, "die Sprache spricht," also reminds us, again and again, that language always consists in the articulation of a substantive form with a verbal event that happens—and first of all, that happens to itself as a purely nominal structure. If Heidegger's philosophical project is nearly always dictated by a "questioning" of Being, then it stands to reason that it will just as often have to be a questioning of this double aspect of language, since language is the mode of Dasein in which the specificity of questioning can take place, or occur historically. Thus, and in a wholly parallel way, the linguistic model will be equally important for the fundamental questioning of thought and of history, or of historicality in Heidegger.

However, it is also necessary to note here, if only in a preliminary and therefore necessarily insufficient way, that very often in Heidegger the *disjunctive* aspect that is eventually revealed by textual history between the power and the signification of a given event appears to be recovered by a further moment of recuperation or of "gathering together" (*Versammlung*). This makes the fundamental relation between Heidegger and the other "symbolists" treated in this book a source of considerable interest and tension. If the insistence on a disclosure of the disjunctive nature of the symbol is *shared* by most of the writers examined here, then this potentially "symbolic" relation formed among them would not be left unaffected by the relation between them and the writing of Heidegger—which is both very similar and very different from whatever can be shared here. Heidegger's contribution to textual history, then, however irrefutable and indispensable for any genuinely historical thinking, is by no means without complications that remain to be analyzed and accounted for.[2]

2. Some of the ways in which Heidegger's relation to textual history would be problematic will therefore be referred to again in the chapter on Blanchot. Whereas certain gestures in Heidegger seem to insist on the continued possibility of understanding the historical event, or *Ereignis,* as a gathering together, or *symbolization—*

The relation of Saussure to a textual model of history, on the other hand, can be outlined somewhat more economically, because of the didactic and discursive nature of his principal text, the *Cours de linguistique générale*. Such a detailing of his contribution to a concept of textual history is all the more necessary in that the notes collected by students from Saussure's lectures on general linguistics are still widely regarded as one of the founding documents of methods of literary, anthropological, and psychoanalytical criticism most often equated with an extreme form of *ahistorical* or *antihistorical* consciousness; that is to say, with the general movement of what goes by the name of *structuralism*.[3] What is problematic about the role Saussure's conception of semiology and general linguistics is made to play within the contemporary scene of the "humanities" (or more broadly still, *les sciences humaines*) is not simply that it tends to be associated with "structuralism." The possibility of such a link is, to some extent, built into his text. Rather, what is most problematic, and worthy of analysis in its own right, is that Saussure's linguistic model is *still* taken as being simply synonymous with linguistic and historical principles whose ambiguous, if not self-invalidating, articulation within his text have *already* been subjected to the most rigorous analysis and questioning. Thus, it is always necessary to reopen the question of Saussure's theory of the sign and textual history, and not just because the radicality of his own text seems to have become so "familiar" to us as

---

sumballein: to throw or bring together, especially in reference to the fragmented pieces of an originary whole or unity—that would unite what is proper to history, language, and thought, Blanchot's thinking of the "symbol" will put this very possibility into question by transferring it into a slightly different, more idiomatic and excessive relation to the event of language. For one place, among many in Heidegger, where language speaks in an act of what appears to be appropriation, see "Der Weg zur Sprache," *Unterwegs zur Sprache* (Pfullingen: Neske, 1959), esp. 254–68.

3. One of the most vigorous, if not best known, critiques of Saussure's "structuralism" on the basis of its purportedly ahistorical premises is to be found throughout the work of Paul Ricoeur. For the most concise presentation of the argument, see his essay, "La structure, le mot, l'événement," *Le conflit des interprétations* (Paris: Seuil, 1969). It is no accident that Ricoeur does not dwell on certain key ambivalences in Heidegger's thinking on language and in Saussure's speculations on synchronic systematicity, for such ambivalences would not be easily compatible with his own hermeneutic enterprise. Of course, the status of "synchronic structures" in Saussure's semiology is a crux for many recent theoreticians of literature as well as of historiography. Some of the more influential examples in this country, not always in agreement among themselves as to the precise "value" to be accorded to a formal principle like synchrony, are Lionel Gossman, Fredric Jameson, Dominick LaCapra, Frank Lentricchia, Michael Riffaterre, Edward Said, and Hayden White.

to be all but unrecognizable. This task becomes even more necessary as those texts written after Saussure that could most effectively intervene in the reception of his semiology are themselves constantly put at risk of being historically neutralized by being taken for granted, manipulated, or ignored precisely in order to preserve such a comfortable, but possibly unwarranted, familiarity with Saussure's text.[4]

What such interventions will always help to suggest, of course, is not only that Saussure had a theory of the sign, but also that this particular theory occurred itself in such a way as to transform once and for all our understanding of the way language occurs and is as a result to be considered historically. By insisting that language cannot in the long run be divided up according to metaphysical categories like sensory experience on the one hand and ideal meaning on the other, Saussure resituates our understanding of the entire linguistic system and all that it touches. For if, as Saussure argued, there can be no question of ultimately reducing language to such categories in order to trace *it* back to two preexisting and independent entities, (for instance, to an empirical and an ideal order, that is, to sounds and meanings), then it follows that the very possibility of such metaphysical *identities* must as a consequence be reconsidered from the point of view of *their* constitution in and through the *differential* relationships that necessarily make up any given language system. If we follow Saussure's thought to its logical outcome, there can be no such thing as a transcendental *referent*—either ideal or material—that would exist outside of language prior to or independently of its implication within a semiotic system of linguistic *reference*.[5]

---

4. In this respect, and speaking from a purely historical point of view, one cannot now simply equate Saussure with whatever is contained in the catchall term "structuralism" without somehow taking into account what also happens between Saussure and the texts of Jacques Derrida and Samuel Weber, among others. See, especially, Jacques Derrida's *De la grammatologie* (Paris: Minuit, 1967) and *Positions* (Paris: Minuit, 1972), as well as Samuel Weber's "Saussure and the Apparition of Language: The Critical Perspective," *MLN* 91 (1976), 913–38, and "Texts/Contexts: Closure and Exclusion," *Institution and Interpretation* (Minneapolis: University of Minnesota Press, 1987). For a group of essays whose implicit, and sometimes explicit, aim is to reestablish contact with or extend such interventions, see *Post-Structuralism and the Question of History*, ed. Derek Attridge, Geoff Bennington, and Robert Young (Cambridge: Cambridge University Press, 1987), especially the essay by Derek Attridge, "Language as History/History as Language: Saussure and the Romance of Etymology."

5. Saussure himself goes out of his way to spell this out with all possible clarity in the chapter on "linguistic value": "Whether one considers the signifier or the signified, language has nothing to do with either ideas or sounds that would preexist the linguistic

Thus, and in another formula that has made history, every sign is a sign with two, inseparable sides: there is no such thing as a *signifié* outside of its constitutive relation to a *signifiant,* and this would apply equally well to any "referent," "perception," or "thing-in-itself" that could be named as such. This means that it would be no more true to say that the *signifié* precedes or conditions the *signifiant* than to pretend the opposite. In fact, if every *signifié* "is" a *signifié* only to the extent that it must always be related to another *signifiant,* then it would be more legitimate to say that every *signifié* is *also* a *signifiant* that by necessity refers to its own constitution within the semiotic system of linguistic differences.

With reference to a historical model like the one we are concerned with here, the priority granted to linguistic signification would mean that historical "events" cannot in themselves be conceived of as wholly empirical realities that would have their own ontological status prior to, beyond, or independently of their transformation into a textual network of semiotic *relations.* An "event" in this sense is never a fully constituted entity—a simple action, or, eventually, an ideal meaning that could correspond to and even replace such an action—but rather is a semiotic element within a constantly shifting "textual field" composed of other elements, themselves formalizable as mutually signifying "agents," "events," "signs," and "meanings." But, and the question is always of more than just academic relevance, is such a formalization of language (and potentially of history) into a differential system of semiotic relations nothing but an empty *formalism*? More precisely, can the kind of formalization that is the founding gesture of semiology be legitimately understood as a mere *reduction* of actual historical forces and events? And would such a "reduction" consist in what, mostly for polemical and strategic reasons, has often been described as a *loss* of historical specificity and a celebration of hypothetically pure signifiers forever at play between the symmetrical poles of merely equivalent, and therefore equally impotent, substitutions? Reading certain aspects of the "application" of Saussurian semiology by Lévi-Strauss to structural anthropology, or by Jakobson to structural linguistics and poetics, or by Barthes to literary criticism, one might be led to think so.

But is Saussure a structuralist in the same way that Lévi-Strauss,

---

system, but only concerns conceptual and phonic differences that are themselves products of this system." See Ferdinand de Saussure, *Cours de linguistique générale* (Paris: Payot, 1976), 166. Further references appear in the text.

Jakobson, and a certain Barthes can be said to be structuralists? The question takes us back to the crucial moment in the *Cours* when Saussure seems to separate his own investigation of language once and for all *from* history, that is, when he insists on the absolute necessity of distinguishing between *synchronic* and *diachronic* linguistics in order to privilege the formal systematicity and coherence of the former over the gratuitous and unintelligible contingencies of the latter (114–40). Obviously, much is at stake in the way we tend to take for granted this gesture, by which Saussure's concept of semiology requires for its scientific development a purely *synchronic* model of language. Such a model appears to restrict the semiotic field to a closed system of purely formal relations within what Saussure calls "la langue," whose own restricted but coherent meaning could be determined at any given moment, regardless of historical or epistemological considerations existing outside or independently of them. In other words, by retaining only the synchronic *structure* of Saussure's linguistic model, the critic (of literature or anthopology, for instance) would be left free to go about the interpretative business of understanding (a given text or cultural artifact) without having to take into account the potentially disruptive *forces* of its past conditions or its future effects, which are both historical and epistemological, in other words, referential, in nature.

The very fact that the *exclusion*, in the *Cours*, of the historical forces implicated in diachronic linguistics is itself an act of some power, and that this act of exclusion takes place during a supposedly formal description and analysis of only *one* aspect of the irreducible duplicity of the entire linguistic system, should alert us to the possibility that the relation between form and force in Saussure's own writing may be less univocally simple than certain of his commentators and so-called continuators have been led to believe or to claim. Just what is the relation in Saussure's text between the formal elements of language and the active forces of history, and where is it in his *Cours de linguistique générale* that the crucial interaction between them is either passed over and ignored or engaged with in a critical way?

At first glance, it is difficult to see how Saussure's semiological analysis of language could ever have led to a structuralism or a formalism that would be wholly closed off and thus sheltered from a critical consciousness of the unruly forces of historical activity. In the inaugural lecture of his course, in fact, Saussure had clearly emphasized how language is to be understood as an event rather than as a mere structure or idea: "the more one studies language, the more one is struck by this fact: *everything* about language is *history*—that is, language is an object of historical rather than abstract analysis" (416). And we should also remember the way in which Saussure's enigmatic definition of "semiology" as a science "to come" is itself oriented toward inaugurating the historical event that it can only announce in the name of that which does not yet exist. Such a *future* event—should it ever come to pass—would consist in producing a kind of knowledge (*scientia*) that could not simply be reduced to or abstracted from other, preexisting systems of formalized thought or science, such as mechanics or physiology: "linguistics has very close relations with other sciences, though the limits here do not always appear clearly; sometimes the other sciences borrow material from linguistics and sometimes they provide it" (20–21). In addition, what Saussure calls semiotics would not only be a *new* science, in the sense that it would take its place next to older, more firmly established ones—it would also be the possibility of radically transforming the very concept *of* science or knowledge itself. As such, it would be the mutation of science as we now know it.

For unlike any other, already existing body of knowledge, semiology, according to Saussure, would be a science that actively *produces* its objects of study as well as its own discourse: "Other sciences operate on objects given in advance which one can then consider from various points of view; in our field, though, nothing is further from the truth. . . . Far from the object preceding the point of view, one could say that it is the point of view that creates the object" (23). This is not to say, however, that such a science could ever simply create its objects of study *ex nihilo* by adopting whatever point of view it pleases, for a science of language has nothing in common with subjective caprice.[6] Rather, it remains for a science of language to produce its proper object of study only because we do not yet have a clear point of view on what language has in fact always been.

---

6. On this point, Saussure never wavers: because " 'la langue' is not a function of the speaking *subject*" in the first place (30), the science of signs, semiology, must proceed by laws that remain irreducible to intentionality, desire, self-consciousness. "For the sign escapes to a certain degree the individual or collective will," Saussure is careful to point out, "and that is its most essential feature, though it is also the one that is least apparent at first sight" (34).

Saussure insists from the beginning that his "semiology" must be so new only because all the misconceptions about the proper object of linguistic study are so old: "Why is it that [linguistics] has not so far been recognized as an autonomous science, having its proper object of study like all others? Because of the following circularity: on the one hand nothing is more proper than language to help us understand the nature of the semiological problem; but in order to pose this problem in an appropriate way, it would be necessary to study language in itself; up 'til now, language has almost always been considered in terms of something else" (34). On the other hand, by asking about the specificity of the linguistic object of study, one comes closer only to the recognition that, taken in itself, language is strictly unapproachable: " 'la langue' therefore exhibits the peculiar and striking trait that it does not consist in entities that could be perceived in an immediate way [*de prime abord:* on the first try, at the outset, without recourse to 'something else'], yet we cannot for all that doubt that they exist and that their play is what constitutes 'la langue' " (149). The specificity of language, which is always and again in danger of being misconstrued and misunderstood, is that it has no specificity that could ever be scientifically observed and verified as such.

Now, it turns out that a science of language, by respecting this peculiar trait of its proper object, will also become historical in an unexpected and truly radical sense as well. For what would be irreducibly specific to semiology as Saussure conceives it is the requirement that it produce its *future* object of study, language, by documenting and accounting for its relation to an ineluctable but inaccessible *past* that is already linguistic through and through. If we do not yet know exactly what language is, this is not just because of methodological carelessness; it is also, and more fundamentally, because language always comes to us only as a legacy from a past so distant that it necessarily eludes direct comprehension: "no matter at what moment we consider it, no matter how far back we go, language always appears as an *inheritance* of the preceding age. . . . In fact no society *knows* nor has ever *known* language other than as a product inherited from preceding generations and available to it only as such" (105, emphasis added). What semiology opens up for the future is a historical recognition that no other science has ever been able to think: all knowledge that pertains specifically to language is historical precisely to the extent that it has to be *secondhand*. Language makes us historical beings because, becoming available only in the mode of ready-made inscriptions or texts—Saussure calls them *empreintes psychiques*—it makes our future depend absolutely on a passive heritage: "language . . . is a product that the individual registers *passively*" (30). A passivity so radical that it belongs to a past that could never have been known to be present to anyone, that is the knowledge that can be articulated only by a linguistic science named in the future mode of that which does not yet exist.

This unique peculiarity of the "science to come" is of course barely audible when Saussure finally promises to conceive the unheard-of object and point of view he calls semiology: "One could therefore conceive of a science that would study the life of signs at the heart of social life . . . we will call it *semiology* (from the Greek *sēmeîon*, 'sign'). It would teach us what signs consist of as well as which laws govern them. Since it does not yet exist, we cannot say what it will be; but it has a right to exist, its place is determined in advance" (33). But what indeed would be the specificity of a science that is thus both determined in advance by the inheritance of the semiotic constraints it will study *and* completely indeterminable, or "unsayable," because it does not yet exist as such, much less in the closure of a formalized knowledge? History. For if there is a systematic structure of knowledge that could be called truly historical, it would be one forever open to the active forces that at every moment condition the possibility of its own forms coming into being. The science of semiology, or of "the life of signs," is therefore conceived by Saussure as that branch of knowledge that, should it one day exist as such—and nothing is less certain—would inevitably bring us back to history, or "the heart of social life." Whatever its hesitations or tensions in other regards—and they are real enough—Saussure's understanding of language as constituting just one part within the general science of semiology could in this respect never be reduced to a *simple* division between a purely formal principle of meaning and a referential historical reality that would somehow lie outside or beyond it.[7]

---

[7]. Of course, the very model of the text would exclude the possibility of ever producing a completely homogeneous structure, intentionally or not, and this principle of differential forces is equally pertinent for those texts, such as Saussure's own, in which it is possible to read of such a model for history. Which is precisely why such texts themselves require reading rather than mere decoding. For the most detailed analysis and commentary on the way Saussure's own text is *also* subject to a pressure to hide from or recuperate some of its boldest and most original gestures, see Jacques Derrida, *De la grammatologie* (Paris: Minuit, 1967).

The future science of semiology would thus, and by definition, be oriented toward registering and accounting for the relations and possible disruptions that occur between all signifiers and signifieds, including so-called "referents," within a textual field of history that is as a result just as much "social" as it is "linguistic." Far from being a simple empiricism or a pure formalism, the semiology of Saussure would be a radical project to think the laws that govern not only the linguistic structures it studies but the actual forces that produce and inhabit these structures in the first place. Undoubtedly the most suggestive section of the *Cours* from this point of view would be the chapter entitled "Internal and External Elements of La Langue" (40–43). It is true, at least from one perspective, that these pages operate under a provisional rule of exclusion—external elements do not belong to a study of "la langue" properly speaking. But it is also true from another, equally valid, perspective that they would sooner or later constitute a necessary, and necessarily related, supplement to the regional study of "la langue" within the larger field of a general science of semiology. The external elements in question here, of course, are precisely those that concern all the social and referential relations that can be seen to hold between language on the one hand, and ethnology, political and geographical history, institutional history, and literary history on the other.

Despite his initial insistence on keeping the "external" aspect of these relations wholly distinct from the closed systematicity of "la langue," Saussure ultimately has to admit that, between themselves, these two "histories"—that of language and that of race and civilization—are inextricably "blended together and entertain reciprocal relations" (40). In fact, the reciprocity of these relations is so far-reaching that, Saussure goes on, "the customs of a nation have an effect on its language, and, at the same time, it is in large part the language that makes the nation what it is." The conclusion, which Saussure himself does not hesitate to draw, is that this highly complex system of relays and relations *outside* "la langue" actually "recalls to some extent the correspondence noted earlier *between* linguistic phenomena properly speaking." In other words, the relations between language and social history, precisely at the moment the *Cours* pretends to exile them from the internal field of "la langue," are defined in such a way that they, too, can be understood only within a semiotic system of differential relations. For the properly linguistic "correspondence" Saussure refers us to at this point in the *Cours* is none other than the one, constituted *inside* "la langue" itself, between *signifiant and signifié*. If it is true, as Saussure will insist in the properly "scientific" analysis of "la langue," that there is no such thing as a *signifié* outside its differential relation to a *signifiant,* then the reciprocal relation here between "internal" and "external" elements could never be adequately treated by a gesture of exclusion pure and simple. Language and history are in fact two sides of the same, semiotic, coin—there is no language without reference to history and vice versa. The rule that excludes from consideration in "la langue" those elements that are referential through and through must itself be considered as being tributary to a larger semiotic principle governing the linguistic constitution of referentiality.

But if this is truly the case, then how could it have happened that Saussure's text has in fact engendered its own reappropriation by structuralism and by countless other formalisms? What is it in the text of the *Cours* that inheritors like Lévi-Strauss—to name just one famous example who has had wide-ranging and powerful effects—have not been able to read?[8] For one thing, they have not always been able to read sufficiently the functioning of the rhetorical figures, metaphors, or *symbols* Saussure's own text must put into circulation in order to illustrate the radically nonsymbolic nature of the science of semiology that, because it does not yet exist, can only be named and illustrated abusively.

One easily and willingly remembers the game of chess, for instance, that Saussure uses to illustrate the two necessary but necessarily incompatible orders of the linguistic system: the *synchronic* order of structural equilibrium and the *diachronic* order of historical change examined in chapter 3, section 4, of Part 1, "The Difference between the Two Orders Illustrated by Comparisons" (125–27). The synchronic

8. For an exposition and critique of the way Lévi-Strauss's mythopoetic anthropology can achieve coherence only at the cost of renouncing a critical engagement with forces that necessarily impinge on it, as its condition of possibility as well as in its own effects, see Jacques Derrida's "La structure, le signe et le jeu dans le discours des sciences humaines," *L'écriture et la différence* (Paris: Seuil, 1967), and "La violence de la lettre: De Lévi-Strauss à Rousseau," *De la grammatologie*. Also pertinent here would be the critique of formalism made by Paul de Man with respect to Lévi-Strauss as well as to another of Saussure's leading "continuators," Roland Barthes. See "Criticism and Crisis," *Blindness and Insight* (Minneapolis: University of Minnesota Press, 1983), and "Roland Barthes and the Limits of Structuralism," *Yale French Studies* 77 (1990), 177–90.

order, Saussure tells us, is like the system of relationships established among all the chess pieces; its differential value, or capacity for meaning, can be determined at any given moment according to formalizable laws. The diachronic order, on the other hand, is like the intercalated moves of individual chess pieces; such moves have no intrinsic meaning in themselves and serve only to destabilize the board's structural equilibrium, but in so doing they also create new systems of synchronic relationships and value upon it.

The figure of the chess game, however, which should correspond here to the ultimate inability of the linguistic system to bring together within a single structure of meaning its two heterogeneous principles, is seriously misleading in at least one fundamental way. For by replacing the actual semiotic conditions of language and history with a board game, whose laws and limits as a game not only can but *must* preserve their coherence by remaining the same before, during, and after each play and even each match, one forgets or suppresses precisely that "wild card" element in the science of semiology that would make it radically *historical* through and through. A board game is teleological by definition; it always has a predetermined endpoint and, therefore, a predetermined meaning, even if there exist an infinite number of ways to arrive at this endgame, and even if, finally, that meaning does not in itself amount to much.[9] The historical dimension that belongs to language, however, and as a consequence to the science of semiology, would have to be different if it is to account for the way meaning actually occurs. In the system of language considered historically it is precisely the play of unforeseeable and irreversible *events* that has the power to condition and to alter once and for all the rules of the game as

9. Saussure himself notes the teleological nature of the chess game, but then he goes on to add: "This rule that is accepted once and for all also exists in the case of language; these are the immutable principles of semiology" (126). Without being able to pursue this particular gesture in Saussure's text in the detailed manner a comprehensive analysis would require, suffice it here to make two remarks: (1) recourse at this point to the immutable principles of a "science" that does not yet exist as such cannot be construed as either simply legitimate or illegitimate and therefore cannot be conclusive; (2) should the science of semiology actually exist one day, one of its immutable principles would necessarily relate to and depend on a "diachronic" field of forces that carries within it the power to alter all that comes before it, including the very "immutable principles" of its own systemic constitution. Nothing of the sort pertains to the principles or the practice of the game of chess. For another perspective on the way the analogy with the chess game upsets rather than confirms the possibility of maintaining a purely synchronic model for Saussure's semiology, see Samuel Weber's "Saussure and the Apparition of Language" (931–33) and "Texts/Contexts" (9).

well as its potential to preserve old meanings and generate new ones among its pieces. No pawn has ever managed to usurp the meaning and authority of a knight in any ordinary game of chess, though such acts of revolutionary force are readily documented and always possible among the identities that comprise genuinely linguistic and political systems.

So it is no mere accident that Saussure, when he finds it necessary to provide an analogy for the specificity of a system of linguistic "values"—rather than of "meanings" pure and simple—passes up the easy reference to chess in favor of one to *political* economy (114–16). But in the sphere of linguistic and political activity, at least as it is conceived by Saussure, one should also be careful not to presume to identify too quickly the specificity of the "agency" involved in maintaining or transforming the system of values that constitutes it at any given moment. Within such a system of values, according to Saussure, the agent of historical activity and change is not to be simply identified with subjective (or collective) consciousness. Because the original concatenation of the two different orders involved in any system of values must be arbitrary and unmotivated, every new displacement of the system will, at least in part, escape the control of the speaking (and thinking) subject implicated in it. "For the sign escapes to a certain degree the individual or collective will," Saussure insists early on, "and that is its most essential feature, though it is also the one that is least apparent at first sight" (34). This is not to say, of course, that there is no such thing as consciousness and intentionality, or that consciousness cannot be a substantial agent of historical activity and change. But within a system of values, that is, within a linguistic and political economy, this agency cannot be restricted to and fully comprehended by the subject of consciousness or desire.

If the semiotic play inherent in political and linguistic systems can still be likened to a game of chess, it could be only with the proviso that, of the *two* players whose necessary and necessarily interdependent strategies determine the movements of the game, only one can truly be said to be following a "strategy" in the first place, that is, a teleologically oriented process of applying cognitive (and tactical) means to tactical (and cognitive) ends. The other player, as Saussure reminds us, is "unconscious or without intelligence," even though its presence in the system is incontrovertible. For this reason, it also plays a substantial role in the system and its history, but it does so precisely by "pitting a *blind force* against the organization of the semiotic system" it helps to constitute (127). The question now becomes: which player is playing with a full deck? When—as is the case of genuinely historical systems like political and linguistic economy—it becomes possible not only to make predetermined moves, but also to prohibit and alter old ones as well as invent new ones as you go along, who can determine with scientific precision which play is systematically meaningful and which is not, or no longer, or not yet? Is it possible to isolate the play of these two necessary but absolutely incompatible players long enough to tell the essential difference between them? This is in fact the question that both conditions and is to be resolved by the full articulation of what Saussure calls the "autonomy and interdependence" of synchronic and diachronic linguistics (124).

Unlike the stabilizing figure of the chess game, then, the "textual history" implied by the future science of semiology would have to take into account the potential inscribed within the system at any given moment to go beyond the provisional limits assigned to the interaction of the forces and structures that comprise it. Therefore, this history would always have to be open to the unpredictability of a future event that could change even the contours of meaning previously understood to condition its own past, though such transformations of understanding could happen in a truly historical way only by respecting the specificity of the linguistic past actually inherited by them. The future can always occur as a mutation of our understanding of the past, but it remains forever impotent to affect in any direct way a past that, because it has been passively inherited rather than consciously experienced or produced, remains inaccessible as such. Semiology, as the science of this absolute past, is thus in principle, and not because of some contingently empirical factor, a science of an absolute future, a science that would be forever "to come." For a science to be truly historical, then, it must be, like history itself, poised between the ineradicable inscriptions that comprise its past and the unforeseeable effects of these inscriptions on the future. As such, semiology can only be a form of historical knowledge that, because it must come out of the production of this future, cannot yet master itself *as* science.

It follows from these remarks that the main burden of reading Saussure's textual history would be to account in turn for the specific ways the *Cours* itself is not able to master the historical effects of its own knowledge of language. Ultimately, this would mean showing how the entire text of Saussure functions systematically first to *open* a space in the general science of semiology for analyzing the necessary production and effects of "diachronic" forces and then to *disallow* consideration of these same forces from the theoretical construct of "la langue," which becomes in this way the reduction of linguistic actuality to a paradigmatic and closed system of "synchronic" structures. A fundamental and far-reaching instance of this peculiarity of Saussure's text comes into view when we compare the way the diachronic and synchronic orders of language are first posited and then later related hierarchically to each other in the *Cours*. If, on the one hand, and as Saussure knows perfectly well, the differential interdependence of these two principles of linguistics is "absolute and irreducible," it eventually becomes nonetheless imperative to consider *only* the system's "synchronic solidarity" in order to maintain the intelligibility of "la langue" as the possible object of a scientific study (114–24). But how, precisely, can Saussure thus take away with one hand what he seems to have given with the other? If the synchronic system does in fact depend initially on a diachronic force, then how is that force constituted in such a way that even the disclosure of its own necessity must itself be forcefully covered over by the science it promises to inaugurate?

The complexity of this structure—which seems to entail the mutual *obliteration* of the system's constitutive elements rather than the preservation and elaboration of their distinctive traits—suggests that we return once again to the now familiar analogy of the chess game in order to determine with more precision, if possible, its relevance in this particular context. Saussure himself, of course, privileges this emblematic moment by insisting that, "of all the comparisons one could imagine, the most demonstrative is the one that could be established between the play of 'la langue' and a game of chess [*entre le jeu de la langue et une partie d'échecs*]. From one end to the other we are dealing with a system of values and their transformations" (125). As we have seen, however, beyond offering the rather limited analogy of its successive "states," the teleologically determined game of chess is fundamentally *unlike* the open-ended play of language. But what should surprise and give us pause here are *not* the individual limitations that affect the capacity of the chess game to illustrate in adequate fashion the linguistic complexities Saussure is in the process of defining and explaining. What is of true theoretical interest and importance is that Saussure finds it necessary at this point in his analysis to make use of a symbolic illustration to explain the properties of a linguistic structure whose most distinctive feature has just been shown to consist in its radically *arbitrary* and *unmotivated,* that is, wholly *nonsymbolic* nature.[10]

In fact, the necessity of articulating the division in linguistic analysis between the synchronic and diachronic orders in the first place is itself the *result* of this first and most important principle of the arbitrary nature of the linguistic sign. For it is only because language is composed of a system of values, that is, a system of unmotivated concatenations of differential relations and equivalences, that the science of linguistics must be sundered (*scindé*) in two (114–17). Because the values assigned within the system are arbitrary, Saussure explains, they must be viewed from the double perspective of their "immutability," or synchronic stability, and their "mutability," or diachronic displacements (104–13). But the double aspect of this one perspective must itself be divided into two "autonomous but interdependent" perspectives if it is not to remain absolutely incomprehensible and thus wholly inappropriate for scientific study (114–40). In other words, it is only because language is fundamentally nonsymbolic in its principles of signification that it requires for its scientific analysis this division between synchronic structures and diachronic displacements, which division Saussure will go on to explain by reference to that "most demonstrative illustration imaginable"—the chess game. But how can any illustration ever adequately illustrate the fundamental incapacity of language to be an adequate illustration of anything? The structure of this complexity resembles not so much the sequential moves of a good

---

10. Saussure, like the other writers examined here, is thus both a symbolist and a nonsymbolist. His theory of language, which emphasizes the nonsymbolic constitution of the sign, is written in a language that cannot itself avoid using symbols to express and analyze this fact, though the ensuing relation in his own text—between theoretical statement and rhetorical structure—could no longer be called simply "symbolist." Saussure's clearest reference to the nonsymbolic nature of language is the section devoted to the arbitrary nature of the sign: "the word *symbol* has sometimes been used to designate the linguistic sign, or more precisely, what we call the *signifiant*. There are drawbacks to this usage, precisely because of our first principle [*l'arbitraire du signe*]. The symbol has the property of never being wholly arbitrary; it is not empty, there is an element of natural association between the *signifiant* and the *signifié*" (101). It is because the illustration of the chess game is not "wholly" arbitrary—or for that matter "wholly" natural—that it becomes such a pertinent and problematic example of the linguistic complexities Saussure must introduce and explain.

game of chess as the aberrant play of language as it simultaneously establishes and undoes the distinction between arbitrary forces and systematic structures that would be necessary for it to come into being.

For if the relation between the synchronic and diachronic orders of language is one of true "autonomy and interdependence," then language is not a simple board game but an *aporetic* structure in which no actual separation (*scission*) of the diachronic from the synchronic could ever be scientifically verified. If the founding principle of all language is truly arbitrary and unmotivated, as Saussure always insists, then it will never be possible to construct a metalanguage (science of language) that could ever be assured of exhibiting none of the unmotivated elements and effects it necessarily inherits from its own object of study—hence the enigmatic "analogy" of the chess game. The game of chess is not *just* a symbolic illustration that can be understood as more or less deficient in its capacity to represent the complexities of language. It is *also,* and just as irreducibly, a *force* that can be imposed on the text in its own right. Thus, when Saussure says that "of all the comparisons one could imagine, the most demonstrative would be the one that could be *established* between the play of 'la langue' and a game of chess" (125), we should be attentive to the connotations of *power* that can always be brought into play around the word *establish*. When a government "establishes" a new tax, for instance, what it actually demonstrates is its power to do so. What is most demonstrative in this respect is that Saussure has in fact established the example of the chess game as a force that can function in his text regardless of whether or not it corresponds in any essential way to the formal division between the diachronic and synchronic orders it was supposed merely to illustrate.

And *this* particular discrepancy, of course—between the illustrative meaning and the actual force inscribed in all linguistic structures—is precisely what the analogy with the chess game was meant to demonstrate in the first place.[11] The game of chess, we should always recall,

11. We should also be careful in referring to "the" analogy with the game of chess since, in fact, Saussure actually deploys this example in two very different, possibly *incompatible,* ways. In the section on linguistic "value" (153–54), Saussure reintroduces the analogy by insisting on the radically unmotivated relation between the figures of the board, a knight, for instance, and the values they constitute within the system. Unlike the earlier "illustration"—which represents the internal coherence in the game between its moves and successive states—this new use of the same example focuses on the impositional power that must establish (*déclarer*) the game from outside: *this* is a

is introduced in Saussure's text only to "illustrate" the fact that diachronic forces have nothing whatsoever in common with the formal coherence of the synchronic structures that would precede or follow them—even if these forces are themselves true "events" only insofar as they befall or produce the scientific hypothesis of such successive states of order. This is how Saussure describes the diachronic event that his own analogy of the chess game actually serves, at least in part, to reproduce: "the displacement of one piece is a fact that is absolutely distinct from the preceding and the following equilibrium. The change operated belongs to neither one of these two states: now it is only the states that matter" (126). It may be only the synchronic states that matter from a systematic and scientific point of view, but how much can that really matter if they are inseparable from the diachronic displacements that alone have the power to occur? At this point, all that remains beyond question in Saussure's model is that language, like history, is a heterogeneous *text* composed of forces *and* forms and that these forms can themselves achieve the systematic coherence of a scientific knowledge only by forcefully excluding all elements of force from their consideration. The formal analogy of the chess game is thus in its very discrepancy a textual "example"—a description as well as an enactment—of how diachronic forces could never be reduced to, nor for that matter abstracted from, the absolute closure of purely synchronic forms.

This double impossibility becomes readable not just in the effects this particular analogy has exercised on most readers of Saussure, but also in the way Saussure himself further characterizes diachronic events or forces as the very *condition* of synchronic structures or forms: "diachronic facts are irreducible to the synchronic system they condition" (127). Such "facts" are always and everywhere capable of interrupting and altering the hypothetical "structures" of synchronic equilibrium because they, and they alone, are the *effective* force of the semiological "law" rather than its merely *expressed* formalism. Diachronic forces are "historical," then, not because they are temporal and successive in nature, but rather because, unlike synchronic structures, which can only be forever talked about *as if* they simply existed, they are the one and only thing that ever actually *happens*. "Di-

---

knight and therefore it may move two squares horizontally and one vertically, or one horizontally and two vertically.

achrony" names language's imperative and historical force rather than its purely formal structure, which is nowhere accessible as such.

Here is Saussure's definition of this linguistic law of history: "The synchronic law is general but it is *not* imperative . . . the simple *expression* of an existing order, the synchronic law *states* how things stand [*constate un état de choses*] . . . [but] the order defined in this way is *precarious*. . . . Diachrony, on the contrary, supposes a dynamic factor by which *an effect is produced,* something *executed*" (131, emphasis added). Synchronic systematicity is precarious precisely to the extent that, unlike the diachronic forces that happen and produce real effects, it may be nothing more than an empty expression that corresponds in no way whatsoever to "how things stand." And because its own unpredictable force will be forever at war with the systematic but precarious forms it was supposed merely to describe, such a historical law of language would itself entail a radical transformation of our very concept of the law: "But the *imperative* character is not enough for us to apply the notion of a law to evolving *facts;* we only speak of a law when an ensemble of facts obey the *same rule,* and despite certain appearances to the contrary, diachronic events always have an *accidental* and *particular* character . . . if we wish in spite of all this to speak of linguistic laws, this term will have to acquire completely *different* meanings" (131, 134, emphasis added).

One of the meanings necessarily made different as a result of *this* imperative of linguistic law would be the one assigned to the synchronic principle and its very capacity within semiology to tell us just "how things stand." For as Saussure has already pointed out, when it comes to language and the epochal possibility of a knowledge that would be specific to it, there *is* no such thing as a simple "state of things" or "existing order." If semiology is to be the science of an absolute future that must create its objects of study as well as its point of view out of an absolute past, then it follows that the "synchronic order" that it would eventually take as its primary field of analysis cannot be said simply to exist as such before the science of semiology actually brings it forth as the closed system of differential relations it is said always to have been. Consequently, if the synchronic law of systematic formalization, of what Saussure in the following chapter calls a "general *grammar*" of language ("Synchronic Linguistics," 141), is itself ever to become an actual historical *fact* rather than remaining an empty formal hypthesis, it too will have to conform to all the "diachronic" constraints of an accidental force. Saussure himself couldn't have been clearer on this point when he delivered his inaugural lecture for the *Cours:* "['la langue'] is made up of *facts* and not *laws* . . . all that seems *organic* in language is in reality *contingent* and completely accidental" (416). But in this case synchronic linguistics would also have to give up the legitimacy of the claim to formal and logical systematicity that defines it as science. There can be no *science* of language without predicating the law of its formal systematicity. But there can *be* no science of language without that same act of predication disrupting its own pretense to scientific generality. At the very moment the synchronic system comes into being, then, its principial claim to formal coherence becomes a kind of *fiction,* since the diachronic act that must establish it as such is necessarily accidental and particular rather than general in nature.[12]

It should be noted, moreover, that the synchronic order becomes in this way a "fiction," or "simulacrum," not because it is itself any the less an operative historical fact, or reality, but rather because, by *having* to occur in the mode of an actual force, this particular historical fact no longer has any *right* to the kind of structural equilibrium and systematic coherence it *by definition* lays claim to. Saussure can originally say that the systematic coherence of semiology has a "right" to exist (33), but his text must go on to demonstrate, as we have seen, that only the accidental force of diachronic imposition can make this right (*droit*) into a necessity (*doit*). The "synchronic" law of systematicity is thus, and despite all illusory appearances to the contrary, "diachronic" through and through in its very capacity to impose itself upon and within Saussure's text. The future science of semiology, which must sooner or later take such a coercive law in language as its own object of study if it is to be "about" synchronic structures in any truly systematic

12. The logical inconsistency at issue here between "diachronic" elements of force and "synchronic" elements of form—an inconsistency in which, ultimately, the specificity of language "itself" might be said to reside—can be retraced throughout Saussure's conception of semiology. A related, but not identical, moment concerns the necessary, but necessarily impossible, distinction between the forms of "la langue" and the forces of "la parole": "Of course, these two objects are strictly related and even presuppose each other: 'la langue' is necessary in order for 'la parole' to be intelligible and produce all its effects; but 'la parole' is necessary for 'la langue' to establish itself; historically, the fact of 'la parole' always takes precedence" (37). It might be more precise to say that what takes precedence, historically, is the necessity that the intelligibility of 'la langue' itself always be established, or imposed, as though it were a mere fact of 'la parole.'

way, would therefore also have to be a textual history. That is, it would have to be a critical analysis of the irreducible ways in which the formal structures it studies in all sign systems are themselves always implicated in a language of power, or force, that lies beyond the reach of every attempt at scientific formalization, including its own.[13]

Such a history, as we have seen, teaches that the crucial separation of the diachronic from the synchronic in Saussure's text does not itself occur as a cognitive form or a structure, that is, as a simple state of things that could ever be described and mastered by any given subject or cognitive science. Rather, and as the *Cours* itself will point out, the founding gesture of this new science *must* occur as a blind force in its own right, though in the oblique form of a systematic decree to do away with its own irreducibly heterogeneous nature: "It is necessary at any price [*il faut à tout prix*] to situate each fact in its proper sphere and not to confuse the methods" (140). But the very diachronic law that imposes the synchronic order by sundering itself from it as (and by) force establishes itself by the same token on the "inside" of the synchronic structure that otherwise would be powerless to occur. The "price" Saussure's text refers to and exemplifies would be simply this: the law that requires the separation of force from structure—of history from language—also makes it impossible ever to fulfill such a requirement, though it remains powerless to make this requirement less binding. This means, among other things, that the mode in which Saussure's textual history can occur is not necessarily temporal in any ordinary sense of the term, since time, as we know at least since Kant, is itself a fundamentally formal principle of organization.

Because the inaugural separation of diachronic forces from synchronic structures can occur only as the result of a necessary, and necessarily "accidental," act of force, the ensuing representation of language as a chronological *sequence* of individual states of equilibrium cannot itself be maintained as a fully "synchronic," that is,

---

13. There is in fact a reference to this sort of critical analysis in the opening pages of the *Cours*. Because it may never lead to a positive knowledge in its own right, its sphere of activity is restricted to a description and analysis of past errors: "What finally is the utility of linguistics? Very few of us have clear ideas on that matter, and this is not the place to determine them once and for all . . . in fact we are all implicated [in the question of language] whether we know it or not—but, paradoxical consequence of the interest this produces, there is no domain in which have originated more absurd ideas, prejudices, mirages, fictions . . . these errors are not negligible; but the task of the linguist is first of all to denounce them, and to clear them up as much as possible" (21–22).

cognitive or intentional, structure. This kind of representation, precisely because it *is* chronological and therefore formal (or, ultimately, "synchronological"), must always be posited, or better, reposited, by a "diachronic" force that exceeds it. The temporality of textual history is therefore not continuous or sequential but repetitive; its occurrence always depends, as Saussure reminds us, on enigmatic forces that remain incompatible with the illusion of sequential succession they constantly serve to interrupt and reproduce.

What this analysis would mean in turn for a straightforward *description* of Saussure's place within a line of writers who could all be said to contribute toward elaborating a concept of textual history is not itself easy to describe or state.[14] On the one hand, there can be little doubt that Saussure's articulation of language *and* history, or of form *and* force, at least the way it is being read here, could with profit be put into contact with the writings of, for instance, Peirce, Austin, Benjamin, Heidegger, Althusser, Blanchot, de Man, Derrida, and others. Much could be learned about the contemporary scene of literary-critical fashions and polemics, for example, by noting how certain "post-structuralists" are actually much closer to Saussure's thinking of a nonformalist and nonsequential textual history than are most structuralists "properly speaking," and that, therefore, understanding these texts according to the chronological principles of change and development already implicit in such appellations are "structuralism" and "post-structuralism" is a very *unhistorical* gesture after all. On the other hand, by treating the concept of textual history as if it could itself be ascertained as a mere "structure" or a "state" of meaning that might then be traced back and forth across an evolving genealogy of writers, we would always run the risk of reinstating uncritically the very model of sequential formal structures that is in fact contested in all these texts.

14. The fact of this difficulty, of course, does not prevent such descriptions from occurring all the time, and with the utmost facility. A representative case in point is provided by the French journal *Le Débat*, which makes "structure" into a prominent but merely transitional *moment* within recent French intellectual history and fashions. See "Notre histoire: Matériaux pour servir à l'histoire intellectuelle de la France, 1953–1987," *Le Débat* 50 (May–August, 1988). But how can the concept of "structure," one of the conditions *of* history as such, be reduced to a mere "moment"—fashionable or unfashionable—*in* history? See, also, Thomas Pavel, "The Present Debate: News from France," *Diacritics* 19 (Spring 1989), 17–32, and *The Feud of Language: A History of Structuralism* (Oxford: Basil Blackwell, 1989).

Is it possible, then, to describe the events of textual history, which are the disruption and transformation of genetic and structural models of language and history, as though they were themselves merely passing moments of a larger, more coherent and comprehensive sequence of historical movements?

It is of course just such a question that serves to bring the theoretical discussion of textual history back to the practical exigency of reading—"symbolism," for instance. And such reading can take place only by charting the specific relations produced by the coming together of given linguistic structures *and* forces in particular texts of symbolism. For no response to the question actually posed to history by symbolism has been more widespread, more systematic, or more violently formalistic than the one that simply ignores "symbolism's" occurrence by subordinating its texts to a simple expression of the very historical and linguistic models that they most effectively challenge. This refusal to read occurs, again and again, whenever we replace whatever happens in these texts by a temporal scheme of understanding that would be able to distinguish clearly between a chronologically determinate moment of Symbolism—infinitely susceptible to refinement by qualifying it as French, Russian, American, poetic, novelistic, etc.—and a more encompassing principle of symbolic organization that would remain in essence the same regardless of its various manifestations throughout history and across genres as well as all disciplines—for instance, symbolism in mathematics, religion, philosophy, literature, law.

Whenever we have recourse to this scheme of understanding, "history" functions as the overarching and homogeneous, as yet undifferentiated, formal principle against whose background innumerable "Symbolisms," in the closed form of discrete but continuous sign systems, can appear and make sense as an evolving pageantry of individual moments. Such recourse signals, on the one hand, that the term "symbolism" is being used only to specify a general semiotic principle whose most valid name would quite simply be "language"; and, on the other, that the organizing principle of "history," insofar as it functions as a typological structure in which all that happens can be described and understood, is also language and nothing else, albeit in the unacknowledged and reductive mode of formalism.[15] But since

---

15. Two pertinent references in this context would be Edmund Wilson's classic, *Axel's Castle* (New York: Norton, 1931), and René Wellek's very thorough article,

true history cannot constitute itself without a founding act of inscription that is material through and through, then *every* actual historical event necessarily depends upon a linguistic "moment" that would exceed the merely formal opposition between historically universal and historically determinable systems of signs, or between symbolism in general and all Symbolisms "properly speaking."

Just as Saussure's semiology must exclude from consideration its own unruly diachronic forces in order to lay claim to the scientific coherence it thereby encroaches upon, so too must literary history banish whatever elements it cannot reduce to a formal system of representation. It does this by positing an all-encompassing historical structure that would lie beyond and comprehend the very linguistic powers from which such a formal history is itself engendered. The only difference, and this is by no means a negligible one, is that the actual historical force of this exclusion is indeed described and accounted for in Saussure's text. The exclusion is inscribed there as the thinking that makes of "diachrony" a historical necessity whose "accidental," and therefore unpredictable, force conditions the production of all "synchronic" structures of meaning, including its own. By the same token, no history, literary or other, could ever legitimately pretend to put "symbolist" texts back into a purely descriptive system of knowledge until it began to register and account for what such texts tell us about and *do to* our notion of history. And the same would be equally true for what we have been calling "textual history." There can be no *history* that would simply relate Saussure's semiology and Derrida's deconstruction to each other or to anything else without allowing itself to be marked and transformed by the actual forces inscribed in all these texts.

"The Term and Concept of Symbolism in Literary History," *Actes du Cinquième Congrès de l'Association Internationale de Littérature Comparée 1967,* ed. Nikola Banasevik. A more recent and self-conscious example of this kind of treatment is provided by Tzvetan Todorov's *Théories du symbole* (Paris: Seuil, 1977): "If one gives to the word 'sign' a generic sense by which it encapsulates that of symbol (which thereby specifies it), then one can say that studies of the symbol belong to the general theory of signs, or semiotics; and my own study, to the history of semiotics" (9). Todorov, of course, will have complicated his use of the term "history" a great deal by the end of the book, but only so far as it can itself take on the evolutionary systematicity of a wholly "typological" and therefore formal structure of language. He can reflect in the end on the relation of "opposition" and "plurality" that is said to hold between *system* and *history,* but not on the more disruptive interaction of what Saussure calls their "autonomy and interdependence," or what is here being called their *textuality.*

The "archetypal" symbolist poet, Stéphane Mallarmé, knew about this impossibility better than most when he wrote his own version of textual history, though he did so not as a discursive project for a future semiology, but rather in the highly elusive form of a semiotic symbol, or *cygne*. Mallarmé's so-called swan sonnet tells the story, if one can safely say that it still tells a story at all, of a kind of bird, a *cygne,* that behaves like a sign, or a *signe*.[16] Because it has a form and a voice, a bird like this can be said to have a history as well. And in this poem, the historical dimension becomes palpable in the *cygne's* anguish, caused, it seems, by an unforgettable but flawed past that also serves, at least provisionally, to block direct access to the brightness of a future.

As such, the poem is a symbolic structure that can be interpreted in any number of ways to tell the same old story of a nostalgia to recuperate the past and of a hope in such a possibility for the future. One of these ways can even include the familiar historical gesture that would turn the present description of a past failure into the very mark of a future success. In this way, the actual symbol *in* the poem, the *cygne* caught in the consciousness of frustration, can be made to prefigure the symbol *of* the poem, the symbolic *cygne* critics of French poetry tend to associate with an entire constellation of themes and names that come together to form the historical moment known as Symbolism: a sometimes exciting but mostly frustrating and anxious moment of linguistic hyperbole and sensitivity that has now been superseded. And the poem itself actually contains both of these *cygnes:* there is the individual cygne that can only "hopelessly remember his magnificence," and then the more general and "allegorical" Cygne that is finally protected from the cold by being "clothed," if only in its own "useless exile." If we read the poem in a linear and sequential manner, it seems indeed as though the little cygne-symbol could ultimately shade into and coincide with the great Swan of Symbolism, thus confirming our own capacity to recuperate the past failure of any given symbolic moment by clothing its uselessness under a historical mantle of distance and understanding, if not outright scorn. As long as we read the poem in this manner, moreover, it remains a distant star that cannot affect us or the way we represent our history here on earth.

But there is of course another way to read the poem and its place in

16. This is the second of "Plusieurs sonnets," whose first line is: "Le vierge, le vivace et le bel aujourd'hui." See Mallarmé, *Oeuvres complètes,* ed. Henri Mondor (Paris: Bibliothèque de la Pléiade, 1945), 67–68.

history. For the text also contains a kind of "symbol" that is neither a "cygne" nor a "Cygne," and therefore it cannot be simply reduced to the formal coherence of either a specific or a general "swan," whether that be construed according to distinctions between natural and ideal, literal and figural, individual and collective, diachronic and synchronic—and the list of oppositions could be extended at will. In fact, this other symbol is what serves to link all possible cygnes within the writing of the poem; it is quite precisely named in the text as their *phantom*. The symbol is a phantom because, like Saussure's future science of semiology, it can occur and be named only as a blind force that conditions the text historically without ever being fully present to it as such, as a perception, an intention, a meaning, or anything else that could be grasped without residue. That is, like actual history, the symbol in Mallarmé's writing is not just a formal principle or state of mind, but is as well, and primordially, the necessity of an impersonal force whose effectiveness is irreducible to cognitive structures of experience and judgment—though it is also inseparable from them. The symbol is a phantomatic cygne because it must always bear within itself all the marks of the arbitrary *signe* history imposes upon it in the very moment of its coming into being. It is, in the words of the poem, a "Phantom that its own pure flash *assigns* to this place [*Fantôme qu'à ce lieu son pur éclat assigne*]." Only by learning to read the flash, the force, or the random assignation that remains the sign of genuine history would it be possible to read what occurs in all texts, including the one we call history. And only through such a reading could the textual phantom of symbolism's *cygne* eventually become a truly historical assignment, that is, something different from the kind of immaterial symbol we mistakenly thought it was or wanted it to be.

2 The Forgotten Figures of Symbolism: Nerval's *Sylvie*

> No degree of knowledge can ever stop this madness, for it is the madness of words. What *would* be naive is to believe that this strategy, which is not *our* strategy as subjects, since we are its product rather than its agent, can be a source of value and has to be celebrated or denounced accordingly.
> —Paul de Man, "Shelley Disfigured"

It is a commonplace peculiar to literary criticism—as opposed to other branches of the so-called human sciences—that attempts at periodization and definition are more often of interest for the tensions and irresolutions they eventually produce than for the tidy but simplistic lines of demarcation they were originally designed to identify and illustrate. What has come to be known as French "symbolism" is an extreme case in this respect insofar as its main representatives—shadowy and all but forgotten figures like Stuart Merrill, Emile Verhaeren, Albert Mockel, and others—are usually mentioned only in order to be simultaneously shunted aside in favor of more canonically recognizable poets such as Baudelaire, Mallarmé, and Valéry. The gesture is of interest not because it excludes Henri de Régnier and Pierre Louÿs from a greatness on which they in fact have little claim, but rather because it points up a potential tension between certain (symbolist) poetic practices and any coherent theory of history. For if symbolism as an actual historical occurrence can be of genuine interest to literary history only in the name of its "precursors" (Baudelaire and Mallarmé) and its "inheritors" (Proust and Valéry), then one should perhaps begin to ask what it is about a literary movement "properly speaking" that resists such historicizing schemes of "before" and "after." Much more threatening to literary history than the mediocrity and marginality of symbolism's chief proponents would be certain having originated or "sprung" from the particular experience of a symbolist literary movement it actually predates—and Eco cites Baudelaire and Mallarmé as its main, post-Nervalian, representatives. Symbolism, as well as Nerval's text, becomes in this way a moment within a general historical sequence, though a moment whose own lack of temporal specificity threatens to disrupt even the most elementary laws of order linking the past to the future.

Small wonder, then, that the actual Nervalian "symbol" Eco chooses to illustrate this aberrantly proleptic symbolism is the famous Renaissance clock in chapter 3. This clock, familiar to all readers of *Sylvie,* is also emblematic in a wider sense of the challenge posed to literary history of understanding the place of symbolism: it is a clock that has become a mere piece of furniture. Such an elaborate but useless knick-knack can indeed illustrate an aesthetic "dance of the hours," but it hasn't been able to register the right time, or actual historical present, in over two centuries. Thus, Eco's first gesture in relating Nerval's use of symbolic language back to a specific historical context is clearly meant to limit what he calls the "irritating" effects of this same language by placing it within and making it subservient to a larger, more comprehensive framework. But it is not clear that such a historical framework, this "clock" composed of sequential literary movements as it were, can continue to run smoothly beyond its necessary encounter with symbolism. Thus, one of the meanings of the Nervalian clock Eco has not remarked and which could easily be added to the list provided by his own analysis is the threat posed to chronological time and to ordinary sequential history by the symbolical use of language. To some extent, then, whatever concept of history becomes apparent in the face of this symbolist clock would be a history that is at the same time "broken" or invalidated by the symbol it requires to symbolize it.

However bizarre this figure of the stopped clock may appear when first encountered, it should by now be recognizable to us as one of the most common figures for symbolism. For the symbolist moment, at least in French literature, is invariably described in terms of an abstract idealism limited mainly to interior and private adventures. As such, it seems to resist coordination with the chronological time of historical continuity as well as with the outside context of day-to-day social relations. Whether it is treated case by case as an individual, psychological phenomenon; or as a local and idiosyncratic version of a larger

symbolist elements already fully present in Mallarmé
in Proust that would make them equally "margina
historical progression they have until now been assun
and perpetuate.

The question has to do, in more theoretical, an
immediately loaded and self-interested terms, with the
of texts that can be received only as all "past" and "
have no recognizable "present." Nerval's *Sylvie* can
such a text, a paradigmatic example that tells the story
ism, however it is conceived historically, can be
something that has already been irretrievably lost.[1] A
be the case even in one of literary history's most com
versions, that is, the classification of texts accordir
principles of theme and formal articulation. While
ridden thematic content harkens back to a French ron
has left behind forever, the self-conscious invention
boles" used to tell this story points forward to a symb
yet to be named. It is precisely at the point where S
textual "present" as nothing but this potential split, d
the theme of disillusionment and loss on the one ha
figurative power of language or symbols on the other,
atic relation of symbolism to history can be approad
plary way.

The complex interplay and eventual disjunction I
historical thinking and the poetics of symbolism is co
trated in a book by Umberto Eco, *Semiotics and t
Language,* which takes *Sylvie* as a privileged exan
calls the "symbolic mode" of language. Yet it is also
text is proposed not simply as a formal model of the s
general—which for Eco has an unfortunate way of d
all-or-nothing alternative for meaning—but rather as
the determinate, that is, historical, mode that is desc
ing from the experience of French Symbolism."[2] C
then, at least within Eco's unquestioned historical
val's romantic use of the symbol would have to

1. Gérard de Nerval, *Sylvie,* in *Oeuvres complètes* 1, ed. A
Richer (Paris: Bibliothèque de la Pléiade, 1966). Further referen
2. Umberto Eco, *Semiotics and the Philosophy of Languag
ana University Press, 1984), 156.

occult and mystical tradition; or as the natural poetic outgrowth of a philosophical inquiry into aesthetics that is said to begin with Kant and culminate in the third book of Schopenhauer's *Die Welt als Wille und Vorstellung*—(or, by passing through Coleridge, Poe, and Baudelaire, as some combination of all of these)—critics of French symbolism tend ultimately to see it as a self-propelled move beyond the surface forms and constraints of the quotidian world, a world so economically represented by the ceaseless ticking of an ordinary clock. And so by pointing to Nerval's unwound clock as *the* privileged instance of symbolism in *Sylvie,* Eco also helps us to identify this text as a story not only made up of symbols but also about symbolism. *Sylvie,* then, can be read as a protosymbolist text that recounts the story of how to understand symbolism. The narrative that describes how a certain conception of poetic language stands in relation to the linear temporality of a more comprehensive history does so by using the figure of a stopped clock to stand for a moment in which literature is itself conceived of as a broken clock.

Thus, the question the "symbolist" hero of *Sylvie* anxiously asks at the beginning of the story as he stands next to his immobile clock, "What time is it?" (247), is also the question that marks this text as a kind of allegory that would tell the story of how to bring symbolism back to a relation with history. Asking for the first time the question that will continue to obsess all subsequent readers of symbolist literature, the narrator is also asking about the possibility of rewinding the stopped clock of symbolism by reassigning it a moment within a new history that could somehow move beyond it.

And yet, would it not be a rather acute form of hermeneutic madness to read *Sylvie,* at best a precursor to symbolism, as though it actually were a retrospective recounting of the completed history of symbolism? Would not such reading make the text into an allegorical response to the question of symbolism before the question had even been asked historically? No doubt, but such an objection can hardly be made to *Sylvie* a priori, since among other things *Sylvie* is also the story of the working through of the "madness" the hero suffers on account of just such metaleptic reversals of "before" and "after," of "cause" and "effect," as is seen most clearly in the narrator's attempt to unravel and reorder his relationships to Aurélie and Adrienne. In terms of an understanding of symbolism, such interpretative madness is not simply an accident; it is its condition of possibility, just as some form of discrepancy or of noncoincidence between conscious and unconscious understanding is the very possibility of opening the hermeneutic circle by way of the process of questioning. As the narrator says in his penultimate chapter, in order to achieve the ideal of reason, "one has to be prepared to enter into nonsense and absurdity" (270). If symbolism marks the moment when the clock of history is put out of order, when the natural order of inside and outside, past and future, is disrupted, then history could never hope to bring symbolism back into its movement without itself first facing up to and traversing this moment of referential and temporal madness. Without somehow experiencing the metaleptic reversals of "cause" and "effect," "before" and "after," history and the form of understanding proper to it can know no Nerval, no *Sylvie,* no symbolism. Symbolism is like a bad dream; it's a shame it has to be there in the first place, but once it gets started you have to take the time to go through with it before you can make any claim to waking up from it.

The shape these problems assume in *Sylvie* is the thematic pressure to leave the private theater of artifice and illusion for the shared context of social reality and the discursive distinction attempted between the hero, whose madness is recounted in the text, and the narrator, who tells this story as his acquisition of experience and reason—in short, a distinction between *histoire* and *narration.* The importance of the opening words of the story, "I was on my way out of a theater" (241), cannot be overestimated in this regard, since their first-person imperfect tense clearly evidences the gradual movement of a subject's emergence from inside to outside at the same time that it prefigures a narrative stance that has already achieved the necessary distance from which it might articulate them. The entire burden of a reading of the text rests on how one understands the final chapter in relation to the first sentence. What is of ultimate import is whether the narrative voice has finally been able to pass beyond its earlier seclusion in the theater, thereby earning the right to say, with all the authority of a self-conscious author looking back over the completed work:

> Such are the chimerae that charm and mislead us in the morning of life. I have tried to set them down without much order [*les fixer sans beaucoup d'ordre*], yet many hearts will understand me. Illusions fall away one after another, like the skins of a fruit, and this fruit is experience. Its taste is bitter, but its sharpness has something fortifying about it. (271)

Michel Jeanneret and Ross Chambers are the critics who have done the most to impress upon us the crucial importance of this narrative gesture by which the loss of reason incurred in the theater is to be recuperated through its aesthetic transformation, or *mise en forme,* in a story of retrospection.[3] In this way, *Sylvie* becomes a bit of hermeneutical therapy that seeks to unite, through an act of understanding, the two I's; the mad I of the beginning and the sadder but wiser I of the end, who has lost his youth but also its illusions. By recounting his recognition of the madness of originally identifying Aurélie and Adrienne (or the past Sylvie and the present Sylvie, or ultimately of all three female figures) without regard to mediations of time, place, and character, the narrator of *Sylvie,* as opposed to its hero, is able to constitute his own social identity as "author." That is, like the narrator in *Aurélia,* the I of *Sylvie* is trying, through writing, to "control [his] sensations rather than endure them," and thus to become someone who is able to give comprehensible form to his madness rather than simply living it. And, as in any genuinely effective hermeneutic model, the original quest for an unmediated identity is replaced through time with an identity on a higher level of consciousness. Whereas the hero sought identification through his possession of an ideal (which in his case is usually a woman who turns out to be a chimera) and in so doing risked his sanity and along with it any identity, the narrator seems to recover his reason and close the gap between the narrating self and the existential self by keeping all three ideal or phantomatic women at a distance in order to understand them better in relation to his own identity:

> Ermenonville! . . . you have *lost* your only star, which shimmered for me with a double light . . . and which was by turns Adrienne or Sylvie,— they were the two halves of a single love. One was the sublime ideal, the other sweet reality. Of what use to me now are your glens and your lakes? . . . . It is *in myself that I find* the fleeting traces of a time when nature was transfused. (272, emphasis added).

3. Michel Jeanneret, *La lettre perdue: Écriture et folie dans l'oeuvre de Nerval* (Paris: Flammarion, 1978), especially 82–83, and Ross Chambers, *Story and Situation: Narrative Seduction and the Power of Fiction* (Minneapolis: University of Minnesota Press, 1984), 97–122. For readings that call such a resolution into question, see Rodolphe Gasché, "The Mixture of Genres, the Mixture of Styles, and Figural Interpretation: *Sylvie,* by Gérard de Nerval." *Glyph* 7 (1980), 102–30, and Christopher Prendergast, *The Order of Mimesis* (Cambridge: Cambridge University Press, 1986), 148–79. I am indebted to all these essays. Further references appear in the text.

We recognize in this story of lost illusions, in the reference to the ripening of fruit and the bitter taste of experience in the last chapter, the classical topoi of the *Bildungsroman* or autobiography. But just as the *Bildungsroman* narrative in Hegel's *Phenomenology* tells us very little about an early nineteenth-century German fellow named "Self-consciousness," the self-reflexive "subject" of the autobiographical narrative in *Sylvie* is as much and more the self-conscious poetic practice of "symbolism" as it is the unnamed and sorry narrator of the text. In addition to the "romantic" story of a dreamy poet's attempt and failure to coincide in an immediate way with any of the three young women, and of his subsequent claim to recover the identity of his self through his recognition of that failure, we should also read here the story, which will later be reappropriated by European literary history, of the linguistic model of the *symbol*. For what the symbol in fact names is precisely this structure of correspondence that is at issue at every point of the narrative. What is thematized as love in the story—and later denounced as a mere "illusion," or "metaphysical phantom"—is the (erotic) desire for a direct correspondence between subject and object, first between the hero and the actress Aurélie and later between the hero and Sylvie. As he says in the first chapter, "I felt that I lived in her, and she lived only for me. . . . For me she possessed every perfection, she *responded* to my every preference" (241, emphasis added). Such a seamless unity, though, is purchased only at the price of a fundamental and phantasmatic negation of *time,* as we have seen in the figure of the unwound clock, and for this reason it cannot be maintained except at the risk of the subject's alienation from the actuality of history. This failure of the symbol to establish itself as an adequate form of correspondence is experienced by the subject in *Sylvie* as an inability to prevent his self-identification with the erotic object from slipping away in a series of temporally regressive and uncontrollable substitutions. Thus, with each interruption of the hero's dream-state of symbolic adequation by the necessarily punctual events of history—beginning in the first chapter with the chance reading of a newspaper (*journal*), itself an apt figure for the printed time and date of actuality—he is thrown into confusion by the gradations and differences that threaten the absolute stability of the one object in which he had hoped to find his ideal, in other words, his self.

The most revealing, though by no means straightforward, example of this complication occurs in chapter 3, "Resolution," in which the hero, midway between dream and wakeful memory, recognizes that behind his supposed identification with the actress Aurélie stands the childhood figure of Adrienne:

> This vague and hopeless love, conceived for a woman of the theater . . . had its seed in the memory of Adrienne, a flower of the night brought into bloom in the pale light of the moon, a pink and blond phantom sliding across the green fields half-bathed in white vapors. The resemblance of a figure long-since forgotten traced itself out from that moment on with a singular distinctness; it was a pencil drawing blurred by time which turned into a painting, like those old sketches of the masters hung up to be admired in museums, and whose dazzling original is found elsewhere. (246-47)

The complexity of this figure derives in large part from the attempt to coordinate a simple metaphorical figure based on resemblance ("the *resemblance* traced itself out") with a doubly articulated process of temporal degradation and development that is made evident in memory ("a pencil drawing *blurred* by time which *turned into* a painting"). Christopher Prendergast (162-63) has analyzed how the founding analogy here between Aurélie (the painting) and Adrienne (the pencil drawing blurred by time) cannot ultimately be founded in any logically consistent way, since the original in this figure (Adrienne as blurry sketch) is less present in and to itself than in its derivative representation (Aurélie as dazzling painting).

Another way to put this logical instability, and one more germane to the text insofar as it is based on rhetorical structures rather than pictorial representations, would be to say that in the symbolic correspondence established by metaphor there can be no question of a true "original" and a mere "copy," since the supposed identification of the two terms that should remain distinct in time and space (Aurélie and Adrienne) is itself only the retrospective construction of a tropological *relation*—between "cause" and "effect," or between "before" and "after"—that can always be reversed in a most unnatural way. What had previously been considered the cause (Aurélie) can always be shown to be determined (through resemblance) by its own effect (Adrienne), and what had been considered the effect (Adrienne) can in turn be seen to determine (through resemblance) its own cause (Aurélie). Nerval, with the literary sensitivity of a poet and the psychological sensibility of a madman, seems spontaneously drawn to a rhetorical structure (metalepsis) that forms the philosophical backbone of Nietzsche's epistemological critique of metaphysics.[4] Once the analogical exchange between Aurélie and Adrienne is put into motion, then, it no longer makes any sense to claim absolutely that the childhood love causes the infatuation with the actress or, on the contrary, that the infatuation with the actress causes him to recall his childhood affection for Adrienne. And so it can be no surprise that Adrienne herself must turn out to be a mere "copy" rather than a genuine "original," since even when the hero "first" meets her she is already an "actress" who not only plays a role from a druidical past but also reminds him of a previous textual model of metaphorical substitutions, Dante's Beatrice.

What is certain, however, is the effect caused by this unhinging of the temporal and logical priority of the categories of "cause" and "effect" and brought about by the subject's metaphorical substitution and identification of Aurélie and Adrienne: what the text refers to as *madness*. Immediately after the evocation of metaphoric resemblance, the narrator cries: "To love a nun in the form of an actress! . . . and if they were the same!—It's enough to drive one mad!" (247). The madness here is the madness of the figure, of metaphor, and of the symbolic correspondence that only pretends to erase all distinctions in order to induce the hero to take Aurélie for Adrienne without regard to their possible discrepancy. But when the hero finally asks, "and if they were the same!," his real desperation is caused not so much by his believing they actually *are* the same as by the impossibility of ever being sure one way or another for lack of any objective criteria according to which he might once and for all determine their relationship. And what is at stake in the uncertainty of this particular substitution is far more than the contingent madness of an unhappy love; or rather, the theme of unhappy love here is itself merely a version of the necessarily radical madness of a self that finds it impossible to constitute itself on any stable ground, that is, a "self" that cannot tell the difference between "same" and "other." For as we know from the first chapter, the hero's love for Aurélie is the condition of his own identity ("I felt that I lived in her, and she lived only for me"), and should he find it impossible to stop the oscillation of his reflected image between Au-

---

4. See, in particular, Nietzsche's analyses of the phenomenalism of the inner world and the "chronological inversion of cause and effect," in *The Will to Power*, trans. Walter Kaufmann (New York: Vintage, 1967), 265–66.

rélie and Adrienne—and with the reference to Adrienne he also opens the circle Aurélie-Adrienne to include an infernal proliferation of other actresses, including Dante's Beatrice—he will have glimpsed by the same token the dissolution of his self into all the impossible fragments of Aurélie's "magic mirror" in which he had hoped to project himself in the first place.

This reference to the magic mirror helps us identify the figural pattern of the analogical symbol at work here as the mythological site of Narcissus. Narcissus is a myth that, reformulated in the texts of symbolism, narrates a conception of poetic language in which it would be possible to constitute the self on the basis of a freely created metaphorical identification between consciousness (I) and a representational ground (Aurélie, Adrienne, Sylvie) on which it could project its mirror image. But in the absence of any form of outside control or regulation, the arbitrary creation of metaphoric identification threatens to degenerate into an overly solipsistic or subjective malady of self-indulgence that can never find complete satisfaction. Christopher Prendergast speaks for an entire line of interpreters of symbolism, extending from Edmund Wilson to Umberto Eco and beyond, when he asks, "in the making of a metaphor, what motivates the relationship between compared object and comparing term? What validates a metaphoric likeness as true, real, or even merely probable?" (165). Whether they valorize such an "unmotivated" phenomenon in a positive or negative way, commentators seem to be unanimous in characterizing the metaphorical identifications of symbolism as "private," "nebulous," "arbitrary," and "subjective."[5] What this means is that the potential threat

5. Proust's remark about Nerval's "madness" is highly revealing in this regard and goes a long way toward suggesting the wider implications of symbolism: "In Gérard de Nerval, the onset of an as-yet-undeclared madness is nothing other than a kind of *excessive subjectivism*, an attachment of greater importance, so to speak, to a dream, to a memory, to the personal quality of sensation, than to what this sensation generally signifies to us all, what is perceptible by us all, reality." "Gérard de Nerval," *Contre Sainte-Beuve* (Paris: Bibliothèque de la Pléiade, 1971), 234, emphasis added. It would be of considerable theoretical and comparative interest to examine this particular constellation of "symbolist" concerns (the self, metaphor, and subjectivity's capricious negativity) in the light of similar issues prevalent in the German theorists of romantic irony. If the relationship of both irony and symbolism to patterns of historical continuity weren't immediately open to being broken by the ironic-symbolist operations it seeks to classify, it would be tempting to suggest that an unbroken ironic (or symbolist) "tradition" runs from Schlegel, Tieck, Solger, and Kierkegaard to Nerval, Baudelaire, Mallarmé, Proust, Gide, and others. The term "symbol" would thus be a kind of French translation used to designate the crucial philosophical problem of subjectivity and its

of incomprehensibility or madness implied in the overly subjective freedom of the self to create metaphors "for" itself, if it is not simply to be accepted or reveled in as such, must be offset to some extent by replacing this creative but arbitrary force within clearly determined limits. In order to guard against the infinite slippage of metaphoric excess, the initially gratuitous and unreliable correspondence between inside and outside, or self and other, must be validated by placing it within a context, that is, by submitting it to the codes and conventions of some recognizable order. If symbolism is a form of metaphoric madness brought on by the absolute freedom of the creative self, then one understandable response to it, and one with a long and fruitful lineage, will be to have recourse to something like a transpersonal consciousness of *history*. With the advent of history, conceived as a reflection on the possible determination and coordination of the individual within a social and temporal order, a cure for the self and its peculiar madness seems to hold itself out to us.

A certain form of history is indeed already present in the passage from *Sylvie* just cited, in embryo, as it were, but it still serves as a prefigurative remedy precisely where the hero is most threatened by the madness of his symbolist identification of Aurélie-Adrienne. We should not ignore the narrator's own care in setting up the figural relation between Aurélie and Adrienne here. They are related to each other not only in terms of the representational medium of painting (pencil/oil, sketch/original) that can then easily be shown to fall apart in the symmetrical reversals of logical and temporal priorities. They are also linked by way of a wholly organic and cyclical model of growth: "This vague and hopeless love, conceived for a woman of the theater . . . had its *seed* [son germe] in the memory of Adrienne, *flower* of the night brought into *bloom* in the pale light of the moon [*éclose à la pale clarté de la lune*]" (246–47, emphasis added). There is a metaleptic reversal here as well, since the flower (Adrienne) precedes the seed

---

negativity, which the German romantics called "irony," or sometimes "Witz." Rather than praising or blaming symbolism as a mere "aesthetic adventure" of rather feeble philosophical pretensions and of limited scope and interest, we must learn to read these texts as theoretical narratives of tensions inherent in any concept of "symbol" or of "irony." That is, we must learn to read them as philosophically legitimate reflections on the necessity and attendant complications of subjectivity's constitutive turn away from the immediacy of the natural world in order to found itself negatively in arbitrarily posited "symbols," "tropes," or "ironies."

(the memory of Adrienne), but unlike the dizzying reversal between original and sketch that follows, this one no longer seems purely formal and therefore ultimately static, and for this reason also not incompatible with certain historical processes of development. Thus, not only must we imagine the love the hero feels for Aurélie as a further flowering of the seed left in his memory by an earlier flower (Adrienne); we must also be prepared to understand the final chapter of the story, where the narrator speaks in his own voice, as the ultimate fruition of the evolutionary process of seed, flower, and fruit: "Illusions fall away one after the other, like the skins of a *fruit*, and this *fruit* is experience" (271, emphasis added).[6]

It could be argued, then, that in the last chapter the earlier symbolist and atemporal model of language as arbitrary image, which had led only to the brink of a mad regress of self-reflection, has been replaced with a more discursive linguistic model based on the temporal unfolding of the plant. Such a move can in fact be read in the very title of the last section, "Last Leaf" ("Dernier Feuillet"), where the cyclical growth and decline of the plant is retained in the reference to the "leaf" and where a model of language as *writing* rather than image (or *painting*) is made evident in these remaining leaves of "printed paper." It is also at this point that we may speak of the writing out of the text as an exercise in the hermeneutic understanding of symbolism and its eventual reintegration within a structure that is both historical and social. Against the background of the dialectical "plant," which has a

---

6. The kind of organicist thinking displayed here is a prevalent theme in German literature of the late eighteenth and early nineteenth centuries, and Nerval's acquaintance with and indebtedness to this tradition is a constant topos in his commentators' critiques. It is true that more than twenty years before writing *Sylvie*, Nerval had translated Goethe's *Faust*, but a reference even more to the point, because less dependent on the contingent issues of purely empirical influence or source, is Hegel's *Phenomenology*. What is at issue in both texts, regardless of how their respective authors may have reached the question, is a distinction between a truly historical and dialectical thinking and a merely representational, formalistic one. One of Hegel's versions of the Nervalian "seeds of experience" is as follows: "The bud disappears in the bursting-forth of the blossom, and one might say that the former is refuted by the latter; similarly, when the fruit appears, the blossom is shown up in its turn as a false manifestation of the plant, and the fruit now emerges as the truth of it instead. . . . [The fluid nature of these forms] makes them moments of an organic unity in which they not only do not conflict, but in which each is as necessary as the other." "G. W. F. Hegel, *Phenomenology of Spirit*, trans. A.V. Miller (Oxford: Clarendon, 1977), 2. Prendergast's otherwise meticulous reading of the original/copy figure in *Sylvie* is marred by his not taking this organic model into account.

history that is also a kind of family genealogy, the symbolist "image," which is neither original nor copy and possibly both at once, stands out like an insane or unintelligible question. Within the prevailing conventions—though perhaps not within the unconscious assumptions—of mid-nineteenth-century French life, the hero's simultaneous preoccupation with an actress, a country girl, and a dead nun is bound to appear somewhat perverse if not out-and-out mad. However, placing the symbolist illusion, or the deluded efforts of the hero to realize his love, into a sequential narrative that becomes in this way accessible and understandable to a wider audience as the misguided attempt to find his ideal self in each of the three women, the text at least allows the original unintelligibility or madness to become comprehensible *as* unintelligibility.

The illusions of symbolism—an aesthetic category that can be extended to include any of the social or economic conventions operative at the moment for which it then becomes an emblem—will never be anything but illusions. But in recognizing them as such one becomes conscious of what had until then been only implicit or hidden. In the process of being brought to light they can thus be made to fall by the wayside when they enter into the sequential and historical patterns of experience they had by definition denied or resisted: "Illusions fall away *one after another* like the skins of a fruit, and this fruit is experience" (271, emphasis added). On an even larger scale, at the level of the experience of literary history itself, we can see this same hermeneutic unfolding take place when the confused mass of individually unintelligible "symbolist" texts or authors begins to fall into a coherent pattern of poetic and aesthetic experiments coming "one after another." Such unfolding takes place, for instance, when we are able to identify Nerval as a *pre*cursor of symbolism only *after* having read Mallarmé and Proust. Like all dialectical processes, this one functions by allowing any degree of negativity—aesthetic unintelligibility or even madness or death itself—to be transcended by granting it a place as a passing aberration within a temporal sequence whose structure includes the retrospective narration of this moment in order to survive it and move beyond it.

At any rate, the pressure toward reading *Sylvie* as the hermeneutic cure of a symbolist malady is very great indeed, if not irresistible. When the narrator finally says, "Such are the chimerae that charm and mislead us in the morning of life. I have tried to set them down without much order [*les fixer sans beaucoup d'ordre*], yet many hearts will understand me" (271), he makes it clear that the madness of symbolism is on the verge of being mastered in an act of retrospective understanding. The means of such a treatment is a hermeneutic concept of history, and the process of recounting the growing awareness of one's "illusions" in order to be rid of them is thematized as a move made possible through the operation of writing. The chimerae are the subject's confused and mistaken attempts to see himself in another, and they disrupt the order of history precisely because they themselves have no order, temporal or logical; they are chimerae for lack of any order. But in revealing their disorder for all to see, in writing the illusions down once and for all, *en les fixant,* the narrator places this purely subjective disorder within a higher form of order, that of a contextualized understanding that *comprehends* by this act of ordering.

Unlike the private and wholly arbitrary chimerae, then, the writing of the understanding is codified within an order that is both temporal and social. That is, it takes place under the revolving light of the sun (as it eventually produces an evening of experience out of the illusory reflections of what the narrator himself calls "the *morning* of life") and in the midst of a community of readers ("many hearts will understand me"). Writing, as the possibility of shared understanding, should be understood here in the most prosaic sense imaginable: as a fully conventional use of language, an absolute conformity to the *fixed* rules of a formalizable lexis and grammar that reduce the originally arbitrary, and therefore *chimerical,* instances of semiosis to recognizable patterns of meaning. And so it is that immediately after referring to the skins of illusion and the fruit of experience, the narrator adds, "forgive me this old-fashioned style," a phrase by which he emphasizes his willingness to give up the arbitrary "phantoms" of overly "original"—in the sense of "subjective"—metaphors (Aurélie, Adrienne, Sylvie) in order to place his writing within an easily recognizable tradition of codes and figures. The old-fashioned style—*style vieilli*—is old because it has *grown* old; like the rhetorical skins and fruits in which it is expressed, the writing of convention sloughs off the bold and misleading metaphors of individualistic paintings, or chimerae, and in its full maturity begins to resemble more and more the living fruit of the natural world.

Such a reading seems indeed to be confirmed in the bourgeois scene with which the text closes, which neatly reverses almost all of the symbolist aberrations of the first chapter into the solid values of the everyday world. Thus, whereas the hero is originally described as being removed from any sphere of possible activity, isolated from the crowd, and drinking only from a metaphorical cup of forgetfulness, the narrator at the end presents himself directly as the author of this text, in the company of a bountiful family, and as the happy guest at a picnic overseen not by a mythological god but by a down-to-earth pastry chef. Undoubtedly one of the most significant reversals here is the juxtaposition of the "ivory tower" in which the hero climbs higher and higher at the beginning of the story with the old and crumbling "brick towers" among which the children play at the end. There could hardly be a more conventional emblem for a rejection of symbolism in favor of historical narrative than this gesture, which, through the agency of time, brings the solipsistic ivory tower back down to earth and at the same time prefigures the reintegration of a purely paradigmatic use of hermetic poetry within the horizontal patterns of conventional prose writing. If *Sylvie* can be compared to a "poème en prose," it is as much by way of this thematic reduction of the skywriting of symbolist poetry into the humble bricks of solid prose as by any stylistic reference to its more lyrical passages.

But since the move from poetry to prose, from private to public, or from chimera to historical reality, cannot itself be an entirely natural process, it will also have to be thematized as a certain form of *sacrifice* and *loss* in this last chapter. Writing for the understanding of a community of hearts rather than for an exclusive love—"many hearts will understand me"—entails giving up the direct and spontaneous correspondence between two hearts and requires instead a mediated process of interpretation open to the many. The one and only time that such a privileged symbolist correspondence is allowed to take place without disruption is marked with the temporal recognition of its irremediably *past* nature:

> Ermenonville! . . . you have *lost* your only star, which shimmered for me with a double light . . . and which was by turns Adrienne or Sylvie,—they were the two halves of a single love . . . you have preserved *nothing* of all that *past*. . . . It is in myself that I find the fleeting traces of a time when nature was transfused. (272, emphasis added)

The communal work of interpretation that leads to understanding Ermenonville as the site of the symbol as a thing of the past is also a process that moves from inside to outside, though it could never become accessible in something like the immediate union of the two halves of the illusory symbol. Rather, one can accomplish the task of understanding only by way of a circuitous and fragmentary route whose temporality is that specific to memory and writing. The narrator's memory does not contain the symbol itself but only the "fleeting traces" of this past, and since these are all he has, he has to dredge them up out of his memory and then write them down again (*les fixer*) so that he himself, as well as many other hearts, will in time be able to recognize them for what they actually are. The detour here is double, moreover: first, writing the "fleeting" traces of the symbol on the memory of the hero and subsequently "fixing" these chimerical traces into the actual text of *Sylvie*. "These days there is no more *direct route* for getting to Ermenonville" (272, emphasis added), says the narrator in a tone of resignation that serves to underscore the necessity of getting to the chimerical land of symbolism only by way of a detour through memory traces that must be rewritten into conventional prose.

Where is it, we should ask, that the "fleeting traces" of the symbol are rewritten in *Sylvie* in codified form? What is the detour that must be followed in order to read this text as a proleptic history of symbolism? Among the various symbolic figures at work in *Sylvie,* none is more privileged in charting the roundabout movement that takes both the narrator and the reader from figure to text, from private symbol to public writing, from chimera to history, than the poetic bird that most often takes the figural form of a swan. The fact that the flight of this particular bird, *le cygne* that always hovers in French between swan and sign, will become something of a cliché in the symbolist poetry of Baudelaire and especially of Mallarmé does not permit us to dismiss its appearance in this text as a *mere* banality. For if it is true that *Sylvie* recounts the history of symbolism as the reduction of a symbolic but chimerical swan (*cygne*) to the prosaic status of the written sign (*signe*), then such a story cannot without further analysis be understood on the basis of our received ideas of symbolism, that is, of precisely this "swan." Rather, insofar as it also tells the story that itself promises to recuperate the madness of the poetic symbol (*cygne*) by reinserting it within a more conventional written system (*signe*) grounded in a temporal and social context, Nerval's *Sylvie* makes a reading of this particular "swan" the indispensable condition of our ever understanding symbolism and its relationship to writing and history.

In order of logical priority—an order that is constantly disturbed in the text in its attempt to remain faithful to the experience of "chimerae" it recounts—the first figural swan in the text is the "cygne sauvage" in the fourth chapter, "A Voyage to Cythera." This wild swan, of course, represents Sylvie herself as well as the immediacy of what will be referred to later in the hero's life as "the real world." The temporal progression of the narrative is disturbed here because by this point Sylvie already marks a sort of regression in the hero's process of self-understanding, an unsuccessful and confused attempt to turn the clock back to a state of nature in which the subjectivity of consciousness would not yet be at issue and in which Being would have all the immediacy of a wild bird in the natural world. The narrator implies as much by admitting that his physical union with Sylvie, the kiss that is awarded him when the wild swan first appears, is possible only by "effacing the memory of another time" (250), his earlier abandonment of Sylvie in favor of Adrienne in chapter 2 (245–46). But this moment of belated and undivided presence found in Sylvie—referred to as a love *sans partage*—is the least stable of all, and it must evaporate just as immediately as it occurs: this wild swan flies away into the setting sun, never to reappear, while Sylvie herself is taken apart by the hero into increasingly discrete units of time and place until she disappears entirely in chapter 6, "Othys," becoming a mere figurine in a genre painting by Greuze. From a strictly formal, as opposed to textual, point of view, we could say that the wild swan of natural immediacy also represents the "romantic" dimensions of *Sylvie,* that is, the traces as well as the critique of a period when it may still have been possible to take the identification between consciousness and nature seriously, and where poetic language set itself the task of coinciding with the actual "world" rather than a derived "image" of it.

The next stage in the hero's development, the truly symbolist point of view that organizes the bulk of the narrative, occurs when the wild swan of romanticism undergoes a figural metamorphosis to become a mythological phoenix. Singing only as it dies, the symbolist swan must become a phoenix in order to survive its own death. This transformation and resurrection of the natural world of immediate perception into a mythological figure is enacted in chapter 7. "Châalis," where Adrienne appears in a passion play in the role of an angel of destruction:

> The scene took place among the angels, among the ruins of this world's destruction. . . . A spirit rose from the abyss, holding a flaming sword in

its hand, and called for the others to come wonder at the glory of Christ victorious over the fires of hell. This spirit was Adrienne, *transfigured* by her costume as she was already by her vocation . . . her voice had gained in depth and range, and the endless fioriture of Italian song embroidered the severe phrases of a solemn recitatif with *bird-like trills*. (257, emphasis added)

No longer linked directly to nature as Sylvie may once have been considered to be, Adrienne, half-phoenix, half-swan, rises up from the ashes of the shattered world of natural immediacy to sing the redemption of subjectivity in the figure of Christ. Or rather, the phoenix-swan sings the symbolist redemption of the world *through the figure,* "Adrienne *transfigurée*." In this use of poetic images both Christ and the phoenix-swan can be understood *as* figures for a self-consciousness that maintains itself in the aesthetic form of song beyond the destruction of the self as mere nature. Rather than finding itself in the empirical world of the wild swan, the self now attempts to project itself onto a metaphorical *figure* (Christ, Adrienne, the phoenix) in order to establish itself as consciousness. But, as we have seen, this symbolist attempt to achieve identity with an image will eventually fail because of the potentially arbitrary element in the necessary play of substitutions. With no outside guarantee or limits, the potential for madness is as great in taking Adrienne for Christ as it was in taking Aurélie for Adrienne, or as it will be when the narrator takes a "different" Sylvie for his "savior." If the natural world "flies away" in its infinite particularity, the symbolist world of metaphor evaporates into the nothingness of groundless fiction. Thus, when the narrator finally says, "in retracing these details I am reduced to wondering whether they are real or whether in fact I imagined them" (257), he is experiencing the failure of the metaphorical symbol to establish an identity that would be anything other than illusory and potentially insane.

However, immediately after questioning the reality of the details of the symbolist process of transfiguration, the narrator refers to another set of details which, he says, are "true and indisputable." These details, unlike the earlier ones, are not part of the theatrical décor of the château, but rather are the quotidian traces of domestic, that is, *historical,* life left in the home of the château's caretaker. These details are marked by the replacement of the wild swan of Sylvie and the chimerical phoenix of Adrienne with a swan that has by this time been fixed into a sign: "We had stopped for a little while at the caretaker's house, where I was very much struck by a *cygne éployé* on the door" (257). What makes the "cygne éployé" impossible to translate here is not so much the play between "swan" and "sign" in the word "cygne"—by now a commonplace that hardly requires translation—but rather the adjective "éployé," which "displays" the play curiously manifest in the very word "cygne." "Eployé" refers to the spreading out of a bird's wings in preparation for flight, and it could have been used earlier in the story to describe literally the outstretched wings of the wild swan that flew off into the setting sun, or even to describe metaphorically Adrienne-Phoenix rising up from the abyss.

In this context, though, there can be no question of the swan flying off anywhere, since "éployé" is being used neither wholly naturalistically nor wholly metaphorically and thus must be read as a kind of rhetorical violence inflicted on the swan in naming both an empirical bird and a poetic figure. One doesn't have to force the reference in the morbid direction of a literally dead swan tacked up for all to see on the door of a sadistic caretaker to notice how the swan is being domesticated in this scene. For the "spread wings" in the term "éployé" belong to the vocabulary of heraldry, and thus must be taken to refer to the bird's appearance on a crest, a codified system of signs and emblems. The swan displayed above the door with spread wings can be an accurate image of a wild swan in flight only insofar as it has already entered into contact with a conventional use of heraldic birds, whose meaning is to be culled from the formalized grammar of manuals rather than simply found in nature or freely invented by individual subjects. By clearly but voicelessly inscribing the movement from a natural (or metaphorical) bird in flight (*cygne éployé*) in the heraldic code of mere signs (*signes éployés*), the adjective "éployé" becomes in its turn a prefigurative emblem for the narrator, who will later "*fix* his chimerae in an old-fashioned style" in order for others to understand him. In other words, the bird *is* the word insofar as it is precisely by *writing* the bird, and the bird "éployé" in particular, that the narrator actually does fix his chimerae into words.

And from the moment there is writing—that is, from the last chapter read as the condition of possibility and retrospective beginning of *Sylvie*—there will be no more room for any swans other than those conventional signs fixed into text: "The ponds which were dug out at such great expense vainly offer their stagnant water to the swan that disdains it" (272). The natural swan of romanticism has flown away for good, and the symbolist swan Adrienne has been banished to the illusory star of Aldebaran. At this point, that is, in the last chapter, which both opens and seals the narrative, the hermeneutic enterprise seems provisionally to close upon itself. The hero, who has by now been disabused of his earlier illusions, is finally allowed to coincide with the mature narrator, who has written these illusions down in the form of *Sylvie*. This act of self-reading and self-understanding also seems to coincide with the inclusion of a wider social and historical context, represented by the final report Sylvie makes to the narrator that Adrienne had died in a convent around 1832. The fact that the actual ending of the story is written in the words of someone other than the identity hero-narrator, and that they refer to a precise historical date for the first and only time, could be taken as a final reminder that the process of understanding is ongoing and cannot be taken for granted.

By citing Sylvie citing the final revelation of a historical past, the narrator seems to demonstrate, albeit obliquely and incompletely, his awareness of the openness of understanding's structure in this text. That is, since it is always possible that new "details"—originating from an "elsewhere" that is both social and temporal—can be introduced into the narrative of self-consciousness already begun by the text, the narrator leaves room to project a new act of understanding into the future by way of the quoted words of Sylvie. This figure of understanding is also a circular figure for its own continual growth through history, since it is conceivable that only later, in a future so distant that it can only be projected beyond but never realized within the text's own voice, could the actual significance of a past date like "1832" be articulated. This infinite process of growth and understanding is in fact already implicitly contained in the narrator's assertion—which can also be read as a wish or a directive—that, now that he has performed the task of setting down the chimerae of his past in written form, a new act of understanding will devolve on others in the hypothetical future of the reading of "Sylvie": "many hearts *will understand* me."

Nonetheless, the narrator's appeal to the heart at this point should perhaps not be taken at face value, since, in this text at least, the "heart" turns out to be something of a loaded term. In a story where the presumed ahistoricity and illusion of the theater is figured by literal actresses who seem to "have no *heart*" (242), and where the genealogical continuity of a motherland and mother tongue is figured by a metaphorical organism that is said to be a kind of clock in which, for over a thousand years, "the *heart* of France has beat" (245), the "*heart* of understanding" ultimately figured by the written text of *Sylvie* becomes something of a puzzle, if not an outright stumbling block to the understanding it promises. As Ross Chambers has pointed out, the renunciation of a discourse of seduction in *Sylvie* can be seen to function as a potential seduction in its own right, since the turn from eros to cognition in this text is accompanied by a new appeal to forces that might themselves lie beyond reason's power (Chambers, 116). The narrator's claim to be reasonable is perhaps never more suspect than when he assures us that "many hearts will understand [him]," for as we all know since Pascal, "the heart has reasons that reason itself knows nothing about." Can we take for granted, then, that we understand just what a heart is and, further, what *Sylvie* means when it says that it is possible to understand written signs by means of the heart?

Before we accept the story of how symbolism is cured of its subjective madness by being recast in an interpersonal situation of storytelling that, like all stories, is susceptible to being understood in terms of a history of human meaning, we should perhaps inquire further into the nature of the human "heart" of understanding that is projected onto a future in this text by means of written "signes." At issue here is an aspect of conventional writing that has continuously attached itself to the narrative movement in *Sylvie* but has not yet been analyzed in its own right: the faculty of *memory*. Memory is what makes the disappearance *in* writing, or the forgetting, of the deadly lure of natural and mimetic figures possible for the individual subject in the first place. But, as the story also tells us, the further preservation of this capacity of memory to forget nature and figure is also what is promised *by* writing in the larger historical context of transpersonal relations, or "hearts." You must remember to forget if you are to recognize the "cygne éployé" as the linguistic sign it was always meant to be. But you must remember too that in order to remember this simple fact of writing you may actually be forgetting all else, your own heart and any other as well. And it is in this double movement of memory that we can finally read the "heart" of writing on which the historical link between past and future, self and other, necessarily depends in *Sylvie*.

In order to determine more precisely the status of memory here, we need to recall once more the trope of tropes in this text, that is, the narrative figure that conveys how poetic figures are supposed to work in *Sylvie*. The trope that articulates the relation of original and sketch with that between seed and flower indeed prefigures the reintegration of the subjective metaphor of symbolism with the conventionalized writing of historical change and growth:

> This vague and hopeless love, conceived for a woman of the theater . . . had its seed in the *memory* of Adrienne, a flower of the night brought into bloom in the pale light of the moon, a pink and blond phantom sliding across the green fields half-bathed in white vapors. The resemblance of *a figure long-since forgotten* traced itself out from that moment on with a singular distinctness; it was a pencil drawing blurred by time which turned into a painting, like those old sketches of the masters hung up to be admired in museums, and whose dazzling original is found *elsewhere*. (246–47, emphasis added)

This concatenation of the seeds of memory with an act of forgetting (figures) is of interest to us for the way that it situates the incipient process of understanding with respect to the consciousness of the subject. What is planted, or imprinted, in the memory, that is, the "original" figure of Adrienne, is *not* present to consciousness as such but is preserved in an "elsewhere" that is not directly accessible to the subject, since he will have to get there by way of a "memnonic" tracing of it (Aurélie).

But, contrary to what one might expect (or want) to happen, the overall movement of *Sylvie* demonstrates beyond any doubt that this unconscious "elsewhere" of memory is not just an unhappy accident that befalls the subject but is actually *necessary* for the subsequent act of understanding to take place. Without being forgotten, Adrienne would remain a *mere figure,* that is, an illusion of correspondence that would eventually threaten the hero with subjective madness. In order for the subject to progress from his youthful illusions to the truth of his experience, the natural figure of the wild swan and the metaphorical figure of the mythological phoenix-swan must be *effaced* from his consciousness, or forgotten, and implanted in his memory. That is, natural and metaphorical figures must be *written* into signs that are preserved outside the subject's self-presence, in an elsewhere of memory to which the narrator (or any reader) can only later return in order to understand them. The subjective disorder referred to in this passage is a result of the hero's continued insistence on preserving a "resemblance" in his memory rather than a conventionally fixed and therefore nonmimetic sign. What the narrator eventually learns, and what separates him radically from the illusions of his youth, is that remembering the word necessarily means forgetting the figure. As we have seen, this process of forgetting the figure for the sake of the remembered word is what contains the ultimate promise of understanding in *Sylvie*. The "detour" through writing that assumes such prominence in the last chapter is in fact a detour through *memory,* and like the narrator's return to his uncle's house in chapter 9, "Ermenonville," it always occurs after a lapse, a forgetting or effacement of the figures such writing was meant to preserve in the sign.

"Er*menon*ville" is the chapter of memory, of self-recollecting Memnon as well as of an entire collective past represented in *Sylvie* by the proper names Montaigne, Descartes, Rousseau, and the narrator's dead uncle. Once inside the uncle's house, moreover, the narrator is able to rediscover his own perfectly preserved past in the metonymic traces of furniture, paintings, old pets, and books that eventually invade the story and replace the seductive figures of the three women: Adrienne, Aurélie, and Sylvie. The fact that we tend to associate *Sylvie* much more readily with these chimerical figures than with the very real but stationary chest of drawers and stuffed animals is indicative of our ideological investment in preserving for ourselves a romantic image of Nerval, and symptomatic of a systematic avoidance of the actual place of memory in this text. For, like it or not, memory is much more like a piece of furniture or a stuffed dog than the kind of man or woman we often like to project into our romantic past:

> Everything seemed to be in the same state as before, only it was necessary to go by the farmer's in order to get the key to the door. Once the shutters had been opened I saw once again, and with tenderness, the old furniture . . . ; on the table, a stuffed dog which I had known living, *former companion* of my romps in the woods. . . .
> "As for the parrot," the farmer told me, "he is still living; I have taken him away to my house." . . . Trembling all over I went into the study, where it was still possible to see the small library full of choice books, *old friends* of him who was no longer. . . . (260, emphasis added)

Like the long-since-forgotten "elsewhere" of memory, the uncle's house remains locked away or cut off from the direct consciousness of the subject, who for this reason must ask for the key from someone else. In this case, the most obvious key is available from the farmer, but it is actually the metonymic proximity of the dog to the narrator's youth that effectively triggers and unlocks this scene of memory and nostalgia, for in recognizing his own past in the preserved traces of the dog, the narrator also realizes that the boy he once was is no longer. Or rather, like the dog, the boy *is* only insofar as he too has been "preserved" in the indirect mode of his own memory.

The dog is able to produce this moment of recognition because, like the writing of a book rather than the barking of an animal, he no longer urges the narrator to romp through the woods. Thus, he no longer risks leading the narrator astray in a chase for the wild swans of nature or the metaphorical birds of symbolism. The dog is finally allowed to enter the house and get up on the table because he is no longer a dog. Rather, the dog has been fixed, like all the other chimerae, into a *text* relieved of all natural urges. He can be left unattended in the living room because he holds only written *memories;* his insides, or stuffing, are composed exclusively of the written traces of the narrator's past. Like the writing in the last chapter, moreover, the dog is an entirely conventional sign here, a pointer indeed, since his place can always be relayed or even taken over by any one of the other "texts" in the uncle's house. What goes into him (the hero's youth) has as little direct connection with this dog in particular as what comes out (the narrator's understanding that his youth "was no longer"). The dog, or the furniture, or the books are figures of memory and writing precisely because they are no longer figures of anything but rather are signs. They are the forgotten figures of writing: the *cygnes éployés, chiens empaillés, chimères fixées* that make up *Sylvie*. This means that, like the alphabet of any writing, they have been effaced as natural or metaphorical figures and memorized as series of foreign notations that are deposited elsewhere—stuffed into the dog, for instance—in order to be recognized not as themselves but rather as signs of the self that can read them. When the narrator comes back to the house of memory and looks with tenderness on the stuffed dog, he doesn't so much *see* a dog as *read* his own past life, though not as a dog, of course, but as a nephew and potential subject in his own right.

It is this distance in fact between boy and dog, consciousness and memory, self and sign, that ensures the ascending link between writing and understanding. In the final analysis, such a distinction between self and sign would safeguard the reading subject from a threat even worse than the one posed by the natural swan of romanticism or the metaphorical phoenix of symbolism, since no self-conscious subject would be left afterwards to recognize itself in the sign and bring it under its control through an act of retrospective understanding. For the subjective madness suffered in the metaphorical identification with the women is still the madness *of* a subject who himself suffers on account of it, no matter how deluded he may be. But where there is only a stuffed dog left to mind the store there can be no question of subjectivity, not even of its forms of madness, much less of its understanding. So, the boy *must not* become merely a piece of furniture, which is also to say that consciousness must not become mere memorization; nor, in principle, should a self become a mere sign tacked up on a caretaker's front door. And the way such distinctions appear to be preserved in this passage, as well as throughout the text of *Sylvie,* is by the mediation of a "heart" that is able to suffuse the impersonal act of understanding with subjective pathos. Unlike the dog's heart, which has been removed and discarded so that the dog can begin to function as a written sign, the "heart" of the reading subject should remain beyond question here, as is clearly evidenced by its capacity to be touched by sadness, to enter into the past "all atremble," and to look on the past as well as its signs "with tenderness." When the narrator finally says in the last chapter, "many *hearts* will understand me," he is using a wholly appropriate expression to conjure up the impression of the privilege accorded the subject in the act of reading, which is ultimately the act of self-understanding thanks to the written signs of memory. And as long as this heart remains intact, the subject who has to forget all the *other* figures in the text in order to remember them as mere signs of the self, can still preserve *this* figure of a reading self, which is also implied in the pathos of one's own heart. With such a heart one is in no immediate danger of effacing one's self in an impersonal and unselfconscious sign.

However, as readers of *Sylvie* rather than of ourselves, we have no choice but to account for the interruption of the inevitable progression from the stuffed dog to the choice books—that is, from the forgotten figures of symbolism to the fixed writing of historical understanding—by the appearance of yet another bird. This bird, unlike the swan or the phoenix, refuses to die off in order to become a mere sign of the narrator's construction of a subjective self. For, unlike the stuffed dog or the emblematized swan, he is not wholly without a heart or the means to express it:

> "As for the parrot," the farmer told me, "he is still living; I have taken him away to my house." . . . "Let's go see the parrot," I said to the farmer. The parrot asked for lunch just as in his heyday, and looked at me with that round eye, bordered with a wrinkle-laden skin, that brings to mind the experienced look of old men. (261)

The dog has to die, the uncle has to die, even the boy the hero once was has to die—all so that the narrator might turn them into written signs of his sadder and wiser self. The parrot, though, does not die; nor is *his* heart saddened as a result of something like the disillusionment of experience. He is still there, and he goes on asking for his lunch just as merrily as ever. Nothing could be more good-humored than this parrot, and so it is no wonder that the narrator is anxious to get away from the stuffed dog and stuffy furniture to go and see him. Moreover, in the spirit of the text, the phrase "quant au perroquet, *il vit toujours*" should also be read in its absolute sense as "the parrot lives forever," since there could be no cheerier thought for the narrator than this, particularly when he realizes that what is still alive in the parrot is precisely that aspect of *Sylvie,* or any other text for that matter, that *cannot* die without entailing its utter dissolution as text. Like any author, the speaking parrot can live on forever because he lives off language as the written traces of memorized signs that can always be projected onto a future act of recognition and understanding.

The parrot, then, to the extent that he actually *says* something understandable, reproduces a recognizable text—"Polly want a cracker," or "May I have some lunch now?" or whatever—that has been committed to memory in order to become available in time to any number of readers: the uncle, the nephew, the lonely caretaker who now lives with him. For this reason, the parrot is a much more adequate figure for the nonfigurative nature of conventional writing than even the dog. The imprinted traces of the narrator's youth, which are only implied in the figure of the stuffed dog, ultimately manifest themselves in the printed pages of the "choice books, old friends," which are themselves introduced by way of the reference to the parrot that serves to link the paragraph of the dog to the paragraph of the book. But once the imprinted traces of language are actually written into these books, the text itself must testify to the fact that books are not merely silent witnesses to the narrator's past but, like the parrot, can always *talk back* to him as well in their own language. It turns out that the dog is man's best friend precisely because he is a silent partner. For once the parrot starts to speak, no matter how cheerful or polite he is about it, there is always the possibility of a confusion as to the origin, or "heart," of this voice of memory, and this deadly confusion is also marked in the parrot.[7]

Unlike the dog, the parrot not only recalls a subject's past by means of a purely accidental, metonymical proximity to his earlier experiences ("his heyday"). He also "brings to mind" (*fait penser à*) in a metaphorical manner the narrator's present activity as a writer *of* experience: "The parrot asked for lunch just as in his heyday, and looked at me with that round eye, bordered with a wrinkle-laden skin, that brings to mind *the experienced look of old men*" (261, emphasis added). At the very same moment that the parrot recites his text, the narrator is forced to note, to mark, to write, a potentially disruptive *resemblance* between the parrot and the man of experience, which in this chapter also means the entire tradition connecting Montaigne, Descartes, Rousseau, the uncle, and of course the narrator himself. If the parrot and his memorized text can remind us of the writer, then it is equally necessary that in some sense the writer of *Sylvie* can bring to mind the mechanical speech of the parrot. Without realizing it, when the narrator looks at the speaking parrot and *reads* "experience" in the wrinkled skin or texture of his eye, he is actually reading about himself and his own, potentially empty and mechanical, speech.[8] And in this

---

7. What is so threatening for the subject about those actresses "sans coeur" his uncle has warned him about, then, is *not* that they in fact have no heart—something relatively easy, and sometimes even desirable, to deal with. Rather, they are threatening precisely to the extent that in their case, as in the case of the parrot, and because their business necessitates an intimate relation to the faculty of memory, one can never determine with sufficient certainty whether they speak with heart or by heart. As such, they are the radical undoing of the possibility of maintaining such distinctions.

8. That the subject is "reading" the parrot is made clear by the interpretative act that allows him to link the parrot to the old man of experience by way of the metaphorical figure of the wizened eye. That reading is a process fundamentally dependent on memory as opposed to reflection or understanding is made clear by the passive role the subject is made to play in the causative *faire* of *faire penser à*. "Thinking" in this sense is the impersonal remembering of previously marked impressions (wrinkles) caused by a reading of more wrinkles, that is, a repetition and not a recollection. That what is remembered or thought here is mechanical through and through is demonstrated by the reader's failure to make the simple but crucial distinction in the figure between the

case, rather than consciously making use of the contingent signs of his past (*chiens empaillés, cygnes éployés, chimères fixées*) to signify a self endowed *with a heart* as well as a mind, the narrator of *Sylvie* would have merely traced out the unthinking process by which the self can claim to understand itself as a thinking subject only by relinquishing itself ahead of time to the wholly impersonal patterns of memorized language: a self *by heart*. "Have a heart," the dog seems to say, but the parrot is always there to answer back, "get stuffed."

The test of such an indecorous possibility can be decided only by a comprehensive reading of the text the self has left behind to make itself comprehensible. Is the metaphorical reference to the parrot-narrator itself merely contingent or is there in fact an entire level in *Sylvie* where the process of meaning can no longer be said to be under the control of a self-conscious subject who promises ultimate self-understanding, but is rather the result of random plays and mechanical effects? The answer will depend in large part on how one deals with such textual examples as the scene in the first chapter where the hero chances upon a newspaper that informs him of a recent and beneficial change in his fortune. The scene is crucial because it has to do with stock market quotations, the *inscribed* economy of loss and profit that organizes the narration, and in particular with the maturation of "foreign securities" that had long been neglected. At the very beginning of the text, then, we are already given a version of the figure for the hermeneutic and linguistic "detour" through which *Sylvie* in its entirety will subsequently attempt to pass. In this case the self must give itself over to some form of *foreign* papers or notation (forgetfulness, memorization, effaced fig-

---

"experience" of a parrot and the "experience" of a man like his uncle, or worse yet, between a parrot and Montaigne, Descartes, and Rousseau. The fact that this scene takes place before the ultimate anagnorisis of chapter 14 can never prevent the "experience" of the parrot in chapter 9 from later "bringing to mind" the experience of the mature narrator in whoever *reads* the wrinkled impressions of *Sylvie*. Thus, the "hermeneutic" circle of the text is broken at every point, since the hero is able to read the mechanical repetitions of the uncle only in the text of the parrot, the narrator able to read the printed nature of the hero only in the first thirteen chapters, the reader able to read the forgotten figure of the narrator only in *Sylvie*, and so on. This process of reading can never be closed off because it is based on a thinking as memory rather than as understanding. As such, it will never be possible for it to achieve enough distance from the textual effects it charts in order to read "itself" adequately. For a parallel reading of a self's reading itself into the text of another "romantic" bird, see Andrzej Warminski, "Missed Crossing: Wordsworth's Apocalypses," *MLN* 99 (December 1984), 983–1006.

ures) in order to come back to itself later with all the profits of understanding and identity, "les *titres étrangers* allaient être *reconnus . . . je* redevenais *riche*" (243, emphasis added). And a reader as astute as Georges Poulet has been able to identify this momentary interruption of the opening reverie on the theater as being the veritable source of the hero's whole itinerary in *Sylvie*.⁹

Yet we must not forget that the sudden hiatus produced by the stock market quotations of loss and gain, and thus the textual detour through which the reading of understanding in *Sylvie* must take place, is itself the result of a purely *mechanical* reading of a *speaking* text:

> While leaving [the theater], I passed by the reading room and looked *mechanically* [machinalement] at a newspaper. It was, *I think,* in order to see the stock market rates. Among the ruins of my fortune there was a fairly large sum of foreign securities. . . . The principal was already quoted very high; I was becoming rich again. . . .
> . . . Was this not just another illusion, a *printing* error [*une faute d'*impression] to mock me? But the other sheets *said* the same thing [*les autres feuilles* parlaient *de même*]. . . .
> . . . My eye skimmed vaguely over the newspaper I was still holding, where I read these two lines: "Fête du Bouquet provincial.—Tomorrow, the archers of Senlis will return the bouquet to the archers of Loisy." These words, very simple, reawoke in me a whole new series of *impressions* [*toute une nouvelle série d'*impressions]: it was a *memory* of the province long-since *forgotten,* a distant *echo* of the innocent festivals of youth. (243–44, emphasis added)

The self that speaks and writes like a parrot is also a kind of machine that *reads* "by heart"; the narrator can only surmise retrospectively— "It was, I think . . ."—that there was any subjective motivation whatsoever in the linguistic machinery that allows him to read the newspaper in the first place. And what he reads in such mechanical fashion, without knowing it, is eventually the foreign, because *imprinted* or memorized, "heart" of all his acts of self-understanding, that is, of all reading and writing.

The "printing error" (*faute d'impression*) referred to here is therefore *not* just the merely contingent one of a misquoted stock or bond. It is also and primarily the necessary error or wandering, the subjective

---

9. Georges Poulet, "Sylvie ou la pensée de Nerval," *Trois essais de mythologie romantique* (Paris: José Corti, 1966), 25–26, 34.

fault or lack *of* printing, the detour of writing or inscription in which the self forgets itself in order to read the speaking sheets of "his" memory. What all the other pages say equally well as the first is that they *are* printing; "the other sheets said the same thing [*les autres feuilles parlaient de même*]" says only that they are a machine of inscription that writes or forgets the "province" of nature and all other figures onto the space of a memory that remains forever foreign to the self and self-control of subjectivity. Such a memory can be retrieved or *reawakened* only by a repetitive reading of more mechanical printing, even if it is of the "simplest" of words: "These words, very simple, reawoke in me a whole new series of *impressions [toute une nouvelle série d'*impressions]: it was a *memory* of the province long-since *forgotten* . . ." (244, emphasis added).

This "waking" of the subject's memory by means of the very simple words of the newspaper is linked to the machine of writing in a double way. First, it is in the *printed words* that the subject's memory of natural and metaphorical figures has once and for all been deposited; the province of the double star Adrienne-Sylvie has long since been "forgotten" by the self so that he can thus become free to read these figures later in the foreign print of his memory. But even the consciously intended, or subjective, memory of the province that is mechanically awakened here *by* the printed characters turns out to be itself nothing but the mechanical repetition *of* printed characters it was supposed to replace. It is clear that what the subject means to awaken by way of the mechanical writing of his memory are the subjective impressions (feelings) of his youth. But what he actually produces at the level of printing, that is, at the level of the letters he must use to awaken the meaning his language is presumed to contain, are not the heartfelt impressions of a subject but the printed impressions (characters), or echo, of memorized letters. The most threatening printing error possible is the one that in fact takes place here and that arbitrarily allows the same letters (*i-m-p-r-e-s-s-i-o-n*) to refer to both the wholly mechanical process of writing and the supposedly subjective faculty of sentiment with which it is incompatible. The printing "error" that in the French idiom allows "printing" to wander on the same page into "impression" is not motivated by any self or self-conscious thought, as is verified by the self's inability to prevent this wholly random error of printing from invading his own subjective impressions. The "echo" that is unavoidably "awakened" here is the imprinted, and therefore mechanical, echo between "faute *d'impression*" and "nouvelle série *d'impressions*," which the narrator is then forced to misread as a "distant *echo* of the innocent festivals of youth" rather than the much less reassuring misprint of mechanical memory. Just as the chitchat of the parrot in chapter 9 made it impossible to determine whether the self spoke with heart or by heart, so the random errancy of the printing press in chapter 1 makes it impossible to determine whether reawakening the "heart of impressions" reveals a self or a machine.[10]

All of which brings us back to the final scene in which the narrator concludes his story by reporting the death of Adrienne through the quoted speech of Sylvie. The quotation marks around the last lines remind us once again that this, like the speech of the parrot and the stock market report as well as the rest of *Sylvie,* is a printed text that the self cites from memory. What is curious here is that the disabused narrator begins the citation with a colloquial expression that reintroduces the question of forgotten figures and their relation to the subject that uses them. Resuming the narration precisely at the point where the hermeneutical circle seems to have closed upon itself in the self's recognition that it will eventually be understood through the recollecting of the text just completed, the subject says, "I forgot to say that . . ." (273), and then goes on to quote himself, remembering what

---

10. E. S. Burt has drawn my attention to the "awakening" of even the so-called innocent impressions of youth thanks to a mechanical effect of the letter: the "or" that is arbitrarily detached from the name "Au*r*élie" weaves itself throughout the chapter until it culminates in the final memory traces of these "resonating" letters: "Ces mots, f*or*ts simples réveillèrent en moi toute une série de nouvelles impressions. . . . Le c*or* et le tambour résonnaient au loin . . . les jeunes filles tressaient des guirlandes et ass*or*tissaient, en chantant, des bouquets *or*nés de rubans . . . nous f*or*mions le c*or*tège avec nos arcs et nos flèches, nous déc*or*ant du titre de chevaliers,—sans savoir al*or*s que nous ne faisons que répéter" (244, emphasis added). Playing on Mallarmé's "Pitre châtié," we could call the repetitions of this "hilare *or* de symbole" another instance of the way Nerval prefigures symbolism's reinscription of the sonorous and aesthetic "impressions" of personal experience into a system of purely linguistic notation and value, like the impersonal monetary system of gold (*or*) that it names and disseminates throughout the text. And the fact that the text calls this moment an "awakening" is also far from being insignificant. For, if to awaken in Nerval is tantamount to recall the play of the letter, then, as Freud reminds us, it is also a form of sleep as well, namely, a *dream*. The concept of dream in Nerval, always reduced by commentators to a psychological or aesthetic state, is in fact a linguistic category, the "impressions" of language conceived as a system of notation rather than as sonorousness or meaning. Dream, for Nerval, and like memory, undoes the polarity between waking and sleeping: "l'épanchement du songe dans la vie réelle" must thus be read as the undecidable question of this poetic "or": "Do I wake or sleep?"

a sore subject for those who think they understand history and themselves as well. As what actually happens, as a text that has been written, the history that occurs in symbolism has little to do with the magic mirrors of correspondence we like to imagine between or within the sexes, between a subject and its self-understanding, or between an event and its cognition—except to show how such mirrors are in fact the stuff of delusion and madness. If *Sylvie* can be said to tell the story of how the literary symbol eventually finds its way into a historical clockworks, it does so by refusing to forget the necessarily mechanical mode that makes such a clock into a speaking face and hands that resemble anything but a self-enclosed human heart. *Sylvie* therefore teaches that actual history is the regular interruption—the inscribed reading and writing—of all of symbolism's figures. As such, it also always returns us to a wholly mechanical bird of poetry that marks out the passing of the hours without being able to tie them together by simply explaining or accounting for them. Like the cuckoo clock in this text, moreover, the history of symbolism can only begin all over again as the reinscription of the same moment it has always been without fully knowing it.[12] And the only thing that would be more insane than such a chanting bird, or *cygne éployé*, would be the deluded belief that we could forget all about it by learning to hear in its ticking a mere song of our own or someone else's distant past.

12. See the crucial question and answer formulated in the chapter called "Resolution": "What time is it? I did not have a watch. . . . I went down to the concierge's, where the cuckoo indicated one o'clock in the morning" (247–48). The nonsymmetrical and noncyclical nature of this temporal pattern finds its most condensed formulation in the sonnet "Artémis": "La Treizième revient. . . . C'est encor la première;/Et c'est toujours la seule,—ou c'est le seul moment," where the ellipses and dash serve to introduce repetitions that do not fully coincide with, and therefore cancel out or complete, what precedes them.

3 Beneath the Lace: Mallarmé, the State, and the Foundation of Letters

> The gowns of these worldly solemnities, such is fantasy itself, sometimes adventurous, bold and almost future, which sees the light of day through former habits. Whoever looks, can read there, blended with the satin, symptoms of a secret that is already revealing itself, beneath the gauze, beneath the tulle, or beneath the lace.
> —Stéphane Mallarmé, "La dernière mode"

Looked at through the prismatic lens of its critical reception, it seems indeed that there is something new to be glimpsed in Mallarmé's text these days. The conventional hemline of literary interpretation that for the first half or so of this century did such a good job of keeping a delicately aesthetic and hermetic oeuvre away from the prying gaze of coarser and more public questions like history, ideology, and politics seems now to be inching its way up, threatening to reveal in the process secrets of a potentially embarrassing and even scandalous nature.[1] The scandal here, though, and as always, lies in the revelation that what passes for the shockingly new and indecent has been there all along, in

---

1. See, among other recent treatments of Mallarmé, Julia Kristeva, *La Révolution du langage poétique* (Paris: Seuil, 1974); Jean-Luc Steinmetz, "Mallarmé, l'Histoire," *Centre International d'Etudes Poétiques* 165 (Jan.–Mar. 1985); Richard Terdiman, *Discourse/Counter-Discourse* (Ithaca: Cornell University Press, 1985); Vincent Kaufmann, *Le Livre et ses adresses* (Paris: Klincksieck, 1986); Ross Chambers, "An Address in the Country: Mallarmé and the Kinds of Literary Context," *French Forum* 11 (May 1986); Barbara Johnson, "Panama: Mallarmé and the Text of History," *A World of Difference* (Baltimore: Johns Hopkins University Press, 1987). The phantasm of an invasion, which is also potentially a defilement and defloration, is obliquely noted by Gardner Davies in his *mise à jour* of the critical bibliography: "the winds of Freudianism, structuralism, deconstructionism and other methodologies which it is sometimes difficult to identify clearly have swept across the vulnerable field of literary criticism, all of them originating in other disciplines." See "Divagations on Mallarmé Research," *French Studies* (January 1986), 4.

the mode of a symptomatic denial and cover-up. In Mallarmé's case, we do not have to wait for a history of reception to register the threat posed to literature's formal autonomy from some sort of worldly outside, for the threat was never far enough outside of the supposedly self-enclosed structures of his texts to begin with. For instance, it would hardly have been necessary in 1899 for Arthur Symons to attach that "subtle veil" to Mallarmé's writing in order to shield it from the desires and disturbances of what Symons called the outside world, if it were not already possible to make out, on the inside of the text and etched in negative as it were, the symptoms of social and critical upheavals powerful enough to rend any and all such veils of protection.

This kind of secret "future," already neatly referred to and anticipated by Mallarmé himself in *La dernière mode,* will of course finally break through the surface of his text in a much cruder form in the journalistic celebration of "Le camarade Mallarmé," as he was baptized in the pages of *L'Humanité* following the events of May 1968.[2] But rather than following a simply linear trajectory of discrete empirical events, the history of Mallarmé reception, leading from Symons's celebration of *l'art pour l'art* to J. P. Faye's symmetrical inversion of this well-known aesthetic slogan into a kind of *l'art pour tous,* constitutes a balanced dialectic of concealment and disclosure. Each of the successive stages in the interpretation of the textual enigma that is Mallarmé's writing can ultimately be shown to bring into relief whatever was only implicitly available or recognized in the others. And while it would be naive to ignore the very different ideological implications at stake in such positions, in the long run they continue to function side by side within the same closed system of clearly demarcated distinctions and choices.

Factional pressures and rhetoric aside, then, reducing Mallarmé's work to a simple polarity between formalism and reference, a private *poésie pure* versus a public *journalisme engagé,* and then seeking to privilege one pole over the other by means of a history of reception might be the least "historical" gesture conceivable. For such a gesture could only repeat in a preconscious, and therefore uncritical, mode a set of questions and tensions whose resistance to final resolution Mal-

2. See Arthur Symons, *The Symbolist Movement in Literature* (New York: Dutton, 1919), J. P. Faye, "Le camarade 'Mallarmé'" and "Mise au point," and Philippe Sollers, "'Camarade' et Camarade," in *L'Humanité,* September 12, 19, and October 10, 1969.

larmé himself identified as one of the principal conditions for a truly historical consciousness. Although he never seems to give up on the necessity of talking about language *as though* it were susceptible to a neat division between the textually self-reflexive and the historically referential, the possibility of actually separating language in this way into its constitutive elements always remained problematic within Mallarmé's own writing practice. We should therefore approach with extreme caution the practically expedient but theoretically questionable attempt to describe, divide, and choose between what may ultimately be the inextricably intertwined modes of poetic and political language. Such attempts appear in some of Mallarmé's prose texts as a mere dream or "desire" whose potential for disappointment and delusion would certainly not be attenuated by its being shared by an entire generation in "crisis"—a crisis, moreover, that is itself political as well as poetical. And as we know from a poem like "L'après-midi d'un faune" the crisis at issue—which is described there as taking place between the imagined and the real—can indeed lead to the committing of a tragic "crime." Such crimes of desire can be seen to result eventually in the inability or refusal to ask critically whether one is in fact talking about, much less participating in, a formalist or referential model of language, a fiction or a history.[3]

But when does a desire, which may start out as a mere poetical fiction, turn into an act that is political through and through? Certain texts by Mallarmé, not so distant in time and concern from "Crise de vers," though not so pathos-laden as "L'après-midi d'un faune," go so far as to suggest the inevitable collapse of any stable distinction between history (act) and poetry (fiction). As a consequence, they also seem to end up turning the first into a simple effect of the second. However, since they do so now in the mode of an absolute truth, they also seem to speak independently of any human desire or agency

3. The texts referred to here in shorthand, "Crise de vers" and "L'après-midi d'un faune," can be found in: Stéphane Mallarmé, *Oeuvres complètes,* ed. Henri Mondor and G. Jean-Aubry (Paris: Bibliothèque de la Pléiade, 1945), 368. All further references will be to this edition. The wish to classify is stated in "Crise de vers": "An undeniable desire of my time is to separate, in view of different assignments, the double status of the word, on the one hand raw or immediate, on the other essential." In "L'après-midi d'un faune," rather than face up to the dilemma posed by the relation fiction/history, which necessarily results from the earlier crime of having "divided the dishevelled tuft . . . that the gods kept so tightly tangled," the faun ultimately chooses to hide from this negative knowledge in the self-imposed numbness and forgetfulness of a simple dream (52–53).

whatsoever. Hence, they remain vulnerable to what continues to function as the easy dismissal of Mallarmé as a verbal contortionist, obscurantist, and political dreamer whose own desire would be not to recognize the actual political status of such aesthetic dreaming. It is true, for instance, that near the conclusion of "Sauvegarde," a short text ostensibly about the place of institutions within the State, in particular about the place of the Académie in France, Mallarmé proposes for consideration the following rather unconventional opinion: "Whereas social relations and their changing measurement strictly or loosely calculated, in view of governing, are a fiction, which is itself dependent on *belles-lettres*—because of their enigmatic or poetic principle—the duty of maintaining the book becomes imperative in an absolute sense" (420).[4] In effect, the proposition that social relationships and their determination are a "fiction" and its corollary that fiction is itself a branch of *belles-lettres* can always be considered variants of Mallarmé's oft-repeated and much ridiculed affirmation that "the whole world exists only to end up in a book" (378). In other words, it seems as if for Mallarmé, as for other oft-quoted but little-read theorists of literary language, *il n'y a pas de hors-texte*.

But are we so sure we know how to read what Mallarmé is saying about political institutions in his text on the Académie française? If it is true, as he says in no uncertain terms in "Sauvegarde," that we do not yet know what we mean when we use such empty terms as "Society"—not because there is nothing to society, but because the *term* is itself "hollow" (*creux*)—then how can we already be certain to understand what he means when he goes on to say that "social relations" are in fact dependent on what he then calls the "fiction" of *belles-lettres*? It may just turn out that Mallarmé's yoking of the social to the fictional/textual in this way cannot legitimately be used as an a priori exclusionary (or inclusionary) principle that would be tributary to what we commonly understand to be the readily calculable *inside* (or outside) of a text. Mallarmé's own writing, for example, may not function according to, or even in complicity with, the simple inside/outside oppositions and reversals at work between *l'art pour l'art* (Symons) and *l'art pour tous* (Faye). For to go on to say, as Mallarmé also does in

---

4. "Sauvegarde," which reflects on the necessity of the poetic or "essential" use of language, was itself first published in a topically journalistic, or "*brut*" context: it was one of the ten monthly contributions, *Variations sur un sujet*, that Mallarmé made to the popular *Revue Blanche* in 1895.

"Sauvegarde," that the calculation of changing social relationships—or history in the broadest sense conceivable—is a function of a poetic principle of writing that is in essence *"enigmatic"* is also to issue a *warning*. Whatever else this text does, it works as a potential "safeguard" against any facile assumptions about what such "enigmatic" textual principles might consist in and what they might leave out. It is precisely because the poetic principle that founds history and fiction remains for Mallarmé indeterminately "mysterious" and problematic that the actual task of the Académie becomes crucial in a sense that is every bit as historical and social as it is "literary." The Academy is itself a social text to the extent that it oversees the fundamental link between language and action that is instituted *by* the historical and the political as such, in what the text itself calls the "bond of Letters that transforms diverse activity [*l'effort divers*] into official splendor" (417).

"Sauvegarde," then, as its title suggests, is a text about how the social order of history can be protected and preserved only by way of watching over its link to letters, or to language. In the hyperbolic and ironic vocabulary of crisis he is so fond of using, Mallarmé describes a situation in which the entire nation of France, the organization of the State itself, is poised on the brink of disaster. Nothing less than "writing"—for Mallarmé the very essence of language—finds itself threatened by treasonous forces: "the Poet calls upon literary Supremacy to lift up a kind of [protective] wing when writing is threatened by high treason or a *coup d'état,* in this case, spiritual" (420). Writing, as what founds a State through the establishment of "the bond of Letters," needs the protection of a State institution, the Academy, against the nullity and mindlessness of factional commotion to which books are always susceptible: "Intellectual [book]bindings . . . open to the gratitude as well as to the jeers of whoever, waving madly about, for or against it's all the same, assumes the status of a stage actor, doubly sham" (419). What makes such factional commotion a mindless sham is not its concrete objectives and the means it employs to realize them. Rather, it is a sham to the extent that, whatever it actually accomplishes, it fails ultimately to recognize its own relation to the book and thus necessarily fails to account for its own "allegorical," or "fictional," dimension. The danger is that political activity, which is in part the product of an unknown and impersonal poetic principle, will be mistaken by ideologues for an autonomous and self-conscious actor or force: "Imagine a government so poorly informed as to mistake itself for the allegory from which it issues" (419). When this happens, the State loses all legitimacy by merely reproducing and even mythologizing the involuntary, and therefore mechanical, aspects of its operation, rather than giving itself the possibility of interrupting and transforming its movements by adopting a critical stance toward them.

Fortunately, for both such a government and its uninformed representatives, the State is provided with a safeguard, the Académie, the highest and most effective institution, since its sole responsibility is to writing: "The highest institution . . . the Academy . . . its aim . . . the bond of Letters . . . everything ends up with or comes back to writing. . . . Our foundation . . . was aware, stepped aside" (416, 417). At times of crisis, that is, whenever writing is being threatened—and as Mallarmé makes clear, this is always and everywhere possible—the poet or writer appeals to the institution of the Academy. But the Académie is not just the highest among many institutions. It is also the institution that becomes the highest only by stepping aside, by *removing* itself from the classificatory system of all other institutions. "The highest institution . . . the Academy," cannot be considered an institution like any other: "its aim, the bond of Letters, makes it totally unique. . . . Our foundation . . . was aware, stepped aside" (417).

Paradoxically, though, it is in cutting itself off from other institutions that the Academy can resist the State's tendency to ossify into mere institutionalization: "I picture to myself, occupying, like a sanctuary, the center of the comprehensive hemicycle, where it consents to sit only occasionally—while that other elite functions according to regular votes—the Academy, which would cut itself off [*se retrancherait*] or keep itself back for some special or rare act, who knows which" (417).[5] Describing the architectural appearance of one of France's most massive buildings, the Institut, Mallarmé suggests the difference the Academy can make by reinflecting the fixed space of its empirical

---

5. This exclusionary status can be taken to refer to the fact that the regular Thursday meetings, or *séances ordinaires,* of the Academy do not take place "sous la coupole" but down the hall in another room. But Mallarmé makes the concept of the Academy depend on its capacity to "cut itself off" in an absolute sense on behalf of writing, rather than on the day-to-day reality of the actual Académie française. We must distinguish between two possible referents that are not necessarily always compatible: the empirical one that can be found on the Quai de Conti and the one that can only be found or founded by reading and writing. The same proviso would apply to every term in Mallarmé's text, including reading and writing.

shape toward the question of writing. At the center of the comprehensive hemicycle, where the semicircular and horizontal curve of the Institut de France is completed and surmounted vertically by its hemispherical dome, there is the occasional "act" of writing operated by the Académie, rare, special, undetermined. Whatever this act is, it is prepared for only when the Academy manages to "cut itself off" or "keep itself back" from the regularized, architectual space in which other institutions are frozen.

The cut is also a kind of military maneuver, then, and the French verb *se retrancher* can also be read to suggest the protective measures that the Academy must take to *entrench* itself against its own placement within the Institut de France. As a single name that refers to a building and to the five national institutions that are housed there—the Académie, the Académie des inscriptions et belles lettres, the Académie des sciences, the Académie des beaux-arts, and the Académie des sciences morales et politiques—the "Institut de France" tends to cover over the "mysterious link" between "Society" and "letters" that is the special province of only one of its members, the Académie. Unlike the other sections, or classes, of the Institut—which can continue to function quite well without ever making the question of the Book a necessary occasion of their very existence—the Académie can come into being only by reflecting on the linguistic "enigma" that founds the possibility of the Institute in the first place—as a social "space" that ensures the link between the empirical (building) and the spiritual (science, political economy, moral and legal philosophy, literature, and fine art).[6] Thanks to the Académie and the strategic operation of the cut, though, the Book remains open. Because spirit itself, along with "its mark, books," is *always* open to the mindlessness of sham factions, the Academy, the protective wing of letters, must always be ready to move aside, to dig down and make the cut from such treasons in order to act on them effectively. The fact that the Academy operates *within* an institutional form it serves to disrupt—

6. The fact that the Academy has since the time of the Convention become one of five sections comprising the Institut de France changes nothing here. Regardless of the empirical status of an "institution" like the Academy, what will continue to distinguish it in a radical way from all other institutions, as well as from the concept of the institution itself, is the nature of its *possibility:* that is, the possibility of the book as the question of writing *as* writing prior to and after all other questions: "To wipe away the dust, of masterpieces, except by calling them to mind, remains an idle act. . . . Intellectual [book]bindings should end up by being notoriously so" (418, 419).

"The Academy, occupying the *center* of the comprehensive hemicycle"—also means that its defensive power of entrenchment is simultaneously an offensive act operated on the inside of what it cuts itself off from. The "wing" of the Academy is a sword as well as a shield. It serves to open and to protect the space of writing, of a dash, for instance, that separates the Académie from all the other, nonlinguistic, geometrical, and architectural institutions.

> The highest institution . . . the Academy.
> This dithyramb, why, in the form of a cupola— (416)

"Sous la coupole" ("Beneath the Dome") is a figure that refers to the Académie française by way of the architectural formality of the Institut de France, a state-run establishment in the center of which the Academy occasionally sits. Why does the Academy appear in such a form, such a figure? To ask this question, at least in the way that Mallarmé does in "Sauvegarde," is to reopen yet again the question of the Book. It is to cut through the superficial layers standing between us and the Institut, the Institution in general as well as the Institut de France, by reminding us of something essential: "wiping the dust off masterpieces . . . by bringing them to mind." What it brings to mind is that the Académie is itself nothing but a book of dithyrambs, that is, a book composed of poetic praises to the Book. An institution of the book to the book, the Académie is thus always under the cupola of the Institute as well as already outside of it. It is the one institution whose task is to question how the state and its institutions are made possible by the book. To ask why the Academy appears in the form of a state building is one way of making a cut from the actual palace. It cuts itself off by inscribing a trench or a dash that asks about writing and its inaugural relation to the state, as well as about the figures and diacritical marks that compose them. The cut and the sword are therefore, and in addition, a pen. When they inscribe these questions they also help accomplish the task of the Academy *as* book: that is, the perpetuation of writing as well as of the "social relations" that are founded by writing.

The reference to continuity, transmission, and posterity implicit here seems to lead to an inevitable misunderstanding in another direction, according to Mallarmé. The Academy, "this dithyramb," is not just a book in an immediate and unproblematic way. The Academy does not just occupy a building the way a meaning might be said, however misleadingly, to inhabit a text. It is also a select society made up of a prescribed number (forty) of living men (and now women), whose sole function is to speak for and to administer the rights and obligations of the Book. And the actual membership of the Académie française has an unfortunate habit of confusing the "eternal" nature of the writing it holds in trust and represents with its own human and social stature: "All the harm can be traced back to this quiproquo: one would like them to be immortal, whereas it is in fact the works" (418). Mallarmé is undoubtedly poking fun in this article at the French practice of referring to members of the Académie as "les immortels," an epithet that has not failed to take on a cynically humorous connotation given that holders of the "forty-first chair," that is, those never admitted to the Academy, include the likes of Descartes, Pascal, Rousseau, Diderot, Baudelaire, and Mallarmé himself. But in a more radical sense the task of preserving the book with the Academy's official seal—"*A l'immortalité*"—results simultaneously in a kind of death sentence pronounced on *any* given subject, no matter how deserving of the title he or she might be.

Thus, it is not just because of the vagaries of the selection process that many academicians have failed to achieve immortality. It is also the case that in order to enter the immortal Academy in the first place they must be forgotten as individuals. Their names will refer henceforward *only* to the Academy, that is, to writing and to the book. As long as they exercise their legitimate powers as trustees of the Book's perpetuity, academicians are not themselves to be considered as living human subjects, but are to be viewed only "from the perspective of eternity, abstract, general, vague, outside any familiarity" (419). Consequently, the book is also a tombstone: "That murmur, rather, that brings to the attention of the elect walled-up in the afterlife . . . the funeral slab of the dictionary" (418). The discussions that take place in the Academy make its members attentive not only to the reviewing and revising of the dictionary: two of their principal tasks. The dictionary they revise also signifies their nonexistence as subjects of desire in their own right; it signifies their immurement as subjects behind the tombstone of its "scattered words" (418). They tend to a book in which they necessarily read of their own encrypted death and preservation as caretakers of the book.

From the specific question of the Académie française, "Sauvegarde" leads along a circuitous itinerary that passes by way of the State, the Institution, Writing, and the Subject, before it eventually winds up by predicating all possible social relations, that is, history in general, on the survival and transmission of the Book. But what kind of economy of gain and loss is this, anyway? The fact that the safeguarding of this kind of writing, as overseen by the Académie, can be achieved only at the price of the living subject—"This Hall. . . . What business do the living have here?" (418)—should give us pause. For it is one thing to say that social relationships are a linguistic "fiction" that must be recognized as such. It is quite another to suggest that once this fiction and the book have been saved from sham factionalization, no room will remain in the social and institutional context for any living subject. In "Sauvegarde" itself, the mortal space of the Academy is survived in the body of the text only by the appearance of a miscellaneous collection of "specters," "shadows," and those who are entitled to enter the Academy only by "hav[ing] no head to fall." How could such phantomatic heroes inherit and perpetuate the writing of the book? And just what sort of social and historical force could they be expected to exert? Questions like these, which eventually threaten to cut open the complicated but otherwise comprehensive and comprehensible logic of "Sauvegarde," become especially acute in those texts where the problematic status, or "death," of the lyrical subject is itself the poetic principle as well as the theme—in such a text, for example, as the highly conventionalized and self-reflexive form of a Mallarmean sonnet.

> Une dentelle s'abolit
> Dans le doute du Jeu suprême
> A n'entr'ouvrir comme un blasphême
> Qu'absence éternelle de lit.
>
> Cet unanime blanc conflit
> D'une guirlande avec la même,
> Enfui contre la vitre blême
> Flotte plus qu'il n'ensevelit.
>
> Mais, chez qui du rêve se dore
> Tristement dort une mandore
> Au creux néant musicien

> Telle que vers quelque fenêtre
> Selon nul ventre que le sien,
> Filial on aurait pu naître.

The last in a series of three sonnets published in 1887 and grouped around the general theme of absence, negativity, and death, "Une dentelle"[7] is considered to be not only the most difficult and beautiful of the triptych, but also the one that progresses from a situation of almost total despair toward a state of qualified redemption for the poetic subject. The question that organizes these three poems is an essential feature of all Mallarmé's writing: How is it possible to transmit intellectual legacies and thereby secure a kind of immortality for the poet? "A l'immortalité" is thus not just the slogan of the Académie française but the essential problem that must be faced by all writers. The real motivation for the text called "Sauvegarde," it turns out, is Mallarmé's own project for the poetic administration of a national "fonds littéraire," an institutional means of overseeing "a treasure [fund, or foundation] left by the classics to their posterity" (418–19). This same concern orients the triptych, where the main theme becomes the challenge and responsibility that devolve on every poet to preserve what the first sonnet in the series, "Tout orgueil," calls "the immortal breath" or poetic spirit which the poet inherits from the language of his predecessors.

It matters little whether one chooses to identify the poetic legator referred to metaleptically in the first sonnet—"The ancient chamber of the heir"—as Baudelaire, Villiers, or even an earlier version of Mallarmé himself, since in any case it is the continuity of a lineage that is the problem here rather than the specificity of its individual links. What is at stake ultimately, named in the last line of "Une dentelle" as a hypothetical "filiation," is the philosophical concept of history, considered here as the minimal possibility of a *future*. For where there is no possibility of extending past experience into some kind of future knowledge, history must remain a truly empty term, devoid of any

---

7. *Oeuvres complètes*, 74. "A lace abolishes itself in the doubt of the supreme Game to half-open like a blasphemy only an eternal absence of bed. This unanimous white conflict of a guirland with the same, fled against the colorless pane of glass, floats more than it buries. But, by whoever is gilded by dream lies sadly sleeping a mandola with the hollow nothingness of music, such that toward some window, according to no belly but its own, filial one could have been born."

sense whatsoever. The question the sonnet addresses, and which is inherited and passed on from one text to another in Mallarmé's entire oeuvre, is whether a historic consciousness is possible beyond something like the death of the poetic subject. We should stipulate that the interruption at issue is something *like* death, that is, closer to a figural death than an empirical death. It is this figural death Mallarmé has in mind when he describes himself after his metaphysical crisis of the sixties as "perfectly dead," and it is with an interrogation of the figural status of death that the poem "Une dentelle" is concerned.

Whereas in "Sauvegarde" the negativity inherent in the preservation of the book is first met by way of the ironic reference to the unfounded pretensions of stodgy academicians, in the sonnet it becomes the very origin of poetry. In order for the poem to begin, something has to be destroyed, eliminated, or at least suspended. Not only has the title of the poem become a blank, but "Une dentelle" itself, which by default is the title as well as the incipit of the text, is dying here, in the process of being abolished. But can we be immediately sure just what this poetic "lace" is? To judge by the commentaries the opening has elicited, the threat to wholeness implied in the verb "s'abolit," which in the context points to an effacement, a pulling away or tearing of the lace, has contaminated not just the artisanal fabric used to adorn as well as to protect windows, beds, and other items, but the intelligibility of the reading process as well. It seems impossible, though necessary, to ascertain whether "dentelle" should be read as a curtain, a natural phenomenon (such as the clouds, the stars, or the sun), a bodily membrane, a self, or even a text. Edmund Wilson, a perspicacious if not overly thorough reader of Mallarmé, suggests in *Axel's Castle* a possible reason for the frustration (or elation) of all subsequent readers of this kind of poetry. He refers to figures like this lace as "metaphors detached from their subjects," with the result that "one has to guess what the images are being applied to."[8]

For Wilson, such metaphors are a sign of the "confusion," even the "insanity," of symbolist poetics, which tears figures from their referents and then fuses them back together willy-nilly without any regard for their natural order. But rather than immediately follow Wilson, as he guesses about the kind of referent to which the metaphors have been

---

8. Edmund Wilson, *Axel's Castle* (New York: Norton 1959), 21. Further references appear in the text.

reattached, we ought first to follow out Mallarmé's thematization of the abolition, detachment, or tear that befalls the figure of the lace in the movement of the poem. Before we ask what the figure of the lace refers to, we must take into account the possibility that it is the capacity of figures to refer unproblematically that is being abolished or torn in Mallarme's writing. It may be that "une dentelle" is not just a figure among others that refers to something else in particular, but also the proper name for Mallarmé's text, "Une dentelle," in which poetic language undoes its own pretension ("s'abolit") to provide a stable ground for the relation of figure to referent.[9]

What is dying in this sonnet, then, is to some extent the received idea of the status of metaphoric language within poetry. "La dentelle," one of the tradition's commonest figures for poetic textuality, is itself passed on directly to Mallarmé by Nerval, among other predecessors. But if this is a poem about continuity and heirs, then what tradition is being preserved and inherited in the place of the torn lace? Is Mallarmé's poem inadvertently abolishing the poetic tradition it inherits instead of preserving it as it ought to? Or is it rather inheriting this tradition only insofar as it manages to preserve poetry *as* the tearing of the poetic figure away from determined reference? And what would it mean to preserve and transmit language as the site of a kind of figural cut or tear, that is, a cut that, because it is merely figural with respect to the actual lace, can indeed become a literal cut with respect to our ability to determine with certitude the crucial link between figure and referent? One definition of symbolism as it is passed down from Nerval and rearticulated in this exemplary symbolist text by Mallarmé would thus be: the literary inheritance and interrogation of a genetic and metaphoric transmission of poetic language. What dies in Mallarmé's symbolism in order to be critically examined by it is the unproblematical link between a metaphor and its subject or object, or between a text and its eventual reading and understanding. Thus, the "fallen trophies" mentioned in "Tout orgueil," the first sonnet of the triptych, and which decorate the "ancient chamber of the heir," also name symbolism as a collection of lifeless *tropes*. That is, symbolism is composed of texts that narrate the "fall" and detachment of metaphors

---

9. For a cogent and meticulous reading of the way the poem refers constantly to the uncertain status of its own power to refer, see Hans-Jost Frey, "Zweifel und Fiktion," *Studien über das Reden der Dichter* (Munich: Wilhelm Fink, 1986), 46–50.

from their subjects—among which can be counted the fall of the common metaphor of symbolism itself as the historical period that links the corpus of romanticism to our own twentieth-century consciousness.

What is the effect of such a poetic fall? The linguistic negativity, fall, or death, which becomes an issue in the lace of the first line of "Une dentelle," is then localized in the second line of the sonnet by the reference to a curious form of "doubt": "une dentelle s'abolit dans le *doute*." But in this poem, writing is both the lace *and* the doubt, both the figure and its destruction. It is first the "lace" that contains the implicit question of the relation of figure to referent, and then the "doubt" that becomes the site where this question is made explicit in the destructive act of a tear. Writing is both figure and the place in which the figure is undone, the self-obliterating relation between the lace and the doubt. It is here—where the interrogation or "doubt" about what writing does to itself as figure or "lace" is carried to its extreme—that the lyric poem radicalizes the journalistic report of "Sauvegarde." In "Sauvegarde" the threat to writing that is being parried by an institution like the Académie is considered as coming to and acting on writing from without. But in "Une dentelle" the doubt produced in writing itself calls into question the survival of what the poem was written to perpetuate. Mallarmé's triptych thus wonders how far it is possible to preserve and transmit the originary tear or cut that determines the social and fictional fabric of language. Who or what is left to inherit when something like the institution of writing, "that fold of somber *lace,* which contains the infinite" (370), tears itself open in the very act of its genesis and retransmission?

The same problem is posed to dramatic effect in another text about literary heritage, *La musique et les lettres,* again in the vocabulary of crisis: "Storm, luminous cleansing; and in upheavals, due wholly to (the) generation, recent, the act of writing scrutinized itself to its very foundation . . . to the point, I would say, of wanting to know if there is any place left for writing" (645). The meaning of the formulation depends on how one reads what Mallarmé refers to as the *cause* of these stormy upheavals, "la génération, récente." Is the cause the very act of generation, production in its most recent manifestation, or is it merely the latest group of contemporaneous individuals who share a given attribute? Mallarmé's phrase can be read to mean either that critical self-scrutiny is a characteristic of the turbulent new generation of (symbolist) writers, or that writing is itself the initiatory storm in which the phenomenon of generation as critical production always takes place. Indeed, it must be read in both ways at once, since what distinguishes the recent generation of writers Mallarmé is talking about is in fact their capacity to bring about, or *generate,* the question of how writing is actually produced. What is odd here, though, is that the condition of possibility of the "generation" of writing is simultaneously unsettled by its own critical examination and is thus threatened by extinction at the moment of its inception. Again, who or what is left for writing after writing generates itself by putting itself into question? The question is asked once more and answered later in the same essay. After the storm, after the explosion, Mallarmé asks, "What is the point?" to which he answers, "A game" (647). So too, in "Une dentelle," the mutually exclusive relationship of the "lace" and the "doubt" becomes the pivotal space in which a certain kind of game is played out: "le Jeu suprême."

The game, though, is enigmatic. On the one hand, it plays for "supreme" stakes, life and death. On the other hand, as mere game or play, it risks going nowhere, remaining only diversion and diversionary. The question "What is the point?" can just as easily be read as a display of frustration as a genuine inquiry. And this question is worked out in "Une dentelle" by developing the implicit tension in the term "generation." For although the sonnet ends with a reference to birth or genesis, this birth seems destined to remain only a hypothetical game, "Filial on aurait pu naître." The term "generation," of course, as well as corollary terms like "conception" and "birth," establishes a metaphorical system in which intelligible activities of the mind, like poetry making, are understood by analogy to empirical sciences such as biology. The question at this point is not whether this figural system is legitimate, for this is the only system available to us for "conceiving" of thought, but rather whether there are elements within the system itself that disrupt it beyond recognition. In other words, is anything introduced by the reference to "conception" that cannot be reassimilated to the literal (biological) or figurative (intelligible) meanings of birth? Should this be the case, then such elements would only serve to "detach" the genetic figure from its intended meanings as creativity and "production." Such a possibility determines the way in which commentators have reacted to an erotic dimension of the poem, implicit in the "game" of line 2 and the "bed" of line 4. The fact that this bed is named as "eternally absent" is most often taken by the critics as confirmation of the successful passage in the poem from the literal, sensuous locale of an erotic game to an ethereal "conception" of poetry's supreme play.[10]

The paraphrastic commentary of the sonnet given by C.F. MacIntyre, one of its English translators, provides a crude though representative example of this sort of interpretation:

> A pair of lace curtains is blown by a breeze, wreathing around each other like lovers. There is no bed, or rather, there is an eternal absence of bed, but you can't stop two amorous curtains, not in a Mallarméan huddle, you can't! The supreme game probably refers to poetry. Now, the sestet: Here broods the dreamy poet, with his *mandore,* his instrument for making poetry, sorrowfully, in a silence that is empty. Now then, he seems to be thinking, if I could only impregnate, fertilize by parthenogenesis, as it were, myself, I could conceive, beget, sire and mother, a son of my own, a poem. Line 12 seems to mean that if he alone could do what the curtains are doing by the pane, the pane meaning also the source of light and creation, why, then he would be self-sufficient and happy.[11]

While we might feel an immediate satisfaction or disappointment in having an elusively hermetic sonnet translated into such an easily comprehensible, because utterly banal, domestic scene, we should not remain oblivious to the somewhat more interesting vacillation between the game's erotic and poetic valences. The stark transition from the bedroom curtains' unstoppable "amorous huddle" and the commentator's enthusiastically ejaculative "you can't!" to the flat assertion "the supreme game probably refers to poetry" is so wholly unprepared that one cannot help wondering why the two references are themselves not allowed to come together. Why keep the erotic and the poetic "conceptions" apart unless, and perhaps in the face of some unnamed threat, it is in order to avoid identifying the initial suggestiveness of the poem's "supreme Game" simultaneously with *both* poetic and amorous ac-

---

10. An interpretation made plausible by reading Mallarmé's own question as a statement of principles: "What good would be the marvel of transposing a natural fact ["le lit," for instance] into its near vibratory disappearance according to the play of the letter [*le jeu de la parole*], though, if it were not in order to derive from it, without the nuisance of a near or concrete reminder, the pure notion" (368).

11. C. F. MacIntyre, *Stéphane Mallarmé: Selected Poems* (Berkeley: University of California Press, 1957), 158.

tivity? Just as with the torn lace earlier, it is not possible to order the levels of meaning in the figure (in this case, poetic first, erotic second) without ignoring what the poem itself is doing with the figure's capacity to mean. The "Jeu" may not just be a figure that refers to both a poetic and an erotic meaning but an actual contest, or "Jeu," *between* two heterogeneous models of poetic language, each of which threatens to interrupt the meaning of the other.

MacIntyre's hesitation in this regard thus becomes paradigmatic for any interpretation of the text. It traces out and then elides a threat specific to the poem's intelligibility. By bringing the game of the solitary poet into contact with the playful huddling of amorous curtains, the reading necessarily opens the door, or at least a window, to all sorts of fantastic shapes and figures, in short, to the "blasphème" mentioned in line 3. This "blasphemy," whatever else it refers to, would also function as a decisive lack of reverence with respect to the poem's entire program of aesthetic conception.[12] For once the erotic component of the "Jeu" in line 2 becomes apparent, it then threatens to extend itself uncontrollably throughout the text and *distract* us from ever coming back to and understanding the poem's supposed lesson about the creative potential of poetic writing. Rather than providing a vehicle for meaning that leads smoothly from literal conception to poetic birth, the erotic aspect of the game may actually deflect the reading from its intended destination and take it in a completely different direction. And without the caution of a transcendental foundation or guarantor of sense, like God and its correlates light and poetry, this is always possible in reading the poem.

The sex in this text, though, is not just a figure for an empirical act that diverts our attention, even if only temporarily, from the serious business of poetry. As is evident in all commentaries on the poem, it is always possible within the tropological system of exchanges that is presupposed to function in the text to reunite biological productivity

---

12. Emilie Noulet, one of Mallarmé's earliest serious readers, cousels against falling into such an impious "trap": in order to make sense of the poem, the reader must resist the erotic temptation here and refer the "Jeu" uniquely to "God, generator of light and life." See *Vingt poèmes de Stéphane Mallarmé* (Genève: Librairie Droz, 1967), 158. R. G. Cohn performs a similar interpretative gesture by tracing all figural registers back to the originary and procreative "light of the sun" (208–9). Leo Bersani does not seem to see what difference such a question would make, and suggests we be satisfied to remain "in the intervals between such alternatives." See Leo Bersani, *The Death of Stéphane Mallarmé* (Cambridge: Cambridge University Press, 1982), 71.

with poetic creativity through the metaphorical figure of "conception." Beyond this system, though, sex is also a subsidiary figure for what, in poetic language considered as an infinite "Jeu" between two different figural modes, ultimately *contests* the figure's own capacity to complete the meaningful link or union between biological and intelligible conception. There is always something a bit kinky about this kind of sex, since by inflecting, tearing, or perforating the final state of balance and equilibrium proper to a unified figural system, it cannot keep itself from actually reopening the question of figure and referent it was meant to fulfill and thus cover up altogether.

In this poem, for instance, there is also the enigma of a game that can be played by one or two. How do we know, in fact, that the game is composed of a "pair" of two *different* curtains? "*Une* dentelle s'abolit," in the opening stanza, and the second stanza explicitly says, "Cet *unanime* blanc conflit / D'*une* guirlande avec *la même*." The erotic "huddle" might have only *one* player, and in this case, the number one would merely relate to itself specularly in order to constitute itself as a desirable "pair." "Conception," literal or metaphorical, never has to become an issue here. The opening scene, a kind of voyeuristic looking in through the lace curtain on the bedroom window—perhaps even onto Hérodiade's absent but imagined and violently desired bed—can become as graphic or pornographic as one wishes. When all is said and done, though, it must be admitted that in Mallarmé the treatment of the erotic remains far from being a simple hymn to the marriage bed, along with its attendant connotations of legitimacy and progeny.

Allowing the "one" in "*Une* dentelle" and "*unanime* blanc conflit" to carry the weight of the lopsidedly erotic figure can therefore also point up the "onanime," or onanistic, aspect of the game. What remains impossible to determine finally is whether there is *more* than one solitary player involved in the onanistic scene, a provocative alternative that "floats" somewhere between the lines juxtaposing "blanc *con*flit" to "*con*tre la *vit*re blême." And such an alternative goes a long way toward unsettling any additive or integrative mathematical principle between "one" and "two," since it is always possible to add another "one" in this kind of series without for all that making any difference to a more fundamental principle of dispersion. It may not be possible, then, to take this game as a synthesizing figure for what we ordinarily understand to be poetic conception, generation, or creativity. What is most shockingly ill-conceived and illegitimate in following the erotic game through the solitary "*c-o-n*-s" and "*v-i-t*-s" of the text, of course, turns out to be the free "play" of the signifier. And this radically linguistic "Jeu" does in fact exceed the conventional metaphorical pattern of biological and poetic conception of meaning by focusing attention on detached letters whose arbitrary power to signify cannot be reduced to a binary model of physical entities and conceptual ideas.

The game, then, is double, and duplicitously double at that. On the one hand, it is the articulation of the double aspect of "conception" with the figural passage from natural genesis to poetic creativity. According to a classical conception of metaphor, a nonphenomenal activity of the mind manifests itself by analogical reference to the empirical world. In this way, poetic production uses genetic reproduction ("le lit") to make itself more concrete for the understanding, though in such a way as to differentiate itself from the merely empirical in which it must appear—hence, the privative "*absence* de lit." On the other hand, the game is also that supplementary aspect of the figure—the erotic elements that do not necessarily contribute to reproduction, or the free play of the signifier, for instance—that can always get out of hand and threaten to subvert or pervert the projected "conception" into the absolute loss of "misconception" and insignificance. There is something in the game's own promise of a passage, transmission, or legacy from natural to poetic understanding that threatens to stand in the way and block access to the very thing that it promises. Without the active presence of such a risk, of course, the game could hardly be called "supreme" in the first place.

It is this element of risk that can also be remarked in the syntactic position of the "doubt" in the sonnet. The "doubt" must now be understood to touch not only upon the figure of the lace given in line 1 but also upon the *outcome* of the supreme game referred to in line 2. In terms of the temporal thematics of transmission and legacy at work in this sonnet (as well as in "Sauvegarde"), the doubt always relates to a historical "past" as well as to a kind of undisclosed "future." The writing that interrogates the legitimacy of any received "figure" also leaves open to question the outcome for history of putting this interrogation into play. Mallarmé poses the same question with regard to the possibility of a future for his (past) friendship with the dead Villiers de l'Isle-Adam: "Do we know what it means to write? . . . [T]his senseless *game* of *writing* consists in undertaking, by virtue of a *doubt*, the task of recreating everything in order to verify that *one is* where one ought to be (since, allow me to express this apprehension, there remains an *uncertainty*)" (481, emphasis added). In the same essay, Mallarmé says of himself what he says elsewhere of the Academy: "whoever writes cuts himself off [*se retranche*]." And the writer is in fact cut off from *everything,* for it is a cutting-off that is "*intégral,*" Mallarmé adds.

Through the operation of "doubt," the writer is removed from all that has been previously instituted and is now presumed natural in order to "recreate" it. That this operation of the cut of doubt is indeed related to a past as well as to a future is made clear in the essay on Villiers. The "doubt" must play over the entire natural and instituted world already given in order to become actual writing, claims Mallarmé. But it is also, in its very "uncertainty" about its own outcome as writing, a new form of doubt concerning the world of the subject that is yet to be determined in the wake of such a process. In the more compressed form of "Une dentelle," the double instability and uncertainty of writing is brought out effectively by the self-splitting syntax in line 2, the locus of the "doute *du* Jeu suprême." Here the grammar, the formalized rules of the game, contribute to produce a structure that is simultaneously retrospective and proleptic. This is a kind of writing that interrogates the past it has inherited, "a lace," in order to open up an unpredictable future in its tearing. For, grammatically speaking, the genitive link between the doubt and the game, "le doute *du* Jeu," can move in either direction. It can either be subjective and retrospective— the doubt belongs to and is controlled by the game of writing: "the supreme Game's doubt abolishes a lace." Or it can be objective and proleptic—the status and outcome of writing is what is cast into doubt: "a lace is rent in the doubt about the supreme Game."

What Mallarmé calls writing, the "recreation" of an uncertain future thanks to a process of "doubt" with respect to the past, is therefore essentially *historical* in nature. It is historical not in the same sense that ordinary empirical events are contingently historical by dint of their mere happening but in the deeper sense that, by instituting an interrogative "cut" into the past, by thus subjecting all of its figures to doubt and rearticulation, writing is the condition of possibility for history to be conceived as a future understanding that could only be opened by critical thought. "Le doute du Jeu suprême" is thus philosophical in nature and Cartesian in structure; it is a formalized activity of methodical doubt that reflects on everything that can be made subject to it, including itself *as* the formal activity (or game) of thought.

As such it can also be understood to be the necessary precondition of any genuinely dialectical development of the mind. Georges Poulet's understanding of Mallarmé in fact moves in this direction when, in speaking of his poetic procedure, he says, "It is the act of negation through which one constitutes one's existence and thought. The Mallarmean operation is thus comparable to 'the internal operation of Descartes.' It is *ultra-Cartesian*."[13] Poulet is commenting on *Igitur* and the narrative struggle it recounts with a philosophical heritage that ends in a form of mental suicide. But "Une dentelle" is not so far from the reflections of *Igitur,* and it holds as well for the sonnet that the nature of doubt is such that it must inevitably turn back on itself to become the doubt *about* the future of writing and thought itself. What makes Mallarmé's procedure "*ultra*"-Cartesian in Poulet's terms, moreover, is the supreme risk it must take by putting its own rules into doubt. For once the connection with philosophical suicide has been made, it becomes impossible not to read the "Jeu" as also containing the first-person pronoun, *je* or *cogito*. But the Cartesian certitude about doubt commonly attributed to Descartes is not simply taken over and adopted by Mallarmé in this sonnet.

Philosophical doubt remains sheltered from the most radical of threats as long it leaves intact the formal structure of the "Jeu," the stable activity of thought that unconditionally links the (doubting) consciousness to a subject. Mallarmé's concept of writing, on the other hand, asks whether this relation between consciousness and self is itself not perhaps a mere game. Writing, for Mallarmé, is a form of reflexive negativity so far-reaching that after allowing all else to be put into doubt it even allows for doubting thought's (or the game's) own "grammar," the formal conditions of the self to come into being *as* doubt. For Mallarmé, that amounts to doubting doubt, to doubting the game and fabric of thought into oblivion, and to opening out onto the doubtful future of one's "own" situation—hence Mallarmé's formulation in the essay on Villiers: "where one ought to be . . . remains an uncertainty."

13. Georges Poulet, *Études sur le temps humain 2: La distance intérieure* (Paris: Rocher, 1952), 333.

This doubt would be a truly "hyperbolic" or supreme doubt. And it can be said to operate in Mallarmé's text wherever the technical aspects of the grammar or syntax, which make the meaning possible, are in themselves insufficient to determine the meaning of the poem's figures, which make the game worth playing. Whether the "Jeu" refers to a philosophically serious operation of reflection (the thinking subject) or to an empirical version of self-reflection devoid of any higher meaning (represented thematically by an act of the not-so-philosophical body), the grammatical ambiguity of the connective "du" casts into doubt the autonomy of the subject referred to. It is not just that the "Jeu suprême" can refer, as any number of critics have noted, to *both* poetic and erotic "creativity." As we have seen, *creativity* is itself a loaded term that gives the game away in advance. For it subjects both dimensions of the text to a specular figure of aesthetic *and* philosophical meaning as a metaphorical model of conception and birth. Rather, in being able to "recreate" nongenetically—that is, from a linguistic model whose operations are no longer dependent on a merely physical nor yet wholly intelligible logic—the "creativity" specific to both thought and the natural world, the free play in writing *necessarily* unsettles the ability of its own grammar to determine once and for all a meaningful reference to either.

Once we notice how the uncertain grammar affects the subjective/objective status of the all-important game, the "Jeu," it is difficult not to ask whether the real conflict, rather than being between the empirical and the thinking subject, is not between the subject as meaning (objectively empirical or subjectively thoughtful) and the subject as writing (the meaningless free play of the *je* as it is constituted in the purely formal rules of the "Jeu"). By making it impossible to decide on how to read the grammatical status of the genitive, Mallarmé's writing also runs the supreme risk of producing an absolutely empty, insane figure—"this senseless game [*jeu*] of writing."

The most effective way of parrying the threat posed by writing's hyperbolic doubt is by treating the radical openness of its outcome as though it could itself be conceived, known, and represented in advance. This would amount to anticipating it as a moment within a larger cognitive process, a moment that, for all intents and purposes, would have already taken place in thought for thought rather than one that remains to be decided. In order to state with any assurance that the text is indeed "about" writing, for example, it is logically necessary to presuppose a discursive perspective or vantage point *beyond* the moment of its own definitional uncertainty. Only from such a perspective would it make sense to thematize writing as the subject of the questions at issue here. "Nothing will have taken place but the place" is the way *Un coup de dés* will have dealt with and resolved in advance the same dilemma of writing's supreme risk. By anticipating a minimal place of intelligible enunciation as the final result of a kind of worst-case scenario for thought, thought's own failure still becomes available to the understanding. When all else fails, one can always try to succeed in telling the story of the failure itself, "if only to disperse the empty act" (*Coup de dés,* 475).[14]

In the essay on Villiers, precisely as a means to shelter the writing subject from the risk of falling prey to an unthinkable "dupery bordering on suicide," Mallarmé will make reference to a mode of writing that would recuperate writing's open-ended risk. In order to pass beyond the constitutive doubt that makes it possible in the first place, writing attempts to recreate and transmit *in advance* the knowledge of the open-endedness of its own operation. It does so through the proleptic reconstructions of theater: "One by one, each one of our conceits, to bring them forth, in their anteriority and to see" (481). Writing is capable not only of creation and production but of bringing anything into being as though it had already taken place, as though its remaking of the world were only a new form of *representation*. As such, whatever writing brings forth for the first time can already be viewed as though it were being recreated in its *anteriority*. By treating the doubt of writing as though it too could be made visible, by bringing forth a sequential representation that would include retelling the past of even that which ultimately abolishes all sequence, writing would attempt to hide from its own dubious future.

In "Une dentelle" this perspective is adopted in the theatrical representation of writing as a play or a game, and it is organized around the poles of light and dark, the sun and the night, knowledge and nonknowledge. Writing, "that spot of ink related to the sublime night," may be what threatens to blacken or "abolish" the everyday world of minds and bodies. But it still plays itself out, at least at the beginning of the poem, on a visual, theatrical, and intelligible stage presided over

---

14. That the "acte vide" would in this way be reduced to a mere moment that could be recuperated by narrating it retrospectively, or, on the contrary, that such a "dispersion" would serve only to disseminate the void of the act along every point of the textual line, remains to be established by a more detailed reading of the text.

by the light of a rising and setting sun of cognition, similar, in fact, to the "private theater" with which Nerval's *Sylvie* begins. The curtain goes up—"une dentelle s'abolit"—to reveal a scene that is accessible to the eye of the spectator through the picture window of the theater. What the spectator gets to see in "Une dentelle" is no ordinary play, of course. In Mallarmé's theater it becomes the dawning light of philosophical reflection as it is made manifest in the Mallarmean concept of writing. Reperforming what he calls elsewhere "the internal operation for instance of Descartes . . . joining theater and philosophy" ("Crayonné au théâtre," 319), Mallarmé's sonnet attempts to represent the philosophical dilemma of recreating the whole world through the unpredictable play of writing. The main character here is writing itself. What it acts out for all to see is the play of doubt as it grapples with and contests the world as we know it. This world put into doubt at the beginning of the sonnet includes the natural light of the sun as well as the cognitive stability of all those philosophical concepts, such as conception and birth, that use the solar system as a model. The Mallarmean theater, through its own step-by-step representation of writing as though it were a character in a play that could be staged retrospectively, seeks to overcome the radical destruction of the determinate and determinable representation that is involved in writing.

In writing conceived of as theater, even the destruction of sequence and intelligibility is susceptible to being anticipated and represented sequentially, "one by one," in a visible and proleptically intelligible order. In a first step of reading the sonnet, the thought that moves out to meet and transform the world through writing seems to destroy all solid entities in order to produce an intelligible figure of itself as the "absence éternelle de lit." In a second, more radical move in the same process, the negativity of the thought can be turned back on its own figures to ask whether the thinking subject is not a mere formal game, produced blasphemously by the free play of writing and devoid of any further meaning. The resulting inability to decide on the status of thought can be represented as a stalemated agon. On the one side is the single-minded introspection that deprives itself of the warmth of the bed, and on the other the onanistically self-indulgent play that single-handedly reduces the poem to pure eroticism. This "blanc conflit" is then depicted sequentially in the theater as the alternating movements of a floating curtain. As such, however, the representation cannot avoid putting into play an aspect of figuration that necessarily enacts or recreates the undecidable openness of its own status as representation. The writing of the theater does this by marking the place of sequential articulation in the poem, the linking genitive in "le doute *du* Jeu suprême," as being itself undecidable by means of any sequential logic, or grammar. Thus, it also prepares the way for the undoing of the semantic determination of a thinking (and feeling) subject in the play of the key word "*Je*u." For, unlike the floating of a curtain, whose movements can be brought to light one by one, the crucial relation between writing as figure and writing as the destruction of figure cannot be reduced to a linear sequence. The priority of the "doute" over the "Jeu," as well as the relation between the self as self-conscious doubt and the self as formal game, is *simultaneously* necessary and impossible to decipher in the actual writing out, rather than the aesthetic representation, of the poem.

As a consequence, the figure of the bed, glimmering eternally in the half-light of the first stanza's conflict between consciousness and sensuality, becomes infinitely more blasphemous when it contests both orders of experience by shading into the uncertain status of the three letters "*l-i-t*" that return to haunt the rhyming words of the second stanza, "conflit" and "n'ensevelit." These letters, in fact, can tell us a great deal about what Mallarmé's "doute du Jeu suprême" does to both the world of sensuous reality and the movement of thought. The wholly graphic, textual nature of the problematic "bed" that is inscribed in certain syllables of the second stanza suggests that writing neither preserves the world naturally, as a simple perception, nor does away with it conceptually through the sheer annihilating power of the mind. Rather, it operates otherwise, through the "play" of letters, *l, i, t,* for instance, that are neither merely empirical nor conceptual, but infinitely suggestive of both at once. As typographical markings, these letters interrupt, disrupt, and keep at a certain distance both the natural, given order of things and the logical transformation of this order into a systematic form of thought. The linguistic disruption is never allowed to become a total destruction and erasure of what it puts aside, moreover, since it also *marks* the interruption it enacts. In so doing it reserves a certain space, a blank, for that world and its transformation into thought, however distanced, deflected, or indirect it may be.

The nature and outcome of the ensuing linguistic relationship between the mind and the world now become the focus of the poem's unresolved question. Because it is written rather than perceived or thought, the "eternal absence of bed" cannot be negated as easily as the natural world or the thinking subject. At least, not without leaving a trace or remainder of its letters. Thus, Mallarmé merely points toward its disappearance in the highly qualified, blinking movement of the French verb *entrouvrir*. *Entrouvrir* means "to half-open," and in this poem the figure of the lacework opens only enough to leave a space. What are thus left to glimpse are an empirical world that cannot ever be done dying or disappearing and a world of conceptual thought that remains unconditionally deferred or postponed. In Mallarmé's "world," lace is thus neither opening nor closing, but a kind of written, typographical suspension of both that hovers *between*, or *entre*. Lace never quite becomes the space of a fully defined and therefore *closed* opening, *ouverture*, much as the hovering apostrophe in *entr'ouvrir*, which qualifies it, marks the place of the abolished letter *e* in the French verb *entr(e)ouvrir*. And it is this mark of the figure's erasure that finally *addresses*, apostrophizes, or summons the very bed which the theatrical scene describes as eternally absent. The question of the "bed" and the entire figural world contained within it returns to haunt the second stanza by way of its written trace in words like "con*flit*" and "enseve*lit*." Such a trace—which summons in an altered state precisely what had been cast into the most radical doubt—should make us careful not to restrict the "blanc conflit" between meaning and nonmeaning to itself mean *only* a uselessly meaningless or sterile form of playful activity in the text. It ought rather to be read here as a supplementary figure for the as-yet-blank, or white, spaces that are opened by and between the play of the letters. In such blanks the undecidable question of the poem's ultimate status, and thus of its transmission and literary legacy, is suspended rather than merely destroyed, "ce conflit . . . flotte plus qu'il n'ensevelit."[15]

The fact that the poem doesn't end there, however, reveals how the pressure to move outside this intolerable suspension or blank of the future works in turn to suspend its own undecidability at the very moment it is named as such. For everything that holds for the quatrains seems to change in the tercets, where the immanent possibility of change is signaled by the conjunctive "Mais," a pivotal term that

15. For a comprehensive reading of the nonnegative, suspensive character of the mark, the remark, the opening, the veil, the blank between the letters, and the supplement of Mallarmé's "writing in white," see Jacques Derrida, "La double séance," *La dissémination* (Paris: Seuil, 1972).

opposes what follows to what precedes. By treating the undecidability of the quatrains as though it were a preliminary negativity that could itself eventually be negated, the oppositional logic of the "Mais" programs a reading of the tercets that would stress by contrast their own positivity. The tercets seem to balance the indecision of the quatrains through the introduction of a symmetrical set of opposing forces, this time valorized in a positive way. The absent bed in the first stanza appears in the tercets as the presence of a sleeping mandola, for instance. Pointing back to the bed because it is "sleeping," the dormant instrument is still able to fill the room with the promise of sexual reproduction that was originally missing or stymied. For the mandola is pregnant, its pear-shaped form a protruding belly that suggests the hypothetical birth that will result "Selon nul *ventre* que le sien." The formal balance achieved by bringing the two opposed thematic moments of the sonnet together into a negative/positive synthesis, a sexual union eventually capable of giving birth to its own "Aufhebung," is as perfect and aesthetically satisfying a version of the dialectical process one could hope for in "symbolist" poetry. Thus, the "*ne pas être*" of the opening absence is filtered across the "mais" of the first tercet before it is picked up again in the "fe*nêtre*" of line 12, and finally re-echoed and sublated in the poem's final word, "*naître*." In what is perhaps the poem's most daring gesture, the conflictual lack of union, or *mariage blanc,* of the quatrains is later overturned in the coming together under the same familial roof—*chez qui*—of the maternal but empty instrument (*la mandore au creux néant*) with the paternal and personalized dreamer (*celui qui du rêve se dore*) in lines 9 and 10.

It is clear that in the movement from the quatrains to the tercets a new mode of poetic language is invoked. From poetry conceived as the critical reception and breakdown of a mimetic model of language that can be figured as *theater,* the sonnet moves toward a more positive conception of poetry as *music*.[16] Music, in this poem at least, seems able to pass beyond the problematization of writing and representation, beyond the undecidable impasse of a negative epistemology to the

---

16. Mallarmé's concept of music is not straightforward. It never appears except in a relationship to other modes of discourse, juxtaposed sometimes to theater, as in "Richard Wagner, rêverie d'un poète français" (541–46), sometimes to poetry, as in "La musique et les lettres" (635–57). It is always organized around a discussion of meaning, subjectivity, history, and politics.

celebration of a liberating and positive form of art. On the thematic level, this move is represented by the replacement of the activity of philosophical "doubt" in the quatrains by that of an aesthetically creative "dream" in the tercets. The implication is that by substituting a poetry of autonomous dream for one of universal doubt, the power of language as voice and melody would somehow be able to replace and compensate for the undecidable outcome of poetic language as the critical reflection on its own statements and cognitions. The question at this point should be whether the aesthetic compensation for the radical suspension of philosophical self-knowledge would not itself constitute something like the "dream" of philosophy. For if it were in fact possible to bypass the inconclusiveness of the question of language as figural representation and cognition in favor of a model of language as pure illusion, as a form of sonorous and verbal play that recognizes and rejoices in its own fictional nature, then it would be possible by the same token to reintroduce the concept of philosophical certainty and truth, albeit in a negative mode, on the far side of its problematization.

Before deciding whether Mallarmé's writing does indeed conform to this model, it is necessary to look more closely at the way poetry as music actually functions in the tercets. One of the most obvious places to locate an aesthetic of music is where the poetic and sonorous resources of the words break in on, supplement, or replace their representational value. This occurs throughout the poem, as we have seen in the reappearance of the figure of the "bed" in the epistemologically suspect form of words like "conf*lit*" and enseve*lit*," but it is not recognized and celebrated as a positive value until language as music and dream is thematized at the end of the poem. Thus, in line 12, the very word that designates theatrical representation, *fenêtre,* breaks open and allows its individual sonorous elements to announce the birth of music that will finally occur in the poem's last word, *naître.* The word *naître* not only *refers* to any and all extralinguistic acts of birth, physiological as well as intelligible; it also actualizes a purely intralinguistic "birth" by bringing into being a new *rhyme,* "fenêtre/naître." Beyond the critical failure to demarcate and control the limits, the birth and death as it were, of the theatrical and representational language of cognition in the first part of the sonnet, there appears in the tercets the musical and fictional, or nonreferential, conception and transmission of poetic language.

Of course, before it performs this promised birth in the ultimate word of the sonnet, "naître," the self-enclosed space of poetic music or rhyme is already introduced into the poem by way of the sleepy "mandore" in the first tercet:

> Mais, chez qui du rêve se *dore*
> Triste*ment dort* une *mandore*

There is nothing new in pointing out the musical act of self-reference at play in these lines. Almost forty years ago Emilie Noulet demonstrated the possibility of creating the fiction of a musical score or partition here by cutting into the words. Thus, "triste" can be read as the tonal indication on which the dream-music should be played, the following repetition, "*ment dort . . . mandore,*" referring only to itself as the "murmured refrain or recitative [*mélopée*] of an ancient instrument" (*Vingt poèmes,* 162). This double internal rhyme performs a kind of symbolic or symbolist "marriage" that also signals the birth of music. On the typographic level, the lines join, unite, or marry detached elements from different word families, "*Ma*is," "*dorer,*" "triste*ment,*" and "*dor*mir," to write out the aesthetic emblem of music in the final word "mandore," while on the sonorous level they actualize a musical refrain by playing on the sounds "dore ment dort mandore."[17]

The tercets seem to confirm that, beyond the breakdown of a philosophical theater of reflection on language as figure and knowledge, there remains the possibility of a new "symbolist" and musical reawakening. And once the instability of the referential link between the figure and the world of natural experience has been shuffled into the background, the potential of awakening the intralinguistic links between *signifiants* (the sounded letters of words) and *signifiés* ("musical sound" as the ultimate meaning of the letters *m-a-n-d-o-r-e*) can become a source of endless aesthetic satisfaction and creativity. Technical resources of language like rhyme seem therefore to allow for the production and transmission of effects of adequation in the way that sounds of words (*ment dort mandore*) correspond exactly to their meaning (the aesthetic play of music). The work thus envisages the possibility of its successful transmission and survival as aesthetic play

---

17. Here, as so often is the case, Mallarmé can be seen to return to and radicalize a "symbolist" gesture already present in Baudelaire: the letters and sounds that finally come together in the *mandore* of this sonnet are like the "longs échos qui de loin se confondent" that are described in "Correspondances."

at the moment it declares the emptiness of its fictional status to be at the furthest remove from anything outside of itself.

It is also at this point that the possibility of a reconvergence of an aesthetic of music with an epistemology of narrative can be reinitiated. For if the positivity of an aesthetic of music can be conceived as the *negation,* or as a fiction, of empirical reference and cognition, rather than as their further problematization, then it follows that such a negativity within literature can itself be understood as being only a temporary stage within a larger continuum that passes beyond it. The alternating structure of opposing moments points toward a future synthesis of both negative and positive elements. This would amount to a final reintegration of the self-conscious choice of a nonrepresentational music, represented conveniently in French literature's own history by Mallarmé and his "symbolism," within a larger historical scheme that could itself lay claim to cognitive dimensions unquestionably rooted in referential and representational models.

This is the principal aim and interest of recent attempts at reading nonmimetic poetic texts by way of an aesthetics of reception, and the implicit project of a critic and historian like H. R. Jauss. Jauss sets himself the task of showing how a history of a text's transmission and understanding is capable of reducing the distance between the formal autonomy of a work and its referential context. To make the demonstration plausible it becomes necessary for him to treat the nonreferentiality of poetic language as though it could be located negatively in a sequence of historical reception—at the end of one model ("une dentelle s'abolit") and as the beginning of a new one ("dort une mandore"). Thus, Jauss is ultimately able to trace in literature a genetic process powerful enough to overcome even the so-called disappearance of literature's own reference to the empirical world. In the aesthetic movement that stretches from Nietzsche to Apollinaire and beyond, and in which Mallarmé's work would occupy a central place, nonreferentiality becomes but a passing moment that can later be theorized and understood as such. Speaking from the retrospective standpoint that recognizes the past necessity of this negative moment while denying it any further validity within our own thought, Jauss can even say with absolute assurance, "In the aesthetic processes of deconstruction and reconstruction, the subject can proceed beyond the loss of its Cartesian self-sufficiency to new forms, and aesthetic experience can compensate for the supposedly irremedial loss of the world."[18] In terms of the Mallarmé sonnet we are reading, this loss of the world that can still be compensated for would mean that the poet simply proceeds beyond all the epistemological uncertainties of representational language by instituting the deliberately determined but wholly independent features of what an avowed formalist like Michael Riffaterre might call a pure semiotics of poetry, "un creux néant musicien."

Jauss's interpretation, which recognizes to some extent the text's actual disruption of the mimetic model of narrative, is able nonetheless to maintain narrative coherence and intelligibility. It does so by reconstruing poetic production as a progressive and self-conscious *negation,* or "hollow nothingness," of representation rather than its undecidable problematization. Can it be claimed, however, that the program of opposing or negating the critique of an epistemology of representation, which begins in Mallarmé's sonnet with the "Mais" of line 9, is carried through to the end of the poem by a coherent and unilateral aesthetic of music? Does the poetic lyre, or symbolist "mandore," remain aesthetically intact until such time as its autonomous dream-song could be negated and broken in on in turn by our own historical outside, whose referential reconstructions could therefore be said to remain safely beyond such questions of poetic and epistemological uncertainty? The answer depends on how successful the figure of music, the mandola, is in eliminating from its aesthetic dream the kind of doubt that impinges on the figure of the lace at the beginning of the text. The dream, as we have seen, would be the adequation of poetic effects with poetic meaning, the use of poetic language to create the illusion of a play of voice and sound in rhymes that can be totally exhausted in their reference only to themselves as music. As mere sound that means nothing other than its own music, poetic rhyme states itself to be a self-referential fiction, or dream, that knows its own hypothetical nature. So long as it is recognized for the fiction it is, poetic music is harmless. And in this spirit, despite what the commentators have suggested, the last line of the sonnet, "Filial on aurait pu naître," should be read as a positive affirmation of the resolutely unrealized, or fictive nature of the poet's "birth." For it is by stating outright that the aesthetic birth can only be one that always "could have been" but never actually was that

---

18. H. R. Jauss, "1912: Threshold to an Epoch," *Yale French Studies* 74 (1988), see pp. 60–61. Further references appear in the text.

the musical poet of the tercets demonstrates superiority over the doubtful "Jeu" of the quatrains.

This picture of the aesthetic dream, or pure fiction, moreover, provides the means for reconsidering how those guardians of the "Book" mentioned in "Sauvegarde" could in fact become the unwitting agents of their own misguided historical and social activity. To the extent that the members of the Académie choose to see themselves as merely fictional subjects operating within the ivory tower of aesthetics, so the story would go, they aestheticize reality rather than cut themselves off, as they claim, from the partisan activities of the marketplace. In the process, they also restrict themselves to playing a wholly negative historical role within it. By now there exists an entire tradition of literary, and not-so-literary, criticism that claims to read in the work of Mallarmé and other so-called symbolist writers just such a turning of history into a mere play of aesthetics, a delusive flight from referential reality that can only prepare and then fall prey to an inevitable collision with those aspects of empirical existence that eventually resist aestheticization, like the abolitions of rights and faculties that are no longer purely figural.

But the fact that the model for language we saw in "Sauvegarde" turned out to be the workaday world of the dictionary rather than the sonorous dream of an aesthetic elite should give us pause, for it serves to reopen in a slightly different mode the question of poetry as music and rhyme. Could it be that the rhyme of a purely self-referential music in the sonnet is itself a fiction of sorts, a strategy that can be used to deflect attention away from the prosaic role that rhyme might actually play in the dictionary of everyday life? If we turn for help in answering this question to the dictionary itself, we find that rhyme is defined there as a "*correspondence* of terminal sounds of words or of lines of verse." Such a definition is of course too pragmatic to be of help to us; it begs the question of poetry's relation to music by itself presupposing rather than accounting for the "dream" of bringing together aesthetics ("sounds") and hermeneutics ("words") into a self-reflexive correspondence. It proves more helpful, however, to ask about "rhythm," the poetic principle of regulated patterns, to which rhyme, as a formal pattern of *sounds,* is conceptually as well as etymologically tributary. Mallarmé himself, of course, always stressed the priority of rhythm within his poetic enterprise: "As for me, I am happy, as a literate, in another way. Namely, to know that there exists in the mind of those who have reflected human being as far as themselves nothing but a precise account of being's pure *rhythmical* motifs, which are its recognizable signs" (345).[19]

In a now famous essay, "La notion de 'rythme' dans son expression linguistique,' Emile Benveniste makes some observations about rhythm in poetry that, however surprising they may still be, turn out to have much to say about reading the music in Mallarmé's sonnet.[20] Most important, according to Benveniste, the term "rhythm," contrary to common opinion, cannot legitimately be understood by tracing its filiation to the Greek root "rheô." When taken without further analysis as the source of the concept of all rhythm, this word, which names in fact the "flowing" movement of rivers, serves only to *exemplify* a linguistic principle of analogy it should rather help us to understand and explain. By projecting the notion of poetic rhythm onto the natural movement of a river, we bypass entirely the fundamental question of how a phenomenal experience (the repetitive motion of flowing water) could be linked to a nonphenomenal principle of linguistic signification (the marked regularity of poetic and semantic units) in the first place. Benveniste argues that, far from constituting something like a "natural" correspondence between sensuous movement and intelligible meaning, the phenomenal reference to the visibility of ocean waves that is invariably associated with "rhythm"—and by extension the more recent association of a sound-perception with patterns of poetic "rhyme"—was actually *imposed* upon, or grafted onto, a more "original" use of the term. Benveniste also points out in passing that this other sense of rhythm has, since Plato, been subdued and all but forgotten in favor of the later genealogy that traces formal rhetorical patterns back to flowing waters.

This is no mere accident, moreover, since "rhythm," at its source, itself names the concept of "form" or "figure" that it always and again has to give to itself to achieve consistency. Thus, rhythm should be

19. This passage, from Mallarmé's "Notes sur le théâtre," is cited by Rodolphe Gasché in his essay "Joining the Text," in *The Yale Critics,* ed. Jonathan Arac, Wlad Godzich, and Wallace Martin (Minneapolis: University of Minnesota Press, 1983). Gasché also points out the pertinence in this context of Heidegger's notion of Being's rhythm, as well as of more recent linguistic and philosophical analyses of rhythm by Benveniste, Derrida, and Nancy.

20. Emile Benveniste, "La notion de 'rythme' dans son expression linguistique," *Problèmes de linguistique générale I.* (Paris: Gallimard, 1966), 327–35. Further references appear in the text.

considered as the logical condition for anything like the "metaphors" it actually engenders, since all metaphorical figures must themselves presuppose the prior constitution of the sensuous and intelligible "forms" they then pretend to link together in a symmetrical correspondence. Rhythm is "form" as it is first *assigned* at an infinitely receding moment; it could therefore never be thought of in terms of preexisting entities but rather occurs by itself inaugurating a field of purely differential relations. Before such an originary conferral of "form," that is, before the necessary act of configuration that institutes "rhythm" as a principle of linguistic patterning, there can be no such thing as the phenomenal or conceptual identities it allows to come into being and replace it. As Benveniste reminds us, rhythm is the giving of form to that which would remain without it formless, "the form of that which has no organic consistency" (333). The "origin" of form is not itself formal but positional: it institutes rather than illustrating anything beyond itself.

As such, "rhythm" names the moment of a first, and nonmetaphorical, figuration. It is therefore a wholly linguistic act by which a purely "formal" set of relations is established in such a way that it can be repeated according to a preordained pattern susceptible to being recognized in its repetition. For this reason, the actual examples of rhythm cited by Aristotle as well as by Benveniste most often refer to the disposition, arrangement, or patterns instituted in the *letters* of the alphabet, the most distinctive example conceivable of a fixed, iterable, nonorganic, and nonmetaphorical, that is, material, "form." As the codified pattern of linguistic notation, rhythm is neither visible like the waves of the ocean nor audible like the chirping of birds. Benveniste says as much in conclusion: "Nothing could be less 'natural' than this notion [of rhythm]," which is the mechanical reproduction of a literal inscription or trace devoid of any immediate and direct relationship to the world we think we see and hear or understand. The preordained aspect of this mechanical pattern, or "rhyme," makes it resemble the grammar of a language considered independently of its semantic function. Mallarmé refers to such a grammatical principle in "Sauvegarde" as "a branch, the nude syntax of a sentence" (418). Rhyme loses its poetic and musical aura in Mallarmé precisely when its "belleslettres" are stripped of their aesthetic integrity and become like the "scattered words" of the dictionary. For the dictionary, it should be remembered, is not just the place where words, units of more or less stable meaning, can be found strewn about like so many beautiful flowers. It is also and especially the place where words, as meaning, can themselves scatter and dissolve into the subsemantic elements of a branch without flowers. Such are the letters of the alphabet dictionary, which are in fact ordered, patterned, and rhymed mechanically, like an empty grammar or a nude syntax, from *a* to *z*.[21]

This changes our ordinary picture of Mallarmé and his concept of poetic music considerably. If the link between rhyme and music is not naturally musical like the sounds of the voice, but is rather grammatical and inscriptional like the letters of the alphabet that compose it, then it cannot be said that the musical model of language proposed in the tercets of "Une dentelle" is any different from the undecidable inscription operating in the quatrains. Instead, vocalized language would itself be an arbitrary and unwarranted representation of the system of voiceless inscription or notation that was there all along, though hidden, sleeping, in the "belles-lettres" of the "mandore." It would therefore not be exempt from the kind of questioning that inaugurates and tears the figure of the lace. Nor would it be possible to subscribe to a reading that, like Jauss's, relies implicitly on polar models to reduce poetic effects like rhyme to a mere aesthetic phenomenon in order to promise historical coherence and understanding on the far side of their most radical negation. On the contrary, by writing out the failed attempt to move away from the situation of doubt inscribed in the quatrains toward the self-enclosed dream of aesthetics in the tercets, Mallarmé's text anticipates its aesthetic reception in order to warn us against it. But, it could be asked, what textual evidence is there that Mallarmé's poem does *not* share the dream of rhyme as a simple metaphorical correspondence between sounds (aesthetics) and words (meaning)? At what point, to use the terms of "Sauvegarde," does the poem actually demonstrate that the link between language and the empirical world takes place as a "fiction," though in such a way that it does not automatically fall prey to a merely aesthetic dream that would

---

21. Two remarkable examples of this effect in Mallarmé are "Le sonnet en yx," where the inexistent "ptyx" is needed for its letters to fill out the rhyme scheme, and "Le démon de l'analogie," where the nongenetic, mechanical production of meaning from the dispersal of letters becomes the source of the allegorical narrative. The most apodictic statement of this effect can be found in "La musique et les lettres": "Anyone who has retained a piety for the twenty-four letters . . . as well as a sense for their symmetries . . . possesses a doctrine as well as a country . . . our fund and foundation, that legacy, spelling" (646).

thereby prevent itself from occurring in a different, essentially historical, mode?

These questions, with their insistence on inaugurating a difference within a signifying system of relationships that are already in place, bring us back to the problem of poetic birth and literary heritage. It is now clear that whatever can be born in this poem must be born out of the womb or *ventre* of music, "Selon nul ventre que le sien." As we have seen, this music must be thought in terms of language as rhyme, language as the repetition of an arbitrary act of giving form to what has not yet either determinate meaning or sensuous form, like the nude letters of the alphabet. The "form" of letters is not originally determined metaphorically as a sonorous or visible manifestation of an inner content, the way the human voice and body can always be taken to be the mere forms of an inner mind or soul. The letters of the alphabet, considered in themselves, cover nothing and mean nothing. They are a "creux néant" whose only "form" is the legibility they eventually promise by means of a conventional system of markings in which each one differs from all the others—these letters constitute what Mallarmé calls elsewhere that "total rhythm, which would be the poem silenced, in the blanks" (367).

However, as the reading also disclosed, rhyme immediately produces an aesthetic version of this blank birth: the aestheticization of rhythm as sensory perception serves as a shelter from the knowledge of rhyme's own constitutive dependence on the unpredictable play of the empty letter. It does so by representing grammatical patterns as a negative moment in a natural genealogy that links the production of meaning to phenomenal categories by way of a determined relation to sounded letters. Rhyme as music thus seems to recover the certainty of perception by negating its constitution in semiotic notation and by presupposing instead a direct relationship to sound itself. But the poem shows that this assumption of an immediate relation to the empirical world is a fiction that has forgotten its fictional nature. Such fictions, or perhaps more accurately, ideologies, attempt to parry the more radical fiction of rhyme as letters, the a priori act of having instituted any relationship whatsoever between the nude syntax of the alphabet on the one hand and either sound or meaning on the other. When Mallarmé says that social relations, society, and by implication the state, are a "fiction," he does not mean that they are not real—far from it. Rather, he means that society is always founded on some sort of minimal linguistic operation of form giving or "rhyme" prior to any determination of its empirical existence or its ideal significance. Therefore, the irreducibly poetic element in the production of a society or state must remain to some extent "mysterious," must fall outside the reach of an analysis derived solely from the opposition between the phenomenal and the intelligible, since the logic of that opposition is itself a result of the very forces it would seek to analyze and control.

The real surprise in "Une dentelle" is therefore what happens when "music" actually sees the light of day in the tercets. For the locus of its birth, the "ventre," does not only conform to a self-deluding aesthetic program, through its reference to the purely phenomenal space of the mandola's sound box. This space, thanks to its visible similarity to a woman's pregnant belly, also manages to reintroduce the theatricality of a traditional "son et lumière" spectacle by infusing the end of the poem with a golden hue: "*se dore* une mandore." In addition, though, the very word "ventre" occurs as and gives birth to an unpredictable and impersonal effect by way of its own letters. And it is the letters of the word *ventre*, rather than the sound or shape of the musical instrument it refers to, that reinscribe an earlier moment of the poem. This is the moment of writing's undecidable doubt and half-opening in the quatrains: "A *n'entr'*ouvrir/*n*ul v*entre*." The word *ventre* can thus be said to repeat the problematic rhythm of the quatrains, the silent rhythm that dislocates the aesthetic program of a purely sonorous rhyme. For "entr'ouvrir," it will be recalled, is the place in the quatrains where writing is not resolved into the symmetrical polarities and specular valorizations of the sensuous ("le lit" as eros) and the intelligible ("le lit" as concept). Rather, this kind of writing results in a typographical suspension, the apostrophe of *entr'ouvrir,* which calls the poem into being by setting it apart from all else.

This apostrophe stands for language's power of figuration, its power to call forth and relate in their dialectical opposition a phenomenal and intelligible "world" of music and poetry, of sound and meaning. But language can produce this figure only by first instituting diacritical marks or letters (*l-i-t,* for instance), which themselves cannot be reduced to mere figures, since the text they write out is neither simply present nor absent, neither purely subjective nor objective. Far from negating the critical question of figuration by substituting for it the dream space of poetic solipsism or subjectivity, the reinscription of the rhyming letters (*entr'*) in the womb of the tercets' own music (*ventre*) shows that the aesthetic dream that also appears in them, whether it is valorized negatively or positively, is always blind (or deaf) to effects of the letter that remain beyond the dream's own power to explain or elude.

We cannot dismiss (or celebrate) the poem for embracing an aesthetic and subjective program that it takes such pains to interrogate and interrupt.[22] The kind of birth "Une dentelle" alludes to must be understood on a different, linguistic, model, if it is to take place at all. It could be prepared only by first going back to and then interrogating the fiction of a determinate relation between letters and sound and meaning rather than by blindly turning away from it. Such a birth, by returning to the wholly arbitrary and mechanical power of rhyme to cut into the semantic unity of music's "womb" (v*entre*), could only occur by somehow waking to repeat—that is, in a mode that defies absolute difference as well as mere identity—the originary and open-ended act of figuration instituted by the fiction of the letter. Such a waking is entrusted to specters who are also readers, those men and women of the Academy who safeguard the dictionary and the rhythm of its letters by overseeing the detached metaphors already scattered there as well as the unheard of combinations to come. To the extent that they must eventually cut themselves off from a mere dream of autonomous meaning by watching over the unpredictable play of its sleeping letters, they also reproduce the dream's original possibility, though this time in such a way that its meaning remains undecidable, a legacy to a pure future. "Filial on aurait pu naître" must thus be read to mean not only that one could have been born but wasn't, but also that one might already have been born without yet knowing it.

---

22. The poem itself always knows how to read an aesthetics of subjectivity, and at the very moment the rhyme wakes up the sleeping letters in poetry's belly, it puts the subjective figure of the poet (or the inattentive reader) back to sleep by showing how the music here has little to do with subjective self-indulgence or stoicism. Whether it is the artist lost in a dream world of self-sufficiency or the critic who thinks it possible to observe with impunity and then redeem such a dreaming artist, the golden sound of the aesthetic instrument is the same from the anaesthetic point of view of the letters: the play of letters is forever poised above a different kind of dream in which new rhymes can always wake to spell out the threat implicit in reading "ment dort une mandore": "*m'endort* une mandore."

4 Ingesting the Mummy: Proust's Allegory of Memory

Je suis le ténébreux,—le veuf,—l'inconsolé,
Le Prince d'Aquitaine à la tour abolie
—Gérard de Nerval, "El desdichado"

If the line of filiation that connects Nerval to Mallarmé and both of them eventually to Proust can be described as a genealogy, it would have to be a curious pedigree indeed, riddled as it is with dead ends, discontinuities, disinheritances, and generally unfinished or abolished constructions. On the level of a genetic imagery that is recurrent in their work almost to the point of the obsessional, there seems to be little chance for the identification, much less the survival, of a family tree, threatened in Nerval's case by the mad chimerae of youth, in Proust's by the disillusionments and sterility of old age, and in Mallarmé's by the improbability of even being born. But this stunted pattern appears to be an insoluble problem only so long as we remain stuck at the naive, elementary level of the image or theme. For once the question of genetic development is enlarged enough to include the specifically textual moment of writing that is implied in the constitution of any theme, no matter how negative or barren, things begin to assume a somewhat different and more promising shape.

It can be argued, and some of the most productive readings of these authors' works have in fact argued, that it is precisely by writing out those images of chimerae that Nerval's text passes beyond them into its maturity, and by writing about the impossibility of being born that Mallarmé's text can overcome this same obstacle to growth in exemplary fashion. Similarly, *A la recherche du temps perdu* could be said to constitute, in its very existence as text, the discovery or recovery of what the text states throughout is lost and must be searched for: the moment of its own conception and birth. The apparent concatenation of theme and structure here is both circular and complementary, the beginning of the writing of the text we have before us coinciding neatly with the end of the thematic search contained and recounted within it. In this way, the actuality of the text would be able to respond to and fecundate the thematic statement of lack articulated by it.

This specular system of relationships established between beginning and end as well as between structure and statement effects a figural and temporal balance that helps to restore the picture of a symbolist family tree of writers that would include unproblematically the specific branch running from Nerval and Mallarmé to Proust. By insisting on the various moments of negativity that must be faced in order to be overcome in the necessary passage from birth to youth, to maturity, to death, and back again to rebirth, Nerval, Mallarmé, and Proust make of the symbolic correspondence between theme and statement, or image and text, a task that is to be effectuated across time rather than something that is given as immediately accessible. "The only paradises worthy of the name," Proust reminds us near the end of his *recherche*, "are ones we have lost."[1] Critical interpretations tend to be ambivalent in their assessment of this brand of symbolism. When the negativity inherent in symbolist poetics is seen as the turning back, by means of a mere aesthetic representation, to what by definition remains buried in the past, it is considered a formalism and a flight from objective reality. But when it is seen as the prelude to an act of understanding that recuperates all the discrepant levels of lived experience by bringing to light the synthesis of a universal meaning, it is considered a necessary step in an ongoing engagement with social and historical realities. In any event, whether they are seen as regressive or prophetic, "symbolist" writers such as Nerval, Mallarmé, and Proust become in this way corresponding moments in a larger family history that includes romanticism as its immediate predecessor and our own modernity and postmodernity as its heritage.

In the case of Proust, one can begin to appreciate the stakes of this genetic scheme more clearly by focusing on the debate surrounding the question of "memory" in *A la recherche du temps perdu*. What is the role of memory in Proust's text, with its concomitant stress on questions of time and especially on time past? Although the general tend-

---

1. Marcel Proust, *A la recherche du temps perdu* (Paris: Bibliothèque de la Pléiade, 1954), ed. Pierre Clarac and André Ferré, 3 vol., 3:870. Further references appear in the text.

ency in the first part of this century was to emphasize those aspects of the Proustian oeuvre that tied it firmly to a past seemingly closed off to everything but nostalgia, of late we have begun to distinguish ourselves from these first readers of Proust by situating the *Recherche* at the furthest possible remove from this sort of nostalgia.[2] Such changes in the barometric readings of literary masterpieces help to remind us that rather than composing a fixed universe of transcendental meanings, the literary canon is itself part of a dialectical narrative whose meaning is not given in advance but produced historically, in large part by way of the evolving sequence of its successive interpretations. Thus Gilles Deleuze, with his avowed interest and investment in the postmodern condition of the contemporary age, seems anxious to align Proust as closely with us as possible by distancing him from a lopsided orientation toward the past when he says that, "no matter how important its role, memory only occurs here as the means of an apprenticeship that exceeds it both in goal and principle. The Search is turned toward the future, not toward the past."[3] The future this particular *recherche* is turned toward starts to sound very much like our own present when Deleuze later credits Proust with having found a truth capable of "displacing" the age-old Platonism of the Logos by turning thought itself into a form of creation, a mode of "production," or a kind of "machine" to be put into public "service" (134, 177, 184). Despite significant differences of emphasis, we find once again the familiar pattern in which the origin or beginning—doubly present in Deleuze's counterreference to the Platonic conception of reminiscences or "memory"—is only a *means,* a necessary, and necessarily negative, detour towards the goal or *end* of a historical process in progress, of which we would be the latest avatars.

The question remains, however, whether any purely temporal scheme can do justice to the complexity of a text that is constantly attempting to articulate the passage of time with the simultaneity of multiple points in space. Memory in Proust is never simply a matter of the before and after, or of the past and future, of a completed entity. It

---

2. For the archetypical reading of Proust as nostalgic recounting of a lost past, see Edmund Wilson's essay in *Axel's Castle,* where he describes Proust's writing as "the last fires of a setting sun" and the Proustian project as the last history of the "Heartbreak House of capitalist culture." See *Axel's Castle* (New York: Norton, 1931), 189, 190.

3. Gilles Deleuze, *Proust et les signes* (Paris: Presses Universitaires de France, 1964), 10. Further references appear in the text.

always includes at the same time the necessary reference to a spatial structure in the process of constituting itself around the mutually dependent poles of an inside/outside relationship. The locus of this differential relation between interior and exterior is of course nothing other than the self-conscious subject itself, which is in turn composed of the delicate interplay between mind and empirical reality. A great deal is at issue in passages such as the one where Marcel claims that, "at last, by *continuing* to follow from *inside to outside* the states of mind simultaneously juxtaposed within me, and before reaching the actual horizon enclosing them, I can discover pleasures of another kind . . ." (1:87). The "other" pleasure that is intimated here proleptically would itself be the subject's ultimate discovery in the work of art of a perfect adequation between temporal duration ("continuity") and spatial extension ("simultaneous juxtaposition from inside to outside").

Drawing attention to the nature and importance in *A la recherche du temps perdu* of this spatializing process of juxtaposition that is eventually said to overtake even the sequential movement of time itself, Georges Poulet has helped to return the problem of *recovering* the self through time to the more fundamental question of *constituting* it as a spatial relation between inside and outside.[4] The emergence from a merely "local" and superficial existence to the more "fundamental" mode constitutive of a genuine subject, according to Poulet, is to be measured in "the act by which the mind *transports* whatever it sees, thus effecting the passage of objective reality into the imaginary" (34). But when Poulet then goes on to quote the reference to Elstir's paintings—"Elstir was incapable of looking at a flower without immediately transplanting it into that interior garden where we are forced to remain forever" (2:943)—we can see that things are considerably more complicated than a one-step process of interiorizing movement. Despite the narrator's tone of discouragement or despair at this point, it is not simply a case of bringing the outside *inside,* unilaterally transporting or transplanting objective reality into the imaginary, even and especially if this segment of the movement first appears as life imprisonment. For unlike Swann, Elstir can become a model for the narrator precisely because he refuses to be confined within this prison

---

4. Georges Poulet, *L'espace proustien* (Paris: Gallimard, 1963). Further references appear in the text.

that seems to separate empirical experience once and for all from the ideal space of a mind.[5]

Clearly, what is of most consequence in the passage on Elstir, and even emblematic for the novel as a whole, is not just the bringing of the flowers into an interior garden—which can always appear to be a defensive strategy of security and protection as well as a form of alienation. What is most remarkable is the indisputable fact that in the act of painting they have in some way been put *back out* into the world again. Only by "bringing whatever [has been] experienced *back out* of the shadows," the narrator insists at the end of the novel, can we ever hope to have access to anything like our "true life, a life finally discovered and illuminated." And the sole means of achieving this exteriorization, of course, is through the "production of a work of art" (3:879, 895). The passage in question on Elstir's painting, in fact, goes out of its way to emphasize the importance of just such an outward, externalizing, turn of thought. It stages a mock confrontation in Mme Verdurin's dining room between the living roses that once provided the painter's model and Elstir's portrait of them. Whereas the "real" flowers are available now only through Mme Verdurin's passive recollection of them, Elstir's portrait, actually there and propped against a chair, serves to bring *la Patronne* and her idealized reminiscences face to face with a painting that is neither simply natural nor yet totally imaginary: occupying a truly intermediate space, the portrait "*almost* resembles them.*" What functions as the centerpiece for the luncheon in question, then, is neither the objective reality of the flowers, long gone, nor Elstir's subjective imagination, since he himself has fallen from favor, but rather this portrait of objectified thought. As such it is "almost," but not quite, equal to both sides of the inside/outside relationship, and so is finally identified by the narrator as an unheard-of flower: "a wholly new variety with which the painter, like an ingenious horticulturist, had embellished the family of Roses" (2:943).[6]

---

5. Claudia Brodsky's interpretation of the *Recherche* is of interest for the way it suggests the inadequacy of the model of memory as retrieval presumed by most readers of Proust, but by using the figure of Swann in order to do so it remains overly tied to the binary structure of experience/recollection it seeks to displace. It may be true that the *Recherche* never manages to recapture anything, but that is not to say that its own writing does nothing to the idea that there was something out there like a natural experience to capture in the first place. See "Remembering Swann," *The Imposition of Form* (Princeton: Princeton University Press, 1987).

6. On the thematic level, the subject of Elstir's painting can be read as a clever reference to those notorious Mallarmean flowers that, regardless of their remaining

Taking a hint from the narrator's own horticultural comparison, it could be argued that the process first described as simply "transplanting" a rose from one soil to another when it goes from objective reality to the imagination next resembles the insertion of an entirely foreign "transplant" when the inner rose is put back out again. The transplant becomes a prosthesis when it serves to enhance, embellish, and transform the family of Roses—both empirical and ideal—it also serves to replace. It would hardly be an exaggeration at this point to say that the operation engaged in by the self when it transplants between inner and outer gardens is at least twofold. It is an interiorization that transports the selfsame flower from one place to another, from world to mind, for instance. And it is an exteriorization that leaves its mark on both regions in such a way that neither inside nor outside would ever be able to remain quite the same. The passage on Elstir's paintings thus seems to confirm in the language of flowers, or rhetorical figures, what we have known all along, or will be reminded of later by Proust. The metaphorical transfers that go from outside to inside constitute a grafting operation as well as a simple transplanting. In other words, the *painting* of ideal resemblances must be supplemented by a nonmimetic *graphesis,* or writing, and it is this kind of writing that the subject will have to learn how to produce for itself if it is to survive at all. But if, as is again the case with Elstir, the result of such grafting is the production of a truly unheard-of variety of flower, a totally "*new* variety of roses which without him would have never been known," then how can we still call that a *survival?* Who, or perhaps better, what, would be the "identity" of that which can only be preserved as something totally different?

One of the most comprehensive interpretations of the *Recherche* from this point of view is undoubtedly that of Gérard Genette, an interpretation that is itself scattered through a number of essays written at various times and in differing contexts but that aims above all at refining and integrating the terms of Poulet's original insights.[7] Thus,

---

absent from all known bouquets, still manage to rise up musically as something else in the cultivation of the poetic act: "I say: a flower! and, beyond the forget into which my voice relegates any particular shape, inasmuch as something other than known calyxes, musically rises, idea itself and suave, the (flower) absent from all bouquets" (368).

7. Gérard Genette, "Proust Palimpseste," *Figures 1* (Paris: Seuil, 1966); "Proust et le langage indirect," *Figures 2* (Paris: Seuil, 1969); *Figures 3* (Paris: Seuil, 1972); "L'âge des noms," *Mimologiques* (Paris: Seuil, 1976). Further references appear in the text.

Genette is able to retain the basic focus on the subjective phenomena of time and space while also accounting for the additional complexity introduced into this dual scheme of phenomena by the passage effected in the novel to an overtly *written* dimension. By translating slightly what Poulet sees as a rivalry between experiences of time and space into the complementary rhetorical structures of metaphor and metonymy through which these experiences are articulated *textually,* Genette is able to accommodate the sequential and diachronic movement of a narrative to the juxtapositioning within it of simultaneous layers of subjective consciousness. Rather than forming mutually exclusive experiences, time and space are necessarily related to each other in a unified system of textual connections produced by the narrative itself between spatio-temporal analogies (metaphor) and spatio-temporal proximities (metonymy). The key to this system is the writing subject, who is nothing but the sequential narrative, or temporal unfolding, of the cumulative analogies that can finally be revealed between all the spatial relations of outside to inside that constitute the experience of the self.

The obvious model for this totalizing coordination of spatio-temporal identities and proximities is provided by Proust's "petite madeleine." According to Genette, the madeleine is both metaphorical and metonymical since it functions both as a temporal identity and a spatial proximity: "the true Proustian miracle is not that one madeleine steeped in a cup of tea would taste the same as another madeleine steeped in tea, and would awaken its memory; it is rather that this second madeleine resuscitates along with it a bedroom, a house, an entire town . . ." ("Métonymie chez Proust," 57–58). The only thing missing from this excellent description of the miracle of resuscitation is the recognition that when the temporal metaphor and spatial metonymy built into this madeleine are then swallowed and taken into the body of the narrator, there is produced at the same time—but "where?" is the question—the supplementary analogy between *inside* (the madeleine-memory) and *outside* (the madeleine-taste) as well as an unexpected proximity between *before* (youthful experiences) and *after* (adult vocation). Obviously, the confused exclamations of the narrator himself at this point—"the essence was not *in* me, it was me. . . . Clearly, the truth I am seeking is not *in* [the steeping madeleine], but *in* me" (1:45)—do not begin to do justice to the complexity of this operation of truth's resuscitation. Where is the truth, then, in relation to the subject that experiences it—in him, with him, or through him?

Had he recognized the answer to this question at this point, the narrator would not have needed to undergo the following three thousand pages of stumbling around in the dark to understand his vocation as author. Closer to the truth than the simple miracle of the madeleine pastry, perhaps, is Genette's characterization of the "auto-illustrative" structure of the novel. Such a structure would, like the madeleine, be able to combine analogies and proximities, but it could be said to come into being only when the narrator had passed from the status of mere personage to that of self-conscious author. This moment would constitute, according to Genette, "the Text, in the full sense of the term."

Still, the task would be not so much to determine whether there is something like a "text," for the existence of the *Recherche* is as undeniable as it is productive of endless critical commentary, but rather to document with as much analytic precision as possible what the text *is* in the full sense of the term. This would entail looking for the actual constitution *in* the text of the claim *by* the text that the dimensions of time, space, and the self can appear in their "truth" ("la vraie vie") only along *with* the completed text. And it would further require an examination of the consequences of such an auto-illustrative claim by the text for the text in order to determine whether the resulting "life" in it is produced as a continuous identity or as a mutant and unrecognizable species. Such, at any rate, is the reading strategy adopted by Paul de Man when, with respect to slightly different claims made in the novel, he tests the aesthetic and metaphysical statements made about reading in the text against the literary practices illustrated by the text read and finds an irreducible discrepancy between them.[8] Such a discrepancy, or nonconvergence, between what the text illustrates and the way it must illustrate it, would in this case also account for Marcel's befuddlement when he tastes the madeleine in "Combray." It could be that this moment of confusion, the overcoming of which constitutes the thematic challenge of the rest of the novel, is of interest for more than just its thematic role of beginning the quest.

For rather than forming the first step in the successfully completed search for self-identity recounted in its wake, this unresolved split in the narrator between what he is and what he can say he is may be the only legitimate thing the text can ever do about what it is trying to say. Only a detailed analysis of specific passages could be used either to

---

8. Paul de Man, "Reading (Proust)," *Allegories of Reading* (New Haven: Yale University Press, 1979).

contest or to bear out such a hypothesis, and considerable care would have to be taken in reading not only the self-assured pronouncements made by the narrator at the end of his vocational itinerary, but also in reading those critics who, like Genette, take these truth claims at face value.[9] The opposition that is itself finally to be overcome between narrator and personage, or at a different level between narrator and author, may not suffice to locate and catch up with the odd voice that finally says: "There is a critical uncertainty whenever the mind finds itself exceeded by itself; when it is at one and the same time the investigator and the land to be investigated" (1:45). There could be no better description than this, in fact, for the auto-illustrative structure of the *Recherche,* which, as text, is both the writing self and the means of access to this self. But the *Recherche* itself, far from taking the status of the auto-illustrative text for granted, warns us right from the beginning that there can be nothing less certain than the outcome of producing such a structure. And "who" after all could be warning us about this radical uncertainty? It could hardly be the personage, who knows nothing of it; nor could it easily be identified with the narrator or the writer, whose very existence is what is said to hang in the balance here. That there should be inscribed in the text itself not only a critical uncertainty about the outcome of its own trajectory, but also about who or what (self) could ever write in this way about the uncertainty of its (own) coming into being, deserves to be taken seriously, seriously enough, at least, to return us once again to the supposed source of the journey.

It was Harry Levin who first pointed out the link between the singularity of the madeleine experience and the traditional figural pattern or topos through which it operates.[10] This pattern, which does not remain unaffected by its rearticulation in Proust's novel, is basically that of biblical exegesis: "the name and shape of that little teacake are traceable to the shells that pilgrims wore on their hats as badges of their vocation. Let us make no mistake; we are at the commencement of a religious pilgrimage" (390). Whatever one thinks of the etymological gesture that attempts to link the name as well as the

---

9. See "Héros/narrateur," *Figures 3*: "the narrator not only, in a wholly empirical way, knows *more* than the personage; he *knows,* absolutely, he possesses the Truth" (260).

10. Harry Levin, *The Gates of Horn* (New York: Oxford University Press, 1963). Further references appear in the text.

shape of the madeleine directly back to the shell and emblematized pilgrimage it stands for, it would be difficult to deny the structural affinity the madeleine scene exhibits with certain easily recognizable topoi of the biblical tradition. Thus M. H. Abrams is wholly within the spirit of the text when he suggests that the *Recherche* is actually "a displaced and reconstituted theology, or else a secularized form of devotional experience."[11] Even French critics, preoccupied as they are with local historical, thematic, and formal concerns, have noted the obvious ritual subtext for the tea-soaked madeleine: "allowing for the numerous religious connotations . . . I am tempted to compare this gesture to the Christian rite of communion: the infusion and madeleine replacing the bread and wine; the aunt officiates and holds out the host: 'this is my body, this is my blood.' "[12]

It becomes an easy matter at this point to reestablish all sorts of historical and generic connections between Proust's text and the rest of the literary canon, constituting in this way a comprehensive system of classification in which the individual text communicates with the universality of the tradition and the unique moment with an entire history. By conforming to the tripartite model of divine creation, paradise lost, paradise regained, the *Recherche* can be seen to participate in an impressive lineage, transforming it along the way by means of stylistic and thematic innovations. Such innovations and displacements would include the formal devices of the autobiographical voice and the figural language used to constitute it which are analyzed by Genette, as well as the highly complex and untraditional forms of sexuality that are suggested by both Lejeune and Doubrovsky. Finally, though, that the madeleine can function simultaneously as an original psychic symbol for Marcel's (or Proust's) repressed sexuality, as a derived metaphysical symbol for the possibility of rediscovering life after death (that is, the transcendence and redemption of meaning), and as a formal symbol for the "symbolist" program of its author merely confirms the symmetrical dynamic of exchange that mediates here between the individual work and its place within a historical and generic continuum of aesthetic forms.

This is substantiated in an unexpected way by the *critique génétique*

11. M. H. Abrams, *Natural Supernaturalism* (New York: Norton, 1971). See especially pp. 65–70, and pp. 80–83.
12. Philippe Lejeune, "Écriture et sexualité," *Europe* (Feb.–Mar. 1971), 121. See also Serge Doubrovsky, *La place de la madeleine* (Paris: Mercure de France, 1974).

much in vogue recently in France. Such a study of Proust's text is able to show how the thematics of the madeleine and linden tea scene are genetically related to those of the hawthorns, which in turn symbolize for the narrator a relation that is split between the church and sensuality, a ritualistic transcendence and its systematic profanation. But by restricting itself to documenting the way a unity of theme develops over time, this kind of criticism is never able to ask the fundamental question of whether and how such a system of antithetical coordination between symbol, mind, and body actually occurs in Proust. That the ritual profanation of Mlle Vinteuil and Albertine's feasting on ice cream cathedrals represent variations on a specular reversal of the eucharistic ritual is of limited exegetic interest so long as one fails to examine the textual operation and effects of both examples. What is at stake in the symbol is not a conflict of one kind of symbolized meaning versus another, but rather the *mode* in which the symbol can grant access to any kind of symbolized meaning.[13]

Such intertextual schemes of coordination that work to link thematic statement and poetic structure are already familiar to us from their implication on the intratextual level of the *Recherche*. And they always manage to bypass the essential question regarding the actual status of this totalizing system within a specific text. They do so by assuming its unproblematic completion within any given text in order to compare with it a number of other texts in the same (or possibly a different) tradition, thereby establishing a coherent system of classification based on the similarities and differences that are constituted between them. The question, once again, is not whether writing the oeuvre is possible for the subject—since clearly this writing has occurred—or whether such writing can communicate across differences of time and geography with all the versions of the same model (in this case, the liturgical rite of the eucharist)—since clearly it does. Rather, what is at stake is whether the passage leading from individual experience to writing, from death-in-life to "the true life," which is promised by the structure of the symbol, can be unproblematically *completed,* that is, whether it can be made intelligible to the subjects whose ultimate definition and identity depend on it. In other words, does the beginning communi-

---

13. See Bernard Brun, "Brouillon des aubépines," in *Cahiers Marcel Proust* (nouvelle série) 12, *Études proustiennes* 5 (1984), 215–304; and Raymonde Debray-Genette, "Thème, figure, épisode: Genèse des aubépines," *Poétique* 25 (1976), 49–71.

cate, or commune, with the end of the work in such a way that the initial question, "what does it *mean*?" (1:45), can be fully accounted for without disturbing the voice that would consume and reverse it in the final assertion, "and I now *understood* that my past life was nothing but the material for a literary work" (3:899)?

As Genette aptly notes, the function of the madeleine is precisely that of providing such connections. And first of all it would connect the incomprehensible and obsessional stutter of the first section of the novel to the three thousand pages that spread out along symmetrical axes from it and eventually redeem it. Until the moment Marcel, now a full-grown man, at the invitation of his mother tastes once again the madeleine drenched in tea, his past is restricted to the repetitive scene of bending to the paternal law by climbing the stairs at Combray to his bed, which means a separation from his mother. Even though there is already in the nightly ritualistic kiss he receives from his mother a prefiguration of a "communion of peace," these opening pages stand clearly under the sway of an arbitrary and *incomprehensible* law of the father. At that terrible moment on the staircase when Marcel is all but lost in the eyes of his mother as well as in his own, the father, who grants a last-minute stay, is compared to Abraham himself: "I stood there without daring to make a move; there he was before us . . . with the same gesture Abraham is making in the Benozzo Gozzoli print that M. Swann had given me . . ." (1:36). And like the Old Testament law represented by Abraham, the law that speaks to Marcel through his own father is like the dead letter separated from it's life-giving spirit, since the boy remains as blind to its ultimate meaning as he does to the source of its power. For, as he says, "when my anxieties had been assuaged, I was no longer able to understand them" (1:43). To be saved like Isaac, then, is to be condemned at the same time to a formalistic, ritualistic repetition of an empty law that awaits its fulfillment in the incarnation, the word made flesh, and the eventual transcendence of meaning.

The figural economy that regulates this fulfillment is a dialectic of loss, or sacrifice, and redemption; and as we have already noted, in Proust, the model for this economy is the eucharistic feast. In addition, though, this eucharistic model, which remains to some extent a filial ritual, displaces the tradition of paternal authority by mediating it through a maternal figure: in Proust there is no access to the recovery of lost meaning without taking into account the crucial place of the mother. The madeleine and the tea, then, are the transposition of the mechanics of transcendence into a nontheological code whose meaning would be conditioned by the place occupied within it by the mother. The reason for this maternal transposition or displacement from the eucharistic ceremony to the partaking of the madeleine seems perfectly clear, moreover, since it is a direct result of the narrator's particular theory of the symbol. The fundamental distinction between the eucharist and the madeleine is that the eucharist, worn down through age-old layers of habit, has become a merely conventional symbol, an ideal object whose hypothetical meaning is totally exhausted in its very appearance. For this reason it cannot provide access to the truth as it actually exists for the subject. The madeleine, on the other hand, a material symbol that has first been experienced independently of its eventual meaning, always preserves some of the reality it originally shared with what Proust will call the "essence" of reality.

The distinction here between conventional and material, which is also a question of sexual difference as well as "essence," can be operative only from the point of view of the thinking subject that is in the process of constituting itself thanks to such "symbols." For, to judge by the wholly conventional link that now obtains for us between the madeleine and Proust's *Recherche,* there is nothing inherently more "material" (or maternal) about the madeleine than there is about the eucharist, except in the consciousness that is able to register it as such.

This process of registration is described near the end of the novel as the writing out of a book whose pages are accessible only to those truths that leave a material trace on them: "This book, the most difficult of all to decipher, is also the only one that has been dictated to us by reality, the only one whose 'impression' has been made in us by reality itself. Whatever idea is left in us by life, its *material figure,* the trace of the impression it has made on us, remains the token of its *necessary truth.* Ideas formed purely by the intellect can only have a logical truth, a hypothetical truth . . ." (3:880, emphasis added). Far from being an aesthetic idealism, then, Proust's symbolism is a *materialism* at the furthest remove from the merely abstract truths of logic and speculation. Truth, as it is being described here, is not simply the formal beauty of an aesthetic object or the logical beauty of a proposition but is in addition the literal truth of what actually happens. Truth is therefore what intervenes in reality with the necessity of a material event that leaves its mark on the world.[14] For this reason, the means of recovering the truth and thereby tasting the joys of what the narrator will refer to as "celestial food" has itself to achieve the materiality of a genuine occurrence, "even if the simple taste of a madeleine seems logically unable to contain the basis for this joy" (3:873).

The madeleine achieves materiality and is allowed to write the truth in the book the narrator will eventually have to decipher as his very own through the repeated communion services Marcel attends on the Sunday mornings of his boyhood in Combray in Tante Léonie's bedroom. The scene, in which Marcel is the acolyte and Tante Léonie the celebrant, ends with Marcel's receiving the bit of madeleine steeped in tea from the outstretched hand of his aunt. Because, just as with the eucharistic service, the ritual preparation of the sacrament is what guarantees the effectiveness of its consumption, the scene deserves quotation in its entirety:

After a moment I would go in to kiss her; Françoise would infuse her tea; or, if my aunt were feeling agitated, she would ask for her tisane instead, and I would be in charge of measuring out onto a plate the amount of linden needed to put into the boiling water. The drying out of the stems had turned them into a capricious trellis in whose interlacings pale flowers opened up, as though a painter had arranged and placed them as ornamentally as possible. The leaves, having lost or changed their appearance, resembled the most disparate things—the transparent wing of a fly, the blank side of a paper label, the petal of a rose—but as though they had been stacked on top of one another, ground together, or interwoven as in the construction of a bird's nest. A thousand useless details, a charming prodigality on the part of the druggist, and which would have

14. The best description of how this concept of truth affects Proust's understanding of the symbol and its relation to a "material" rather than an ideal beauty remains the following passage on Giotto's frescos, cited and read by Paul de Man: "But later on I came to understand that the overwhelming strangeness [*l'étrangeté saisissante*], the peculiar beauty of these frescos consisted in the important place taken up in them by the symbol, and that the fact that it was represented not as a symbol, since the thought symbolized was not expressed, but as real, as actually endured or materially handled [*effectivement subi ou matériellement manié*], lent to the significance of the work something more literal and more precise, and to its teaching something more concrete and striking" (1:82). Proust is not here denying the existence of logical truths or "immaterial symbols" in which the symbol would itself coincide with the thought symbolized in it. Like the distinction between voluntary and involuntary memory, this one involves the question of the material effect or effectiveness when something occurs as an actual "event" rather than a mere "idea."

been left out of an artificial concoction, gave me, like a book in which one is astonished to find the name of a personal acquaintance, the satisfaction of realizing [*le plaisir de comprendre*] that these were actually the stems of real lindens, like those I had seen on the Avenue de la Gare, modified, precisely because they were not replacements, but themselves, except that they had aged. And each new character being nothing but the metamorphosis of a previous character, in the little gray bulbs I would recognize the green buds that had not come to term; but especially the rosy gleam, soft and lunar, that made the flowers stand out amid the delicate forest of stems in which they were suspended like little roses of gold—the sign, like the glow that still reveals on a wall the place of an effaced fresco, of the difference between those parts of the tree that had been "in color" and those that had not—showed me that these petals were the very ones that before adorning the druggist's package had lent their fragrance to springtime evenings [*ces pétales étaient bien ceux qui avant de fleurir le sac de pharmacie avaient embaumé les soirs de printemps*]. That rosy candlelight was still their color, but half-extinguished and drowsy in this diminished life that now belonged to them, and that is like the twilight of flowers. Soon my aunt, who relished the taste of dead leaves or wilted flowers in the boiling infusion, was able to steep in it a petite madeleine, from which she would hold out to me a small piece when it had become soft enough. (1:51–52)

What becomes immediately evident at even the most cursory glance at this passage is the disproportionately small place allotted in it to the madeleine. Stranger still, perhaps, is the fact that the passage itself, a passage to which all the other passages in the *Recherche* can be said to point as to their origin and key, is not marked by the narrator in any distinctive way. It is merely retold as just another of the links in a long chain of associated memories. But this chain, it should be remembered, was itself set off several pages earlier by the recognition of the capital importance of precisely *this* madeleine and *this* cup of linden tea: "And as soon as I had recognized the taste of the piece of madeleine steeped in linden tea and given me by my aunt . . . all of Combray and its surroundings . . . came out, town and gardens, of my cup of tea" (1:47–48). A scene in which the formalized mystery of transubstantiation is itself transubstantiated into a material symbol that leaves its indelible mark on the subject of narration is of obvious exegetic interest. Not only can this scene of symbolization be considered paradigmatic for the functioning of all material symbols contained in the text; in addition, it should also help to reveal whatever aspects, if any, of its own marking operation must remain unremarked or inaccessible to the subject that undergoes this mysterious operation.[15]

The all-too-obvious madeleine, it turns out, is itself just a cover-up for a deeper layer of symbolic functioning at work here. The identity of the two madeleines—and therefore of the narrator-personage as well—is not only a metaphorical structure that is tied to the metonymical links radiating outward from the center of Combray. It is also, and more important, linked to and conditioned by a more fundamental metaphorical principle put into play by the *linden tea*. Genette's characterization of the Proustian "miracle" as a symmetrical and reciprocal *alliance* of metaphor and metonymy can now be completed by remarking that such symbolist alliances must themselves be grounded in a metaphorical correspondence. What is truly miraculous is that a metonymy could ever be said to correspond to a metaphor in terms of a "symmetry" and a "reciprocity" that is itself the foundation *of* metaphor. Thus, the madeleine is not just the symbol that prefigures the narrator's future identity by a mere metonymical juxtaposition of the sensual and the spiritual—"the little scallop-shell of pastry, so richly sensual beneath its severe and devout folds" (1:47)—it is also a figure that recalls the underlying symbolic mechanism that conditions such a reciprocal relationship between inside and outside as an alliance based on a metaphorical symmetry and adequation. This mechanism, which is fully developed in the description of the linden tea, is first signaled by the casual reference to the infusion of herbal tea, which establishes the entire procedure as one of *internalization* and *fusion*. Moreover, the French term, "infusion," is an especially felicitous choice here, since its semantic range covers the chemical process of maceration as well as

15. There is a natural tendency on the part of critics to relate and valorize individual moments in the *Recherche* in terms of their proximity to the text's most far-reaching insights and accomplishments. For instance, it would be easy to imagine enlarging the present discussion by tracing the figural operation of the madeleine to the many versions of transcendence that take place in and around the sacramental space of "the church," itself merely a prefiguration of the aesthetic truth to be found in "writing," a truth whose disclosure begins, we should remember, with the description of the steeples of Martinville and ends with the completion of the entire *Recherche*. However, to the extent that the only "ultimate" textual principle involved here is that of tropological substitution *between* terms, it can never be established *in advance* which specific figures occurring in the narrative are to be privileged over the others. Every figure must thus be thoroughly tested in its capacity to refer not only to all the other figures of the text but indeed to the text's own principle of figurativity. The figures of the madeleine and linden tea remind us of this truth as well: only when we recognize *this* (and in this every other) figure in the text can the *Recherche* finally become what in fact it always has been.

the theological concept of a divine imparting of grace, uniting in this one word for interpenetration both poles of *matter* and *spirit*. What the passage attempts is nothing less than the reconciliation by an act of the mind of the transience of organic nature and the permanence of artistic representation—a reconciliation, it should be recalled, on which the entire *Recherche* depends for its own intelligibility.

Such a reconciliation can only be the result of overcoming a natural process of loss and increasing entropy. By themselves, those qualities of nature associated here with summer, blossoming flowers and trees, youth and objectivity in general, seem unable to preserve their freshness, much less their own identity, as when it is stated that "the leaves, having *lost* or changed their appearance, now resembled the most *disparate* of things." The passage of time, from summer to winter and concomitantly from outside to inside, is first perceived as nothing but a degradation. The passage of time is a constant wearing away that reduces even the metonymical links of natural experience to a state of dissolution and isolation, in this case, a rather unappetizing collection of dismembered flies, empty labels, and dispersed flowers. The human counterpart that immediately comes to mind for this insuperable process of loss is of course Tante Léonie herself, a shriveled and wilted version of natural life, reduced to a state of skeletal rigidity and trapped inside the colorless and stale tomb of her two adjoining rooms. But this extreme limit of decay also turns out to be closest to the reversed image of its renewal, for shortly afterward, aided by her library of medical and spiritual manuals as well as by "a statue of the Virgin and a bottle of Vichy-Célestins," Tante Léonie becomes the explicit figure for the promised resurrection into eternal life.[16]

The intervening step that prepares and allows for this reversal to take place is the transposition of nature, whose dominant figure in this passage is the linden blossom, into a *text,* "a book in which one is astonished to find the name of a personal acquaintance." It would be impossible to overestimate the importance here of recognizing this familiar name, since the possibility of maintaining a nominal identity

---

16. It is in the second paragraph immediately following the one quoted here that Tante Léonie is described in the terms that made Gide, one of the readers of Proust's manuscript when it was submitted to (and rejected by) the NRF, doubt Proust's ability to use figurative language: "She held out to my lips her sad brow, colorless and tasteless, on which, at this hour of the morning, she had not yet arranged her artificial hair, and from underneath which the vertebrae stood out like a crown of thorns or the beads of a rosary" (1:52).

throughout each of its stages is what ensures that the genetic process that leads from what can be described only retrospectively as natural perception to the "now" of textual representation can be effected without radical loss to the subject, who has staked its entire future on it.

The strength of this claim to an unbreakable tie between nature and the book, between a natural process of organic decay and its recuperation in a textual act of understanding, is made to rest solely on the possibility that the blooming linden flowers will be able to find their way essentially unaltered into Tante Léonie's cup of tea. Such a claim is made explicit when the narrator speaks of *reading* and *understanding* the dried blossoms as though they were the written characters of a book: "And each new character being nothing but the metamorphosis of a previous character, in the little gray bulbs I recognized the green buds." The relay is helped to some extent by the fact that the one word *caractère* can be made to function simultaneously as an index of both natural "properties" and written "ciphers," exemplifying in an economical way the very "metamorphosis" that is being attempted here. At any rate, the persuasive value of the passage finally appears beyond question when the narrator speaks of his satisfaction at realizing (*le plaisir de comprendre*) that what he has before his eyes are not mere substitutes or replacements (*non des doubles*), but rather the very *same* linden blossoms, though in a different, more permanent and useful form. Thus, and in spite of an occasional note of dissonance—introduced for example in the odd reference to an "effaced" fresco—there is a one-to-one correspondence established between nature and its transformation into a recognizable and intelligible text. This correspondence, it is important to notice, is itself modeled on a natural process, of what is called "aging" (*elles avaient vieilli*) in the passage in question. If frescos, books, names, and characters can redeem trees, streets, flowers, and petals, it is because, in essence, they can all be made to depend on the same, ultimately organic laws of aging and growth. Mechanical effects of repetition or simulacrum are therefore downplayed to the advantage of natural cycles of change and progression, and if reference is made at one point to the ornamental technique of a painter, it is quickly reassimilated to the natural scheme of things when the narrator then assures us that this can be no mere "artificial concoction" (*préparation factice*).[17]

---

17. The genetic model that ensures the link between the growing plant and the writing of the text, which Proust inherits from Nerval, moreover, becomes even clearer

The consequences of this self-enclosed system of correspondences between the living blossoms and the dried blossoms are far-reaching, moreover, since it is capable of infinite expansion in time and space. Thus, and always according to a balanced economy of figural exchanges and reversals, it would finally be able to include even the "present" act of writing the text as well as its own reading, which is projected onto some hypothetical "future." It is also possible at this point to confirm Poulet's observation that the role of memory in the *Recherche,* which is present here in the figure of the "drying" or "preserving" of the objects of nature for future use by the mind, is *proleptic* as well as *retrospective.* The narrator is presently remembering an act of recognition that took place in his own past (the identity between the living blossoms and the dried ones), an act of memory that simultaneously prefigures the future recognition (the identity between the experience of the boy and the writing of the man) that is to take place only after the novel will have been written and read.

The writer who is "now" telling his story thematizes in this way a remembered scene of preservation and assimilation that both looks back toward a "past" boyhood experience *as well as* forward to a "future" preservation and assimilation of the man by the writer, who will be able to read this meaning in his own text. It is as if the linden blossoms—insofar as they are both a past experience (already swallowed by the boy and remembered by the man) and a future figure (yet to be employed by the writer)—were themselves saying: "As often as you do these things, in memory of me shall you do them." The "me" in question, of course, is the identity of the boy, the man, and the writer, and it always remains to be confirmed yet again in the "now" of reading by reassimilating these three stages of "true life" to their mutual proximity in the textual memory. The proof of the system's efficacy is that each element can be substituted for any one of the others without entailing a loss of intelligibility for its overall functioning. Thus, the past can become present and future as easily and reversibly

---

at the end of the novel: "In this way my whole life . . . would and would not have been able to be summed up under this title: A vocation. It would not have been able to inasmuch as literature had played no role in my life. It would have been able to inasmuch as this life . . . formed an inner reservoir identical to the albumen that is stored in the ovule of plants and from which the ovule extracts the nourishment required to transform itself into a seed. . . . So too was my life in contact with that which would be accomplished through its maturation" (3:899).

as the green bud and gray bulb become specular figures for the green boy and gray writer as well as for the green (naive) reader he once was and the mature (gray) reader he will one day become.

The figural law of this system of transformations is the process of interiorization that is established analogically between the textual layers comprising the blossoms, the boy, and the writer. Just as the blooming linden can be dried and brought inside the house without loss, so too can the dried linden be recognized by the boy as the past summer evenings he now consumes as an actual beverage. Finally, the novel would be the making available in linguistic "characters" of the whole internalizing process that leads to the ultimate identity of the self, which occurs as an act of consuming, or reading, its own writing. In this way, the text becomes the manifestation, on the outside as it were, of an inner experience of the writer remembering himself as a boy, a boy, moreover, who had brought the outside of nature inside his body by swallowing the tea that contained the preserved linden blossoms. Such spatial reversals of inside and outside that are then temporalized into a sequence are familiar to any reader of Proust. By not taking sufficient notice of the full extension of their symmetrical crossings, however, one runs the risk of mistaking what is in principle a dialectical and genetic structure, whose endpoint is already implicitly contained in its starting point, for a series of entirely separate but related fragments. Thus, for instance, Deleuze, whose principal concern is to isolate and protect the realm of art from all the other activities described in the novel, is able to attribute to it a spontaneous freedom only by positing an "opposition" and a radical "break" between a "philosophical" and historical *past* and an autonomously "artistic" *future* toward which the *Recherche* is moving (*Proust,* 131–34). In order to do so, of course, he also has to establish a linear hierarchy of discrete moments between what he calls the signs of memory (the madeleine), of imagination (the steeples of Martinville), and of art (the *Recherche* itself). But for Proust, there would be no more opposition between such "material symbols" than there is between the linden blossoms and the residue of the textual leaves Marcel learns to read in the cup, and out of which he eventually writes his novel.

At any rate, the system of analogies set up between the change of seasons in nature and the transformation of the boy into the writer has become so resilient by the end of the passage that the narrator is able to cross back and forth between the antithetical regions of life and death, nature and art, outside and inside, without the least hesitation or obstruction. The long climactic sentence that begins with the recognition that each new character of the linden is simply a natural metamorphosis of an earlier one winds its way in typically Proustian fashion through the intricate comparison of the flowers' rosy hue with an old fresco and finally ends in the demonstration that these dead leaves were indeed the very same linden petals that had once participated in the rites of spring. It is noteworthy that the proof of this identity is itself given in the form of an additional figure when it is further said that these were the same petals that, before *adorning* the druggist's package with a shape, had *graced* the springtime trees with a perfume. For by insisting that, whether dead or alive, these are lindens that share at least one essential property, this extra figure reinforces yet again the metaphorical link and possible substitutions between the living blossoms and the dried petals. In this case, it is hardly fortuitous that the property shared by blossoms and tea just happens to be that of a kind of "flower" that, independently of its empirical status, is still able to "bloom" as a rhetorical figure of embellishment.

This flower, which therefore graces Proust's text as well as both the druggist's package and the linden tree, is almost impossible to detect in translation. It is dependent for its full flowering on the idiomatic use of the French verbs *fleurir* and *embaumer* to mean "to enhance" or "to grace" by means of a shape or a scent. What this passage claims to demonstrate in French, then, is that "ces pétales étaient bien ceux qui avant de *fleurir* le sac de pharmacie avaient *embaumé* les soirs de printemps." The loss of grace entailed in a more literal and unidiomatic translation of the phrase is a first indication of what is ultimately at stake in such figural crossings: "these petals were the very ones that before *flowering* the druggist's package had *embalmed* the evenings of spring," where the meaning aimed at in both cases is clearly "to embellish," thanks to either a beautiful appearance or a pleasing fragrance. But what is so effortlessly achieved in the French—the figural meaning of a visible or odoriferous "grace" that allows the dead and the living flowers to function in an analogous way and thus to be said to be "the same"—becomes much more difficult to swallow in the English translation. The respective meanings of the transitive verbs "to flower" and "to embalm" are anything but gracefully assimilated in our language, where their interpenetration conjures up the antiseptic atmosphere of formaldehyde and mortuary preparations as much as the balmy freshness of spring promenades in the country and aesthetic invention. The double meaning in the French can be no mere accident in a passage that claims to translate and reconcile outer experiences with inner recognitions, the foreign with the domestic, by means of an act of interiorization. That the restorative linden tea should produce a case of dyspepsia (or dyslexia) by being translated into English may itself be a symptom of a further-reaching disorder.

For the transposition of the linden blossoms into a foreign idiom merely brings out, in the same way that within the thematic description the delicate forest of stems highlights the suspension of rosy flowers, a figural play between foreground and background that was already, though more subtly, operative in the original. If the flowery glow of the original's figural meaning has a difficult time making it across to the English, it is equally true that what is underscored in its place by the translation is the literal spine of meaning that remains judiciously covered over by the figures, or "flowers," that are specific to the rhetoric of the French. To some extent, then, it is the very coarseness of the translation's insistence on a *literal* process of "flowering" and "embalming" that serves to remind us that, beneath and beyond the shared attribute of "gracefulness" common to the living and dried flowers, what is essentially at issue here is precisely the possibility of substituting those living blossoms that literally "flowered" with these dead leaves that have been literally "embalmed." And it is only after we have been reminded that all such flowers *can* be substituted for one another that it becomes possible to notice that the passage has indeed already switched the literal attributes so that the preserved leaves are now said to be "flowering" inside the package while the "embalming" of the living blossoms has already occurred outside in nature. Such a switch, of course, is just one more example of the kind of chiasmic exchanges from nature to mind and to text out of which the entire passage is constructed. In addition, though, this particular reversal from organic growth to artificial preservation is what remains to be *explained* by the passage, rather than merely taken for granted in it. What is the status of an explanation that uses what is to be proven as just another example for the truth of its argument?

In order to suggest an answer to this question it is necessary to look more closely at what happens in the passage when the attributes of nature and art are exchanged in the figure of the linden's flowering and embalming. First of all, the dried, dead flowers come back to life; they are resuscitated in a more permanent and accessible form than the fleeting blossoms could ever be considered to possess. And unlike the natural flowers, the preserved blossoms can be articulated into a fixed pattern; constructed or "woven" (*tressé*) like a text, moreover, they can be measured according to fixed conventions and finally consumed by the hero. As such, the reflowering of the linden tea becomes the prefiguration of the narrator's own resurrection, which is prescribed at the end of the novel as the production of just such a textual work of art.[18] But as is also noted at the end, and in conformity with the symmetry required by the chiasmic exchange of properties, it is possible for the dried leaves of the text to resuscitate only when the living blossoms of nature are made to die, are sacrificed in their place. Quoting the scriptural text, "unless it die . . . ," the narrator will of course finally have to recognize the necessary connotations of death and burial that were implicit all along in the verb *embaumer* (3:1044). Clearly, "embalming" is a metonymy for death in the passage we are reading, since it names a process or a ceremony that presupposes a death and a corpse upon which to operate its preservative function.

In the terms of the Christian allegory that is mimed throughout the novel, the "madeleine" is also a proper name, Magdalene. As such, it has a specific role to perform in this sacrificial structure: "At that time, Mary Magdalene, Mary the mother of James, and Salome, brought spices, that they might go and *anoint* Jesus" (Mark, 16:1–2). The madeleine, then, already names the faculty and the agent of the anointing and embalming it performs on the narrator's boyhood; through its homonymy with Mary Magdalene it smears the natural corpse of Combray with the perfumed oils of linden in order to preserve it ritually. The ceremony of the eucharist, which for the hero is the partaking of the linden-soaked madeleine, therefore works as well for a prefiguration of the writer's resurrection as for a commemoration of the boy's own death and burial.

The coherence of this system of death and resurrection seems to be guaranteed by the privileged status accorded in it to *memory,* conceived here as the intermediate space between organic nature and subjective

---

18. In the drafts, the trelliswork of the linden blossoms is compared to an antique lace, or "dentelle": "most of them . . . had turned the golden, almost russet color of an antique lace that is a bit shabby [*fripée*]" (*Études proustiennes,* 5:242). In the symbolist genealogy at work here, Nerval's lace metaphor must be torn by Mallarmé before it can find its afterlife in Proust.

thought. This is the faculty thanks to which nature's death can be anointed and preserved while it awaits a resurrection in a future knowledge to be made available in its transfiguration into a work of art. Proust could not be clearer on this point when he has the narrator ask: "So then, wasn't the recreation by the memory of impressions that would later have to be elaborated, illuminated, and transformed into intellectual equivalents, one of the conditions, in fact, the very essence of the work of art as I had just conceived it?" (3:1044). As the condition and essence of what is described in the same passage as an "art of thought," this kind of memory must be considered to determine the self-conscious subject it subsequently allows to come into being. That is why, not only in Proust but in the entire tradition to which his text constantly makes reference, the preservation effected by memory is always figured as an *anthropomorphic* ceremony or a ritual, a participation by the human subject in the death (of natural experience) that is thereby preserved in a material impression.[19] The necessity of this human agency will also account for the crucial distinction Proust makes—complicated by the paradoxical and potentially misleading epithets he attaches to the mnemonic faculty—between *mémoire involontaire,* which presupposes the full engagement of the subject in the sacrificial ritual of preservation, and *mémoire volontaire,* which functions as a disengaged, disinterested and formalistic memory. For Proust, then, there are always *two* kinds of reality (and thus of self, of memory, of experience): one that is *material* and remains to be uncovered or recovered by dint of an active process of reading and writing; the other a superficial and false, one could say *ideological,* version of the first. Insofar as the *mémoire volontaire* does not take the implication of the self in the operations of memory seriously enough, it would also be like the merely "possible" truths of abstract and formal intelligence, if it were not oriented toward some imaginary *past* rather than a hypothetical present or future: "Of course, it is possible to

19. In this respect Baudelaire condenses the whole tradition in just a few lines of his poem on subjective memory, "Spleen II": "mon triste cerveau. / C'est une pyramide, un immense caveau, / Qui contient plus de morts que la fosse commune. / —Je suis un cimetière." Of course, Baudelaire is also a key intertext for Proust in associating the subjective faculty of memory with the sense of smell—an association especially remarkable in poems like "Le flacon," "La chevelure," and "Le goût du néant." However, what is of interest is not so much the simple fact that both authors make use of the same thematic articulation between odor and memory, but rather *how* such an articulation functions and is constituted textually.

extend the spectacles of the *mémoire volontaire,* which no more engage the fibers of our very selves than would leafing through a book of *picture images."* (3:873).[20]

Like the readability of the proper name that guarantees the truth of a book, the ritual of *mémoire involontaire* must include a material trace of what, in the linden tea episode, are called the "thousand useless details" that mark a given event as actually being "real" for the subject who thereby registers and appropriates it. As such, the mark is also a kind of *signature,* and it always belongs to a "me" in whose memory the dead past is promised a future resurrection through the work of writing it out: for instance, through the second coming, as text, of Christ, Madeleine, Marcel, or any recognizable signatory whatsoever, the distinction being elusive at this stage. Near the end of the *Recherche,* the narrator will insist that it is only thanks to the "somewhat aberrant particularity" that shapes the individual's own paraph, or signature, that the truth of an author's thought can become universally valid and available to others as well. This is so because the reader of such a signature is none other than its very own author, even when it seems to belong to someone else: "Actually, each reader, when he reads, is his very own reader. . . . The recognition that the reader makes, in himself, of what the book says is the proof of its truth, and vice versa" (3:910, 911). Books always say the same thing, then, and this is the survival, beyond the death of all natural experience, of the proper name: "a book is an enormous cemetery," Proust has his narrator say at one point, and learning how to read amounts to recognizing in it the construction of a monument to one's own name (3:903, 904).[21]

We are led back by the logic of this conclusion to the passage involving the hero's infusion of the madeleine and linden tea, since that is where the mechanics of the preservative power of the *mémoire involontaire* are most fully worked out. As the place where an initial

---

20. The richest, though by no means simplest, discussion of the wobbly distinction operative in Proust's concept of memory occurs, interestingly enough, in Benjamin's essay on Baudelaire, "On Some Motifs in Baudelaire," *Illuminations,* trans. Harry Zohn (New York: Schocken, 1969), 157–63.

21. "In fact, if it is often said that his loves and losses have benefitted the poet, have helped him to build his oeuvre, if strangers who would least of all have suspected it . . . have each contributed a block of stone toward the erection of the monument they will never see, then it remains to be considered just how the writer's life does not end with this oeuvre" (904).

recounting in *Combray 1* of the memory of a material impression made during the subject's childhood (1:47–48) is then recomposed in *Combray 2* into a much more elaborate scenario (1:51–52), this passage can legitimately be taken as a model for the work of art that is called for by the writer at the end of the text. As such, it is itself an exemplary "elaboration, illumination, and transformation into intellectual equivalents" of the way involuntary memory functions as the unconditional principle of any art of thinking. The passage is, then, in strict accordance with Proust's own description, an *allegory* of memory, and it must therefore contain within itself all the elements required for the passage from experience to thought as well as their possible recombination in the ultimate construction of the *Recherche*. We have already examined how this allegory works as a process of continuous internalization that moves from the flowering and death of nature to the preservative embalming of memory, upon which any further flowering of textual reproduction and recognition will depend. The only element in this functioning of memory that remains to be located and accounted for is that of the human agent, who must at every stage underwrite and sign its own participation in the sacrifice of nature.

For in order to guarantee that the art of thought that resuscitates on the far side of natural experience can be understood as a thoroughly human work—rather than an unheard-of species of monster—the subject of memory that initiates it must indeed be recognizable as what the narrator refers to as "une *personne* de connaissance," a *personal* acquaintance. Such accounting hardly seems necessary, since in the scene of ritual ingestion the overwhelming presence of the boy himself, as well as of Tante Léonie and the helping hand of the druggist-artist, should more than suffice as a gauge of human participation. Nonetheless, the premature and unexplained figural crossing of the attributes of life and death, traceable in the chiasmic substitution of the lindens' "flowering" for their "embalming," cannot fail to be somewhat disturbing. In strict defiance of the genetic logic of cause and effect it lays claim to, this crossing occurs just *before* the proof concerning the linden flower's essential identity in life and death is concluded, and it thereby alerts us once again to a potential complication in memory's capacity to complete the trajectory from death (nature) to life (art) it assigns itself. For what kind of (rhetorical) trick would it be to switch "life" for "death" *before* these very terms have been allowed to acquire their full ontological significance for the human subject, which can be defined solely in relation to them? How would it then be possible to resuscitate what has never actually died? Or conversely, what could it mean to kill something that has never actually lived?

These questions remind us that what is at stake in reading Proust is the possibility of establishing and maintaining a genealogy, though they do so in such a way that it becomes difficult to avoid the interference of a palpably ethical tonality. At what point can it be said that this became inevitable and not just a mere importation from outside the text? Certainly the intertextual reference in the *Recherche* to the figural pattern of the eucharist can never be completely isolated from the context of interpersonal violence that necessarily surrounds the sacrificial death commemorated in it.[22] The crown of thorns to which Tante Léonie's skull is compared thus makes her a prefiguration not only of an eventual resurrection but also of those other calvaries for which the narrator will later feel himself personally responsible, in particular the sufferings of his mother and grandmother. One even begins to suspect that the analogy he will eventually make between a book and "an enormous cemetery" may possibly have been dictated by similar feelings of guilt at having failed himself to live up to ethical responsibilities involving the welfare of others. In themselves, however— and no matter what the extent of the individual's turpitude, which in this case, and for the purposes of the story, seems to have been magnified to somewhat hyperbolic proportions—such feelings of personal guilt would *not* be able to account for the more radical question of how it is possible to establish the sacrificial difference between life and death in the first place. And this question becomes unavoidable from the moment Proust's text uses nature, the natural cycle of the seasons and the organic process of the seed's maturation, as an allegorical figure for the embalming and preserving operations of the *mémoire involontaire*. Which makes it from the very beginning an ethical question or rather *the* ethical question: what constitutes true "life," and

22. This is made abundantly clear in the parodic and dissonant juxtaposition of roles in which the celebrant of the sacrifice, in this case Françoise, can appear, depending on whether it is seen from the perspective of the kitchen or the dining room altar: "When I came down [Françoise] was in the process . . . of killing a chicken which, by means of a desperate resistance that was completely understandable, . . . tended to throw into relief the saintly gentleness and unctuousness of our servant less than it would have at the following day's dinner by means of its skin embroidered with gold like a chasuble and its precious juice drained from a chalice" (1:121–22).

"who" (or what) can determine the circumstances under which this process may be (rightly) interrupted?

The allegory of memory in Proust is also a story about how the natural development of life, the growth of a seed, is interrupted and brought to a halt before it can complete itself. As a consequence, it is an allegory of what can thus be called "abortion," and it includes the ethical dimension necessarily engaged by this term. In order to make the linden tea in this text, nature must be "preserved," but in order to be preserved, the natural process of maturation must be interrupted somewhere *short* of its endpoint: "in the little gray bulbs I recognized the green buds that had not come to term."[23] It is at this point that the status of the signature, of the assurance of a "personal acquaintance" or *human* agent who would be recognizable as such throughout the process, becomes absolutely crucial. The interruption at issue here would work in an understandable and acceptable way only so long as it is construed in terms of a *sacrificial* economy that always takes natural life away in order to turn it into an allegorical language signifying something else, something *higher* because more "elaborated and illuminated . . . *true* life." This claim can of course be made when some*one* endowed with consciousness (and potentially conscience) intentionally makes use of nature, uses it up, exploits it, and even erases it in order to nourish the life of subjectivity with it cognitively and aesthetically (physiologically as well). The (ethical) problem would arise only when the line that *must* be drawn to separate the "life" that is said to be merely "natural" from the one that is determined as being, more or less, consciously "human" becomes open to genuine questioning.

In the same way, to suggest that the allegory of memory is also an allegory of "abortion" could, at least in principle, be understood as the deployment of a rather innocent, if striking, figure. It becomes (ethically) problematic only when, as in reading Proust, a question arises

---

23. The insistence on an interruption of the organic process at every point short of "completion" is even clearer in the drafts of this passage, where the anthropomorphic reference is also not elided: "With very little effort one could recognize in a little yellow shell a bud that was going to open when the plant had died, in an anemone-red capsule a fruit that had not come to maturity, this bouquet of little bulbs that dreamily lays its heads one against the other, *like the heads of tender children,* are the seeds that did not come to maturity" (*Études proustiennes,* 5:245, emphasis added).

with respect to an understanding of the status—human or nonhuman —of the "buds" and "flowers" that are actually *referred* to within the allegory and that are cut down before they are allowed to come to term. The question of what is human, the ethical question, has brought us back to the question of the figure, or of what is rhetorical, that first disclosed the "human" *as* a question. This is what Paul de Man means when he says that ethicity is the *referential* version of a linguistic predicament: that is, ethicity is the ineluctable pressure to decide between literal and figural meaning when the *reference* at stake includes the line dividing "human" from "nonhuman" as well as the necessarily concomitant value system of "right" and "wrong."[24] In the passage in Proust we have been dealing with, the interference of the ethical values of right and wrong with the cognitive determination of the rhetorical status of "bud" and "flower" would become truly problematic—and simultaneously imperative—were the line between human and nonhuman (in this case, the "budding flowers") somehow to be crossed. Is there in fact a point in this text where it becomes impossible to distinguish the behavior of the (nonhuman) flowers from that of the human subjects?

There are indications outside the passage that this may indeed be the case. It could be rather unsettling, for example, to place the linden blossom episode side by side with the final "illumination" of what constitutes, in *Le temps retrouvé,* the narrator's "vocation" as writer: "Thus my whole life . . . the memories of its sorrows and its joys, formed an inner reservoir identical to the albumen that is stored in the ovule of plants and from which the ovule extracts the nourishment required to transform itself into a seed. And this at a time when no one knows that the plant's embryo is developing as the site of respiratory and chemical phenomena that are no less active for their remaining

24. See "Allegory (Julie)," *Allegories of Reading* (New Haven: Yale University Press, 1979), 206. See, also, "The Epistemology of Metaphor," in *On Metaphor,* ed. Sheldon Sacks (Chicago: University of Chicago Press, 1978), 1979: "One now sees that the figure is not only ornamental and aesthetic but powerfully coercive since it generates, for example, the ethical pressure of such questions as 'to kill or not to kill.'" In this case, de Man's formulation of the problem is derived from Locke, where the specificity of the example is "the predicament (to kill or not to kill the monstrous birth)" that can appear either in the guise of a "logical argument" or an "ethical issue" (17–18). For a slightly different, more extended and original, reading of this gesture toward ethicity in de Man, see Werner Hamacher, "LECTIO: De Man's Imperative," in *Reading de Man Reading,* ed. Lindsay Waters and Wlad Godzich (Minneapolis: University of Minnesota Press, 1989), esp. 183–87.

secret. So too was my life in contact with that which would be accomplished through its maturation" (3:899). For one thing, reading the two passages together reconfirms the complex spatio-temporal structure of memory: it is an interiorizing process that evolves throughout the novel, absorbing into itself along the way the physiological functions of nourishment, fertilization, and even reproduction.[25] Memory, in this novel, is an internalization powerful enough to link the acts of ingestion and generation in an eroticized phantasm whose extreme form would be cannibalism: memory is a faculty that swallows the entire world and then tries to reproduce itself from out of its own stomach.

Yet even here, where the writer's interpersonal relations are seen retrospectively as so many opportunities for self-reproduction from the fecundating traces left on the imprinted surface of his memory, the critical distinction between human and botanical (or animal) forms of life does not appear to be seriously threatened. As long as the writer, *as human*, remains the unquestioned "ground" for the metaphor, the "vehicle" of the plant's (or animal's) functioning can itself be assimilated into a figural balance achieved between two fully constituted and separate entities. More troublesome, from this point of view, is the fact that the second passage on the writer's vocation must presuppose the accomplishment of its own future, as a written text, on the basis of or by analogy to a *prior* knowledge of how the "natural" maturation of the plant works. But it is precisely such a *natural* process of maturation that is categorically denied to the (linden) blossoms in the earlier passage. As we have seen, the organic model referred to late in the text actually occurs beforehand by way of a disruption of organic development. Thus, the entire text is written from the logical point of view of a premature intervention into the natural process without which the

---

25. Thus we see once again that the actual reversals of inside and outside, which mark the most basic physiological functions with the processes of memory and thought, describe a möbius-like structure that would be anything but "formal" or "formalistic" (that is, metaphorical) in Deleuze's sense. Walter Benjamin's insight in this regard remains exemplary: Proust's image not only functions *metaphorically* like a rolled-up sock that can figure its own content ("gift") and form ("wrapping"); it is also and at the same time *another* thing—namely, an ordinary "stocking." See, "The Image of Proust," p. 205. The analysis that is being undertaken here of figural, mnemonic, digestive, and botanical processes would therefore also have to be extended to the entire network of sexuality in the *Recherche,* especially as it relates to the laws of sociability and society, of sexual difference and "inversion," of fecundation, generation, and genealogy, both "natural" and "figural," and of the law in general. Obviously, the opening pages of *Sodome et Gomorrhe* would be essential ones for this question.

preservative powers of memory would be inconceivable. We seem to end up with the same kind of circular reasoning between the beginning and end of the novel that could already be found operative within the space of a single sentence in the earlier switch between the "flowering" and the "embalming" of linden blossoms. The proof of the founding analogy between the genesis of a plant and the vocation of a writer *cannot* be made by presupposing the analogy as its own evidence, no matter how far such "proof" is extended and multiplied through the narrative development.

There is, however, a slight but decisive difference to be remarked between the two passages, and thus between the beginning and end of the novel. The orientation of the power of memory has shifted subtly from a perspective on what actually has occurred in the past to what, as a result, *can* happen in the future. Where the earlier passage insists that the preserved tea petals are the very same as the blossoms that *once* began to flower, the later passage claims only that the transposition of the writer's "life" into his "text" thanks to memory *will be* like the "maturation" of the plant's seed. We cannot rule out the possibility that the later analogy, which makes explicit the relation between the budding plant and the writer, and which is only hinted at in the earlier episode, is saying something far more complicated and less easy to assimilate than a casual reading would suggest. For there is no a priori reason to suppose that the concluding passage on the writer's vocation is in any way blind (or deaf) to what has already been written in the earlier section on the writer's apprenticeship. On the contrary, there is every reason to believe that we can be said to "read" a text only when we allow our understanding of it to be governed in this way by its own, rather than our, premises and development.

By finally claiming that the role to be played by memory in the writer's future is to be understood by analogy to the seed's maturation—which the text itself has already structured as a radical *disruption* of the process of organic development—the later passage may simply be reminding us that, *until* we have allowed this textual "abortion" to redetermine whatever is meant by "nature," "seed," "maturation," and even the concept of "future" itself, we have not *yet* sufficiently read the earlier version. In fact, since what is at issue is historical temporality as such, we should not even say that this version could in any essential way be "earlier" until it will have been read. Until the reinscription of nature that occurs in the text is read, nothing whatsoever can take place materially—early or late. What if this text were therefore writing about the possibility of a future that could *only* take place once our reading registered and moved beyond the interruption of the natural order it has itself already produced? As such, the maturation of the future would be the least natural event imaginable, and it would remain before "us" only as a secret possibility, requiring a kind of time and a kind of embryo different from anything "we" now know: "a time when no one knows that the plant's embryo is developing as the site of secret respiratory and chemical phenomena that are no less active for their remaining secret" (3:899).

And since, only a few pages after describing his own vocation as writer in these terms, the narrator appeals to a genealogical line that would also include Nerval and Baudelaire, this reminder about what remains to be read would apply equally well to their texts.[26] Of course, we would as little be able to continue to understand such a "genealogy" in terms of unbroken lines of conception, birth, and filiation as we would now be able to continue to understand "nature" in this text in terms of a simply natural maturation. The traditional concept of genealogy would thus be open to disruption at every point by being reinscribed within such a "tradition" of writers, whose textual production of a future would remain to be read not only in these texts but in other, nongenealogical, that is to say, noncanonical, texts marked with the most heterogeneous signatures as well. "What remains to be read": such would be the formula for what, still in embryo, could only occur or be produced in a text beyond the shattering interruption of the (natural) plant's embryo and all that it conditions, including the philosophical concepts of "filiation" and even "abortion" itself. If there is still to be a history that could ever contain this ruptured genealogy—comprising at the very least Nerval, Baudelaire, Proust, and by implication Mallarmé—it would be one that could be given only as a *future:* history would be the as-yet-to-be-accomplished "maturation" of what has already taken place in these and other writers as a textual "abortion."[27]

26. "One of the chef-d'oeuvres of French literature, Gérard de Nerval's *Sylvie* . . . has about it the same kind of feel as the taste of madeleine. . . . And in Baudelaire, of course, these reminiscences, which are even more numerous, are obviously less fortuitous, and as a result, decisive in my opinion. . . . So I would try to remind myself of those pieces by Baudelaire whose basis was the transposition of such a feeling, in order finally to get myself back into a *filiation* as noble as that one" (3:919–20).

27. One should not forget in this context that "abortion" is a political issue of some urgency as well as a "mere" rhetorical structure deployed and interrogated in Proust's

The implications of this conclusion for a reading of the episode of the linden blossoms are considerable, from both a rhetorical and an ethical point of view. First of all, it has the effect of making "us" responsible, as readers, for this textual abortion. We should not assume too quickly, however, that such responsibility can be adequately understood, measured, or prescribed in the subjective or intersubjective terms in which the concept of responsibility is by tradition assessed, although we cannot simply afford to disregard these terms. By far the most curious thing about the linden blossoms in Proust is that their organic development is not checked or aborted by the intervention of a *human* subject already assured of the attributes of consciousness and conscience. It is rather nature her- or itself that functions as an incomprehensible intervention into its own process of natural growth—which is also to say that nature is not primarily natural in this text. The "responsibility" thus becomes the burden of determining with as much precision as possible just how it is that our own future as "living subjects" is made to depend on a kind of nature that is itself the source of unnatural acts, and first of all, the inhuman signing of its own death sentence. The petals that announce the flowering of spring cut it off in the same breath and, through a ritualized abortion, preserve it for future use in a state of suspended animation. One can hardly believe it, but where the symmetry of the figural crossing between art and nature would require only that the springtime blossoms be embalmed by the druggist before they

---

text, although it may be a naive (or strategic) gesture to pretend that urgent political issues can be considered, much less decided, without reference to or interference from rhetorical structures. Barbara Johnson is one critic who has written thoughtfully and provocatively on the complex relation between figurative language and the question of mothers and abortion. Her remarks on the necessity of considering the gender of the mother whenever the question of "abortion" is raised would have a wholly salutary influence on a reading of Proust's text. Instead of asking if Albertine is really a male (Albert) portrayed as a female figur(ine), it would be more to the point to ask how Proust's abortive signature can be read maternally. This should not be taken to mean that there is no (empirical) difference between a male and a female (writer), nor that there is nothing absolutely irreducible in the significance an "abortion" can have for a "woman." Rather, the displacement of the mother in Proust's text suggests that a straightforward *negation* of the metaphorical and conceptual system in favor of empirical reality (or vice versa) would still remain too much within the same (paternal or patriarchal) structure it attempts to unsettle. For this reason, it would also be inadequate to account for the "truth" of history, that is to say, what Proust's text discloses as the mater(n)iality of what actually occurs in history as the abortion of the future. See Johnson's "Apostrophe, Animation, and Abortion" together with "Mallarmé as Mother," *A World of Difference* (Baltimore: Johns Hopkins University Press, 1987).

are allowed to flower inside his package, reinforcing in this way the proximity of the human subject to nature throughout the internalizing process of memory, the text actually demonstrates, beyond any doubt, that "these petals were the very ones that had embalmed the evenings of spring *before* they flourished in the druggist's package."[28]

And whether we like it or not, it is the logic of the text that is consistent here, since according to Proust, true "life" can never be consciously present at its own conception and maturation. Rather, it can only be *re*cognized or *re*discovered by the subject, who must always stumble across it belatedly and as if by accident—after a radical break in consciousness or self-presence—much like the narrator in the courtyard of the Guermantes, when he finally loses his balance for good and becomes a writer. What makes such recognition possible is memory. But that same memory, as the aborted intersection of mind and nature, is itself nothing but this "moment" of losing control, or of stumbling, which is preserved in the material traces of Proust's text. It is the fall in which nature is no longer natural and the subject is not yet human.[29] This means, of course, that the reason *la mémoire involontaire* is involuntary is not because it is not controlled

28. Proust's sentence "ces pétales étaient bien ceux qui avant de fleurir le sac de pharmacie avaient embaumé les soirs de printemps" must have seemed so incomprehensibly unnatural to his English translator, C. K. Scott-Moncrieff, that it was corrected, even at considerable cost to its grammar, to something like, "ces pétales étaient bien ceux qui, avant de fleurir, le sac de pharmacie avait embaumés les soirs de printemps," since his translation reads, "these were the petals which, before their flowering time, the chemist's package had embalmed on warm evenings of spring." *Swann's Way*, trans. C. K. Scott-Moncrieff (New York: Modern Library, 1928), 63. Petals can "embalm" (or embellish) natural flowering with a scent only because they can "embalm" (or preserve) natural flowering as an unnatural material trace: the condition of possibility in both instances is a law of figural supplementarity. There is nothing natural in making the scent of flowers function as though it were an embellishment that could somehow be added to (or for that matter subtracted from) a more basic condition of natural growth.

29. The episode in question involves the narrator's loss of equilibrium when his foot seesaws between two unequally positioned paving stones (3:866–67), itself a figure taken from empirical experience to illustrate Proust's definition of "reality": "What we call reality is a certain relation between those sensations and these memories [of vague hopes and projects]" (3:889). As the only access we have to the relation between sense perceptions and a formalized system of meaning or intentionality, the material traces of Proustian memory are like the inaugural concatenation, in a semiosis, of the two heterogeneous "surfaces" of perception and signification that result from it. The *gap* between these two paving "stones," because it is still represented within the homogeneous space of empirical experience, is therefore itself an inadequate or hobbled symbol for Proust's concept of the hobbling symbol.

by the subject; it is involuntary because in it the "subject" in control is not itself human or dependent for its power on human intentions or desires. As such, as this possibility of turning away (from a nature that is no longer there naturally) and of turning toward (a human subject that cannot yet be present to itself as such), *mémoire involontaire* can only be language considered as pure figuration. Memory, as this power of radical turning in language, is thus the unnatural and inhuman album(en) where an abortion of nature is written down and stored as the embryonic promise of a human subject that is not yet there.

To be responsible for memory's abortion, then, cannot be taken to mean a simple return to a concept of human or natural responsibility. This would be to refuse to be reminded of the necessarily rhetorical dimension in ethics, in the mistaken belief that we already understood fully the difference between nature and culture, and thus what it means to be human. Rather, as a responsibility oriented toward the future "maturation" of a textual abortion in which both nature and culture and all their distinctions founder, it would be one that, in ways yet to be determined, allowed this unnatural and inhuman element within our own memory to be written into history as what "survives" nature and culture.[30] It would mean to produce a genuine genealogy precisely by "elaborating, illuminating, and transforming" this inhuman and unnatural element in which the language of memory outlives the impossibility of both getting back to nature and getting on with being human. And this would be the truly critical aspect of Proust's text. For by reminding us of the necessarily linguistic structure of symbolism's history, by reminding us that the turn to history must no longer be conceived on a natural model but that it cannot yet be founded on a purely human one either, Proust's text helps to neutralize the place of usurped authority that is occupied whenever the representatives of so-called natural and human or moral law do not take into account in a critical way the inhuman and unnatural element of which they too partake.

History, as the future of this memory, must be written, can in fact only occur as writing. But such writing becomes illegitimate from the

---

30. In the drafts for the passage on the linden tea, Proust had considered having his description of the legible "characters" left in the preserved blossoms culminate in a "burst of flowers that detaches them from all the rest, painted in gold with the thread of their stamens as though on a chasuble, that is *survival*" (*Études proustiennes*, 5:245). The kind of survival at issue in Proust would not be incompatible with what Jacques Derrida has written about "living on." See "Survivre," *Parages* (Paris: Galilée, 1986).

moment it is read as a simple prescription whose coherence could ever be given or retrieved by symbolic recourse to natural or human, and therefore transcendental, principles. In Proust, the coherence of the prescriptive rule is torn irremediably when the blossoms of memory interrupt their own flowering. In doing so they abort their natural development by inscribing it within a system of textual notation whose rhetorical principles remain in part irreducible to either organic or human models of genealogical development, though such principles cannot be made wholly independent of them either. Ethics, or ethicity, can begin to occur historically only when, in addition to filling mere (human) prescriptions, it goes on to register the marks of this inhuman tear. It is by a prodigality that exceeds the measure, by remembering the "thousand useless details" left by the inscription of the deadly blossoms, that the pharmacist in Proust shows us how to be a reader and writer of history as well as a filler of prescriptions and, beyond all the dismembered flies and flowers, how to make room in a text for the future of a blank album.

5 The Duplicitous Genre of André Gide

> In point of fact, the past few years have seen the rise of a new literary genre, which has enjoyed immense success, and which could be called the "defense" or the "alibi." Its common theme, more or less, would be: "the author will show, despite all appearances to the contrary, that he is not an author."
> —Jean Paulhan, *Les fleurs de Tarbes*

With the advent of André Gide on the French literary scene, it appears as though some real progress had finally been made with respect to the dead-end and hothouse atmosphere of *fin de siècle* aesthetics. What is ushered in by Gide—beginning around 1897 with the publication of *Les nourritures terrestres* but already prepared by the symbolist parodies of *Le voyage d'Urien* and *Paludes*—is nothing less than a new line of French letters, the rebirth of French literature in the twentieth century. Or rather, what appears in Gide is the twentieth century *as* a birth that could finally be more alive, more real, more historical, than just another elusive symbolist dream or obsession. Such, at any rate, is the thematic and chronological scheme of self-analysis and evaluation that had become firmly embossed on the face of French literature by the time Gide died in 1951, and that was begun in the critical writing of the period as early as 1913, when Jacques Rivière used Gide as the model for inaugurating what he called the genre of the *roman d'aventure*.[1] According to Rivière, at that moment in French literature something had died and disappeared that would never be seen again, and any writer who wanted to live beyond this death would have to be disengaged from it: "Symbolism . . . has hung

---

1. See "Le roman d'aventure," *Nouvelles études* (Paris: Gallimard, 1947). Further references appear in the text.

on for a long time after reaching its zenith, but now it is dead and there is nothing left to do in the line opened up by it" (235).

There is a call to action here, and it is one that has become distressingly familiar in the domain of literary studies since Rivière's formulation of it on the eve of the First World War. For the action referred to here is the turn away from literature itself, in this case a turn from what is considered the hyperconsciousness and inactivity of symbolist formalism to the extraliterary world of action itself: "this sudden youthfulness makes every one of our contacts with the world a delicious one; it is enough to look around us to find any number of pleasures: the pleasure of being in the midst of events, or in the midst of people. And first of all the pleasure of being someone to whom something happens" (247). It is itself no accident that the gratuitous, accidental nature of Gide's famous *acte gratuit* will always be characterized by its commentators as precisely that of an extraliterary *action* or *event*, of something that, beyond the morass of a self-reflexive literary tradition, at last and no matter what the consequences, can and will *happen* in the world of immediate experience.

Gide himself, of course, participated actively in forging this literary myth of which he became the most recognizable authorial emblem. In August 1921, while he was working on the only text he would recognize as rich enough in events or happenings to belong to the genre of the *roman, Les faux-monnayeurs,* he wrote the symbolist epitaph that remains for the most part unquestioned even today: "The symbolist school. The greatest objection to it is the little curiosity it showed toward life . . . they were all pessimists, renouncers, resigners, *las du triste hôpital.* . . . Poetry became for them a refuge, the only escape from hideous realities. . . . Disenchanting life from all that they considered only a lure, doubting that it was worth the trouble to 'be lived,' it is no wonder they weren't able to produce a new ethics . . . but only an aesthetics."[2] The adventure of the twentieth century, what allows contemporary literature to be born or reborn, is what remains unformulated or incomplete in symbolism: the implied link that could eventually lead from a textual "aesthetics" to a lived "ethics." And so when Edmund Wilson writes his classic history of symbolist literature, which is nothing less than the genetic narrative of how literature once

2. André Gide, *Journal des faux-monnayeurs,* in vol. 13 of the *Oeuvres complètes,* ed. Louis Marin-Chauffier (Paris: Gallimard, 1937), 37–38. "Las du triste hôpital," of course, are the opening words of Mallarmé's poem, "Les fenêtres."

again became historical in the twentieth century, he uses Gide's indictment to situate his own concluding chapter.[3]

According to such a developmental scheme, aesthetics and ethics would themselves be distinct "genres" of literature, though what they would represent as genres would be the ultimate possibility of isolating the formal element in literature in order to move squarely beyond it into the direct experience of a world of historical reality and action. Such schemes of coordination between a literary form and a historical experience, which are always predicated on and from the perspective of the modern, the postmodern, and the contemporary, presuppose a concept of historical process and progress that implies that literature could at certain moments transform and overcome itself through its own means. Literature could thus become truly historical, according to this common perception, only by producing in itself an ethics (or lived content) that would be perfectly contained and reflected in its aesthetics (or literary form). The aesthetic theory of such a genre would be so permeated by the ethical force of its literary formulation that it would no longer be simply aesthetic. Gide's own aesthetic trajectory, which runs roughly speaking from *Le traité du Narcisse* (1891) to *Thésée* (1946), would be the perfect analogon or "symbol" for this mythological itinerary *from* symbolism *to* history, since it plainly traces the passage from the death of Narcissus's aesthetic interiority to the founding of the ethical space of Theseus's polis. That Gide himself was not wholly blind to some of the deeper tensions that might attend the passage from formalism to history by means of a thoroughly formalistic device, or symbol, can be seen in his perennial struggle (and failure) to achieve a literature of total "sincerity" or "authenticity."

But through a kind of twist or reversal that is always possible in the consciousness of failure, one is tempted to add that it is precisely by representing so doggedly this struggle to achieve sincerity in his writing that Gide can become the very model of the sincere and engaged author. It is this sort of dialectical reversal of opposing terms that must have motivated Sartre's comment, in March 1951, that it could only be at the moment of Gide's actual death "that we discover just how much he remained alive."[4] The fact that it is Sartre speaking here about the

---

3. Edmund Wilson, *Axel's Castle* (New York: Norton, 1931), p. 257. This last chapter treats Rimbaud, who is said to have fled symbolism "to a life of pure action" (283).

4. Jean-Paul Sartre, "Gide vivant," in *Les temps modernes* 65 (March 1951), 1537.

life and death of literary figures is not inconsequential. For a philosophy and literature of existence and commitment like his own would in many ways be among the most legitimate heirs of Gide's literary project, and they would therefore depend on Gide's presumed ability to rescue literature and thought from what Sartre also refers to in this article as the "symbolist rut." What is thus endorsed at the moment of his empirical death is the capacity of Gide's writings to rehabilitate or regenerate a nineteenth-century literature of dead formalism by re-establishing in its place an aesthetic proximity to the activities and adventures of "life." Such an event of palingenesis is the very figure of Gide's accomplishment in French letters, moreover. It functions not only as the crucial *biographical* turn from the stifling *cénacles* of Paris to the open roads of North Africa, but also as a *textual* figure that recurs from one end of Gide's oeuvre to the other, from the theme of *Les nourritures terrestres* to the title of the autobiographical *Si le grain ne meurt*.[5] The specular structure thereby suggested between the *ethic* of a life and the *aesthetic* of a literary vocation confirms yet again the figural pattern of inside/outside turns that comprise any historical development that is based on organic and genetic models. The passage described by Gide's turn away from the past (Mallarmé) announces an eventual turn toward the future (Sartre); and this turn should also be read as being more or less equivalent, on the referential level, to the aesthetic evolution that actually takes place in his writings from the solitary figure of Narcissus to the social art of Theseus.

This game of mirrors, where the texts seem to reflect what is happening in the life so that the life can then reflect what is being described in the texts, resembles nothing so much as the fullest extension conceivable of Gide's most notorious and least understood legacy to the field of literary theory: the *mise en abyme*. In its casual usage, the *mise en abyme* is regularly taken to refer to a (potentially endless) process of self-reflexivity or autoillustration, which would characterize

5. Gide left for North Africa for the first time in October 1893; it was there that he experienced the revelation of his homosexuality. *Les nourritures terrestres* was published in 1897 and was meant to purge literature of the "risk" represented by symbolism's separation from life by "hurling it into an *abyss* of sensualism." See Yvonne Davet's *Autour des nourritures terrestres* (Paris, Gallimard, 1948), 18–22. For Gide's description of the stuffy aestheticism of the symbolist *cénacles*, one has the choice of reading a parodic transposition in *Paludes* or an autobiographical version in *Si le grain ne meurt*. Gide's experiences, or experimentations, with communism would provide an analogous example in the overtly political realm. See his *Retour de l'USSR* as well as the *Retouches*.

the self-enclosed modernist text. As it is described in the *Journal,* moreover, the "mise en abyme" does in fact first look like an ordinary intratextual mirror:

> I have a distinct preference for those works of art in which it is possible to find, transposed onto the scale of the characters, the subject of the work itself. Nothing illuminates it better, nothing more surely guarantees the proportions of the whole. Thus, in certain paintings of Memling or of Quentin Metzys, a dark little convex mirror reflects in its turn the interior of the room in which the scene being painted takes place. . . . And in literature as well, in *Hamlet,* the scene of the play, and in many other theatrical representations too. In *Wilhelm Meister,* the marionette scene or the castle festival. . . . None of these examples is absolutely right. What would be much more exact, what would illustrate better what I was looking for in my *Cahiers [d'André Walter],* in my *[Traité du] Narcisse,* in *La tentative [amoureuse]* is the comparison with that technique of heraldry that consists of putting into one part of the shield a second one "en abyme." (*Journal 1889–1939:* 41)[6]

But we should not overlook the fact that precisely *this* reference to a purely formal and internal "mise en abyme" is itself part of a larger, extratextual "shield" under whose aegis all the self-reflexive pages of the *Journal* have in fact been written. For "la mise en abyme" occurs in the *Journal* only as a further illustration of a more comprehensive "abyssal" structure that would put the writer's *text* into direct contact with the existential production of the writer's *self:* "I wanted to indicate, in this *Tentative amoureuse,* the influence of the book on the one who writes it, and during this very writing. For in coming out of us, it changes us, it modifies the course of our life" (*Journal,* 40).

    6. It is symptomatic that the term *mise en abyme,* a technical term of heraldry coined as a metaphor for the specificity of the way Gide's own texts functioned, is used today almost as a cliché synonymous with the kind of formalistic self-consciousness and self-reflexivity often assumed to characterize the development of literary modernity in general. It is symptomatic for two reasons: (1) without the specific reference to Gide, it is used as though Gide's presence in this development were so pervasive that it need not even be mentioned by the entire age or aesthetic for which it becomes emblematic; (2) it is used as though its articulation in and by Gide's texts presented no real problems of exegesis and thus as though its meaning (of self-reflexivity) could itself be taken for granted by us *as* a (self-evident) cliché. For two representative studies that do more to exhibit than to analyze these symptoms critically, see Bruce Morrissette's article, "Un héritage d'André Gide: La duplication intérieure," in *Comparative Literature Studies,* 8 (June 1971), and Lucien Dällenbach's book, *Le récit spéculaire: Essai sur la mise en abyme* (Paris: Seuil, 1977).

The movement at issue in Gide's writing can start in either direction, then, but it always seems to lead to a final turn from letters back to life. Thus, a book can actually be written by artfully describing what it is like to write a book that does not as such exist (*Les faux-monnayeurs*, for instance). Or, a life can in fact evolve by experiencing what it is like to write about an imaginary experience (Gide's depiction here of *La tentative amoureuse*). In both cases there is a play of difference and similarity between separate though mutually supportive entities. The book that is eventually written will have to differ from and yet reflect the experience of the writer who produces it. And the life that is experienced will of course be changed by how that same life is imagined and written about in the book. However, in neither case would the reflexive relation between book and life be radically altered by its *mise en abyme*. This is so because what is always being assumed here is that a book *can* be written the same way one lives an experience and that a life *can* be lived the same way one writes a book—hence, the master figure of palingenesis. In Gide, palingenesis would ultimately name the writing self's ability to develop its fundamental identity by rising up again the same after each new (writing) experience thanks to another one—much in the way that the character Michel, in *L'immoraliste*, understands his own rebirth by analogy to the reading and writing of a palimpsest.[7] Like the "recent" authors mentioned by Paulhan in *Les fleurs de Tarbes*, Gide would be a writer who always seems to be writing in order to prove to himself and others that he is not really a writer.

The assumption of such an adequation between the principles governing both books and life, or aesthetics and ethics, is of course not in itself a foolish or illegitimate one—on the contrary. But the fact that it relies ultimately on *differential* relations to constitute closed structures of reflexivity, that is, that it tries to establish and maintain meaningful identities by means of mirrors and metaphors, serves to remind us that we may be closer to perpetuating the myth of Narcissus than we had at first been led to believe. For what has "happened" in this version of the passage from symbolism to history is merely the extension of a formal

---

7. See *L'immoraliste, Romans, récits, soties,* ed. Yvonne Davet and Jean-Jacques Thierry (Paris: Gallimard, 1958), 398–99. Further references to this edition of Gide's prose works appear in the text. Also of interest in this regard is Gide's statement in the "Postface" he wrote for the second edition of *Paludes* (1895), which was also to serve as an "announcement" of *Les nourritures terrestres:* "It is necessary to defend oneself against every new book" (1477).

and intratextual complementarity between text and ideal meaning to a referential and extratextual complementarity between text and what is here being called real "life." That is to say, nothing has really happened at all in this call to action, unless we could call it a more serious relapse into the very symbolist malady that it was intended to cure. Not only has the new specularity between text and world not changed the original formal structures it was meant to replace; it has not even examined in any critical way the premises and functioning of the formalist thinking it unknowingly reproduces on a larger and more serious scale. Theseus, it seems, has not only *not* emerged into the daylight from the labyrinthine forms of Narcissus's mirror; he has not even yet encountered the actual Minotaur hidden within it.

This, at any rate, is the implication of a reading of Gide's itinerary from symbolism to sincerity that would not simply align itself with Sartre by affirming the successful and unquestioned *completion* of such a passage as its own mirror image. An example of such a reading is provided by the reading and writing of Maurice Blanchot. Because Blanchot does not take lightly the possibility that a book can be *written* the same way one lives an experience, or that a life can be *experienced* the same way one writes a book, by the same token he does not take for granted the easy specularity of these categories within the structure of the *mise en abyme*. Nor does Blanchot accept uncritically the suggestion that the passage from Narcissus to Theseus, which does occur as a "chronological" advance within the evolving career of Gide's own writing, would be "historical" in any essential way. And it is precisely because Gide's Theseus is *not enough* of a Narcissus, not enough of a formalist or a "symbolist," that is, that he and his history can always be suspected of fraud. As Blanchot himself puts it in his essay on Gide:

> When we see Theseus come out of the labyrinth, glorious victor in a battle no one watches, it is only right to suspect him of cheating or trickery. For there is only a labyrinth for the one who is put to the test by it, and the test is real only for the one who is truly lost in it, and the one who is lost in it is no longer there to attest to his loss. . . . That is a dilemma for which there is no out. Theseus rediscovers his route because he remains tied to something secure; but because he has not cut the thread, he remains the one who has not known the labyrinth.[8]

---

8. Maurice Blanchot, "Gide et la littérature de l'expérience," *La part du feu* (Paris: Gallimard, 1949), 219–20. Further references appear in the text. Blanchot's response to

To break the thread, "rompre le fil" or "abolir la dentelle," is what Theseus does *not* do, according to Blanchot, and therein lies his deceit, his "illusion," or "supercherie." He is not deceitful because he is unethical; he has not yet reached the genuinely ethical possibility, because his encounter with history is only an illusion. Blanchot, who in this respect is much closer than either Gide or Sartre to being an actual descendant of Mallarmé, suggests here that only by cutting oneself off is it possible to enter the labyrinth and to make of the labyrinth an experience or event that would have the status of a genuine occurrence rather than of an empty fiction or illusion. As long as the labyrinth is circular, as long as one can come out of it the same way one has gone in, one has not broken the thread, which is also a barrier that keeps anything whatsoever from happening.

But then what about Gide's *abyme* or abyss? What is the relation between the rhetorical structure of the "mise en abyme" and the thematic "labyrinth" that Blanchot describes as a "dilemma for which there is no way out"? Isn't the abyss, after all, also a kind of labyrinth, a place in which it is possible to be swallowed up and lost irremediably? Like the labyrinth, and still following Blanchot's rearticulation of it, the abyss could be encountered as an actual experience only if it can be entered into without the security of an uncut thread or cord. To be put into the abyss, "la *mise* en abyme," could only happen as an event if it is not taken as a circular, specular, or self-reflexive structure thanks to which, and by means of a mini-detour through writing, one ended up at more or less the same place one started out from. Gide's own description of being put into the abyss—perhaps because it is so straightforward, so prosaic, so banal—makes it difficult to take so seriously: "I wanted to indicate, in this *Tentative amoureuse,* the influence of the book on the one who writes it, and during this very writing. For in coming out of us, it changes us, it modifies the course of our life. . . . It is therefore a method, though an indirect one, of acting on oneself which I have offered there; and it is quite simply a story as well" (*Journal 1889–1939,* 40–41). Blanchot, after quoting once again this famous passage, notes the unexceptional character of the *mise en abyme,* but then he insists on something else as well:

---

the ideology of a literature of "action" is detailed at length in "La littérature et le droit à la mort," also in *La part du feu.*

It is easy to affirm: literature is an activity through which the one who is made to go through it tends not only to produce works that are beautiful, interesting, instructive, but tends also to be put absolutely to the test, not in recounting, expressing, or even in revealing oneself, but in pursuing an experience in which will be uncovered, with respect to this one and to his world, the sense of the human condition in its entirety. It is easy to repeat: writing, for the one who writes, has the value of a fundamental experience; one says it, and repeats it; but in the end what is repeated is nothing but a formula, illusory and without substance, that cannot stand up to analysis except by eluding the critique whose essential value it nonetheless affirms. One of the traits of Gide's *oeuvre* is that it helps us to understand these difficulties from which it stems itself. (211)

Blanchot insists on two important points in this passage—a passage that is itself not easy to read without immediately reducing it to the kind of empty formulae against which it warns. First of all, the *mise en abyme* is essentially double if not unthinkably duplicitous; it recounts, expresses, reveals, embellishes, instructs, and therefore *represents* whatever one expects or desires from an object of art; but it is an *act* or activity as well—"agir sur soi-même"—that, beyond any aesthetic function it may serve, has the power to put the world and one's place in it to an absolute test.[9] Secondly, this fundamentally double experience of writing—which is "quite simply a *story*" as well as "an *activity* of absolute self-trial"—has in addition a further propensity to (re)lapse into an empty formula that cannot stand up to the critical analysis it necessarily calls out for. Unless writing can maintain itself as story *and* act through a new act of what Blanchot calls critical analysis, it becomes a mere illusion, an empty and repetitive saying without substance. In other words, then, in order for the duplicity of the "mise en abyme" to happen at all, to occur itself in all of its historical heterogeneity, it must somehow cease to elude the kind of critique it demands *and* resists, resists *by* (merely) demanding. Blanchot's commentary is indispensable as a prolegomena to any reading of Gide because he is the only critic who has so acutely formulated the neces-

---

9. This duplicity informs all of Gide's work, from one end to the other, and thus to the point of making it difficult, structurally speaking, to tell one "end" from the other. The difficulty of construing the Gidean oeuvre as an itinerary, or "voyage," is already readable in the tension that splits an "early" work like *Le voyage d'Urien* between the dictum "it is always necessary to *represent*" and the recognition "we were tired of thought, we wanted *action*" (18–19).

sity of taking into account the nonspecular, self-obliterating, and labyrinthine structure of the "mise en abyme" from which he reminds us, all of Gide's writing stems.[10]

In order to read what is written in Gide, then, we must learn to give up merely repeating Gide's *mise en abyme* as a mechanical formula and begin to read it differently. If the *mise en abyme* is anything at all other than an empty illusion, it is something other than a self-reflexive and self-evident aesthetic experience that always ends up by reflecting the familiar desire to see our own self-image. By critically examining the *mise en abyme* of writing, we also begin to put ourselves to the test in it insofar as we allow the abyss to become the fundamentally disorienting experience it has to be. By the same token, we would also cut ourselves off from Gide's Theseus, who was not sufficiently able to cut himself off from the protective thread of an illusory labyrinth and thus could not expose himself to the labyrinth's actual threat. Only in this way would we have any access to the nonillusory and therefore genuinely *historical* element in Gide's writing. Such a history, which is also a "mise en abyme" of traditional historical schemes of development, is equated by Blanchot in his essay on Gide with the capacity to produce one's own past by giving to old words the future of a new meaning: "By his oeuvre and the manner in which he tied it to his life, Gide gave a new meaning to the word *essay*. One can find precursors in our entire literature, but what does that matter, since it is none other than Gide

---

10. There is something in Blanchot's insight into the self-resisting poles of Gide's writing that is reminiscent of Valéry's understanding of his own relation to Mallarmé, as well as of the relation between "aesthetics" and "ethics." See Valéry's "Lettre sur Mallarmé" in *Variété:* "In literature it is by *refusals* that hard work is revealed and accomplished. It could be said that it is measured by the number of refusals. . . . The rigor of the refusals, the quantity of the solutions that one rejects, the possibilities that one does not allow oneself, reveals the kind of scrupulousness, the degree of conscience, the quality of pride, and in the same way, the modesty and various fears one might feel about the future judgments of a public. It is at this point that literature intersects with the domain of the ethical" (*Oeuvres,* ed. Jean Hytier [Paris: Gallimard, Bibliothèque de la Pléiade, 1957], 1:641). No study of symbolism and history can afford to overlook entirely the important place that would be occupied in it by Valéry. The present chapter can thus also be taken to suggest that, just as we must learn to reevaluate Gide's "move beyond" the nineteenth-century symbolism of Mallarmé to contemporary history by actually reading his texts, so too must we learn to rearticulate the odd place Mallarmé holds within Valéry's writings, especially within the problematic articulation between his poetry and his critical and historical writings. A first gesture in this direction is provided by Werner Hamacher's "History, Teary: Some Remarks on *La Jeune Parque,*" *Yale French Studies* 74 (1988), 67–94.

himself who serves to illuminate this parentage by giving to those writers he relates himself to the new meaning that would justify such a filiation. One could say that he has *produced* those from whom he is *descended,* and that they owe him all that he himself owes them" (209).[11] This would be a concept of history, of the event and its tie, or "*fil*iation," to a meaning, that would be very different indeed from the linear trajectory we saw earlier, which runs from Narcissus to Theseus, from aesthetics to ethics, without a hitch. For history would not be temporal and sequential in any ordinary sense at all, since by giving itself the debt it always owes to another it could in no way be said to include one's own present as its natural endpoint or origin or anything else.

Rather, it would be a textual history, insofar as it is produced only as an event of reading and writing. History in this sense would be the continuous work of producing those from whom one is descended by means of a textual filiation. One breaks the thread of illusion and enters the labyrinth, Blanchot suggests in reading and writing his own debt to Gide, only by *tying* one's life to the abyss contained in the literary act. By exposing oneself to the actual risk in writing, one breaks with an empty concept of "experience" and joins oneself to all those who, like Gide, have already made the break by experiencing the abyss themselves. But as we also saw, such an abyssal event is always threatened by a relapse into the mechanical repetition of empty formulae and formalism, like that illusory victory of Theseus, who never goes anywhere. In order not to fall back all too quickly into the trap of an illusory and formulaic labyrinth, it would require not merely discovering, describing, teaching, or representing what Blanchot has to say about Gide's *mise en abyme,* but also critically examining how the abyss is actively put to the test in Gide's own writing. Where is it in Gide that we would be able to test Blanchot's affirmation that the *mise*

---

11. One thinks immediately that Blanchot must have Montaigne in mind here, especially since Gide had in fact pointed out this filiation between Montaigne and himself. Later in the essay, however, Blanchot makes it clear that he is also thinking of another kind of genealogy: "Having issued from symbolism, [Gide] does not give up his faith in the idea of perfection, in the virtues of a finished form and a polished style" (211). Rather than simply replacing one line of filiation ("les moralistes français") with another ("les symbolistes"), Blanchot's rearticulation of Gide's self-displacing debts of literary genealogy serves to reopen the question of all these lines, since it would now become necessary to test in what way our understanding of Montaigne's discursive "essai" is disrupted by putting it into contact with Mallarmé's poetic "essai."

en abyme actually does occur in this way? In attempting to shed more light on this question, we should ask first of all whether the *mise en abyme* in Gide is itself a theoretical concept that, much like classificatory concepts such as genre and period, would allow one to distinguish between one kind of text and another, particularly when it is a question of historical self-definition. Does Gide have a *theory* of the *mise en abyme?* Is it possible to know for sure when the labyrinth or the abyss has become a mere illusion and when it is still a genuine test?

Given the remarkable diversity of Gide's oeuvre—which includes novels, *récits,* the so-called *soties,* lyrical prose pieces, theater, politico-anthropological essays, autobiographies, and the *Journal*—it comes as something of a surprise to note the relative absence in it of properly theoretical texts. Aside from a small number of occasional pieces he wrote for conferences and in response to journalistic inquiries around the turn of the century, some scattered considerations in the *Journal* he kept for over half a century, and perhaps certain sections of the *Journal des faux-monnayeurs,* the more abstruse and theoretical questions of literary production seem to have concerned Gide in only an oblique way at best. Indeed, one of his more theoretically self-aware statements is his own admission, "it matters much less to me to theorize about texts than to write them." While the work of his early mentor Mallarmé and his exact contemporary and friend Valéry were characterized by sustained and often esoteric reflections on the practice and even the possibility of poetic language, which account for a good deal of the interest the two writers continue to elicit in contemporary criticism, Gide had a tendency to move in a different direction altogether. Rather than tracing the literary experience *back* to its theoretical underpinnings and complications, Gide preferred to look *forward* from the actual existence of literary texts toward the links they might be capable of establishing with the outside world.

One is therefore not likely to consider as being on the same level of theoretical awareness statements like Mallarmé's teasing definition of poetic figure, "the Idea itself and suave, the (flower) absent from all bouquets," and Gide's urgently existential admonition to the reader at the end of *Les nourritures terrestres,* "now is the time to throw my book away. Emancipate yourself, leave me" (248). This apparent urgency—if not outright naiveté—is what also accounts for the considerable confusion that ensues whenever one tries to situate with any precision the theoretical impact of Gide's oeuvre, since such straightforward appeals in the literary work to an extraliterary world that would exist beyond it serve only to mask the deeper tensions of his writing behind the smooth contours of its surface. For this reason, it has always been easier and more convenient for critics to class Gide among the French *moralistes* than to risk unsettling his reassuring image by juxtaposing his work with that of poeticians and theorists like Mallarmé and Valéry. It is true that Gide's abundant reflections on those subjects most susceptible to the changing winds of fashion or scientific belief, such as psychology, sociology, politics, and sexuality, have not withstood the test of time very well. Since they always seem governed by the existential priority of an individual's place at a particular moment in a particular world, they may no longer be of immediate interest to us, and in Gide's case many of his more overtly theoretical reflections—which are directed toward these topics—do indeed appear rather dated and superfluous today.

Nonetheless, the very fact that Gide's work *is* so diffuse, so splintered, so torn between such a large number of genres—among which no single form of writing or subject is allowed to keep the upper hand for very long—should alert us to the possibility that the dissemination of genres is itself a theoretical gesture of no little interest.[12] Thus, the closing "Envoi" in *Les nourritures,* "throw my book away; remind yourself that this is really only one of thousands of possible *poses,*" in addition to encouraging a purely existential form of "availability," can itself be taken to refer to a displaced theoretical project in Gide whose deeper motivation would be the aim to proliferate, expand, and displace the borders commonly drawn between canonical literary genres and poses. One of these borders, of course, is the one that would presume to delimit the internal precinct of literature from all that lies beyond it; namely, theory, criticism, and the entire realm of extraliterary experience and activity. But if, following the self-reflexive gesture of *Les nourritures,* the pose of existential engagement that figures so

---

12. See Gide's comments on the necessity of putting all his works into "dialogue" in order to assess the significance of any one of them. For instance: "Those who like my *Immoraliste* cannot forgive me for *La porte étroite.* I cannot in my own mind separate the two books, however; it was together that I brought them into being; together they make a pair; it is in the excess of the one that I found a kind of permission for the excess of the other" (1549). That the part "in excess" of any one form of textual closure may be the most "theoretical" dimension of all in Gide's work, is the working hypothesis of the present argument.

prominently in all of Gide's writing is itself just another "genre" among others, then how would it be possible to decide whether *this* pose is dictated by literary, theoretical, or empirical constraints? It cannot be a priori certain that the Gidean concept of personal and social *disponibilité* would be any less the "effect" of a fundamental, though necessarily implicit theory of abyssal literary genres than the other way around. What would it mean, for instance, to read Gide's well-known thematic and autobiographical equivocality in matters of sexuality, politics, and religion in terms of their relation to theoretical considerations of a primarily poetic or linguistic nature? Were such considerations in Gide actually made available to us, then their effect on the traditional reception of his entire authorship could not be reduced to the status of a mere accident. Or rather, this accident that would then befall Gide's place in the modernist canon would have to be understood as having all the necessity of Gide's own *acte gratuit,* which is itself the most rigorous condition for something to occur as anything more than the mindless routine of illusion.

There can be no theory of the *mise en abyme,* then, since the *mise en abyme* is itself the possibility that, in every genre and at every moment, the text to be read is nothing but the allegorical narrative of its own coming into being *as* text. There can be no theory of the *mise en abyme* that could ever assure that a text was anything more than simply the story of how it was written and how, being something that was written, it will have an unpredictable effect on the one who writes it. There can be no genre of the *mise en abyme,* because the *mise en abyme* is itself what ruins the concept of generic classification by being the pure possibility of all genres being simultaneously *represented* and *activated* in every text. This possibility is implicit when Gide writes:

> It seems to me that each of my books was not so much the product of a new inner disposition, but rather, on the contrary, its cause, and the first provocation of this disposition of mind and spirit in which I had to maintain myself in order to complete its elaboration. I would like to express this in a very simple way: that the book, from its very conception, disposes of me absolutely, and that, for its sake everything in me, including what is most profound, is orchestrated. I no longer have any other personality than the one that is appropriate to this work—objective, subjective? These words lose all meaning at this point; for if it happens that I use myself as a model (and sometimes it seems to me that there can

be no other accurate kind), this is because I have from the beginning become the very one I intended to portray. (*Journal 1889–1931*, 737)

There would be no way to be sure of distinguishing between the writing about (theory) and the enacting of (literature) a textual feature that manifests itself only by producing itself independently of anything that is prior to it, including the identity, personality, or intentionality of its "author." In fact, to be an author in this sense is to be the one that can only come into being as a result of this very textual operation. What would be the fundamental principles of a *theory* of literature that could never appear as such, since what it would theorize, "la mise en abyme," is also what would always risk turning itself into an *example* of what it was meant to describe, explain, or teach?

The first text that Gide published under his own name, *Le traité du Narcisse (Théorie du symbole)* (1891), is not only an example of just such a "theoretical" work; it is also a narrative reflection on its own "genre" of theory. As such, it could not legitimately be considered a simple "theory" of the symbol, even though that term does in fact appear in its subtitle. Rather, it would be the story or "allegory" of this "theory," the second-level narration of the *mise en abyme* that is Gide's self-degenerating genre of theory. This allegorical function is signaled by the "title," which is really two headings between which the text struggles to situate itself, and which would depend for its power to signify on the two irreducible genres it names and falls between: *Le traité du narcisse* and *Théorie du symbole*. Narcissus may be the myth that is supposed to tell the story of the self as it constitutes itself as its own mirror image, but the two headings of Gide's text—which juxtapose a reference to classical *myth* with the promise of a *theory* of linguistic symbols—do not necessarily relate to each other in a similarly specular way. Thus, being neither completely the same nor simply polar opposites, myth and theory cannot constitute themselves as a single head, face, or self to which we might give the symbolic name "Narcissus."

This text, then, is neither a simple theoretical examination in purely discursive language of the literary "symbol" nor a wholly figural and therefore "symbolic" version of an archetypal theory of the self. Rather, it is a hybrid or monstrous genre that is simultaneously a representation of the symbol in the form of a myth *and* a theoretical reflection on the way that myth is able to function symbolically. As such, it is a kind of *mise en scène* of one particular symbol as well as of the power to symbolize in general, and it therefore opens up a theatrical space between "myth" and "theory." This space is and is not theater at the same time; it is not simply a representation *of* something, but it is theoretically *of* or *about* representation itself. It is something like the theater of the possibility of theory, or a metatheatrical text of literary theory in the form of a mythological figure. Rather than theater, it would be the *mise en abyme* of theater by theory. It would be theater, but in the form of a representation of itself *as* theater rather than as a representation of something that could exist outside it, independently of any implication in it, like the presumed autonomy of subjective or historical reality.[13]

Formally, we have little trouble noticing the *mise en abyme* dimension here, since the introduction to the text spells it out in no uncertain terms: "All things have been said already; but since no one is listening, it is always necessary to begin over again" (*Romans,* 3). Each of the episodes contains within itself this gesture of beginning all over again, but at the same time it is clearly marked that they do so from within a structure generated in a previous episode. So, the pictorial emblem for the *mise en abyme* (the dutch cocoa box on which there is a picture of girl holding a dutch cocoa box on which . . . and so on) is in this way transposed to a purely textual space: a text that recounts a new beginning that recounts a new beginning that recounts . . . and so on. And to the extent that this example *is* textual rather than representational or mimetic, we might suggest that *Le traité du Narcisse* is a more appropriate example of the *mise en abyme* as a literary device than are Gide's own remarks about it two years later in the *Journal,* which themselves

---

13. This aspect of radical dependency—which implicates the critical act in the very object of its study—is what makes Gide's "abyssal" treatment of Narcissus—or Mallarmé's Narcissus figures of Hérodiade, Hamlet, Pierrot—so different from the innocently parodic versions of the same "myth" that are found in the work of poets such as Jules Laforgue. If we insist on using terms like "symbolist" and "decadent" to distinguish between these two groups of writers—an insistence that is at best provisional—it might only be in order to emphasize that for the "symbolist," unlike the "decadent," the distance established between what the text is (language) and what the text is about (the delusions of language) could never result in a simple demystification, or finally, in a subjective detachment and superiority. If it is true that "Narcissus" becomes the perfect emblem for the self-enclosed play of language, it is also true that some writers took this play seriously enough to go beyond simply repeating or mocking it. It is not enough to take Narcissus seriously; it is also necessary to take his disarticulation in and by Echo seriously.

relapse into a pictorial representation taken from Dutch painting (*Journal 1889–1939*, 41). But the *mise en abyme* here is present not only in a formal sense but also in the thematic development of the text. For precisely at the center of the text the operation of the symbol is compared to a descent into an "abyss": "and let there come a time of tacit darkness, when denser waters descend: in the imperturbable *abysses* secret channels will flower" (7). What this means, of course, is that the *narration* of the "abyss," of the symbolic process of descending into the abyss, is told in the *form* of an abyss, in the figure of a structural *mise en abyme*. We could say, then, that the form of this text is a *mise en scène* of its theme, or that the theme is an unfolding, a *mise en scène* of its form. In either case, we seem to be dealing with a text in which form and theme are mirror images of each other, a self-reflexive text that represents its relationship to itself as text. That is, it is an interweaving of structure and theme, theory and myth, thought and description, in the form of the self-reflexive mythological hero Narcissus. The structure of this text relates to its theme in the same way that Narcissus gazes into the mirror of his own eye. But can any text that involves the duplicitous structure of the *mise en abyme* be that simple? To the extent that the myth of Narcissus is as much the story of the undoing of the subject of self-reflection as of its constitution, is it not somewhat unsettling to take this particular myth as the theoretical symbol of the potential of all symbolic language to achieve adequation between its own theme and structure?

Le traité du Narcisse, in any case—despite Gide's own ostentatious self-consciousness and the well-known fact that the text is to some extent the result of an actual conversation Gide had with Valéry one evening in the botanical gardens of Montpelier—is *not* primarily an autobiographical text. Nor is it, at least not in the first instance, a text that is about the self, self-consciousness, or subjectivity. Rather it is all that *as well as* a figural dramatization of the theory of its own language, a *mise en scène* of the very possibility of writing with symbols, and what it eventually stages is a sequential pageantry of the several different conceptions of symbolic language in general without which no self could come into existence, much less be written about. For this reason, rather than simply repeating the classical myth of Narcissus, this text makes theoretical use of the mythological self by having it serve as an emblem for the figural dimension of *all* poetic activity, including its own writing. In particular, it makes use of Narcissus as an emblem for the possibility of a specular relationship between what a text says (its theme) and the way that a text must say it (its rhetorical structure). What is put into the abyss, or put to the absolute test, therefore, is the possibility of bringing together the subject's experience of language and the knowledge the subject can have of that experience. For the sake of convenience, and in order better to measure the "dramatization" of theory which this text is, it would even be possible to divide the narrative movement of the text into the five acts of classical French theater. First, there is the introduction, which makes the classical reference to Narcissus and asks about the necessity for a new version. Then, the second act recounts the search for a mirror and the beginning of Narcissus's dream of lost paradise. The third act contains the story of Adam and the loss of paradise. The fourth act introduces the possibility of regaining paradise thanks to poetic creativity. And finally, the fifth act echoes the first by asking again about the text's *raison d'être*.

The main narration of the text begins with Narcissus, who is alone in the middle of a deserted landscape—"no more bank nor source; no more metamorphosis and no more reflected flower" (3). He initiates the movement of the myth when he then sets off in search of an appropriate *image,* that is, a phenomenal appearance or shape for his *soul,* in other words, his nonsensory interiority. This first conception of poetic language is therefore easy enough to recognize as a more or less classically metaphorical theory of the symbol: a structure in which there is perfect *correspondence* between inside and outside. Of course, the main representative of this conception of the symbol—the perfect adequation between body (*corps*) and soul (*esprit*)—would be Baudelaire. As such, poetry would be a language that could synthesize perception and imagination with no great difficulty through the mediations of a metaphorical chain of substitutions by resemblance. For example, when the text says that "[Narcissus] wants to know finally what form his soul has; it must be, he feels, excessively beautiful, if he judges it on the basis of its long shivers" (3), such a metaphorical conception of language has already been put into place. For to describe the motions of the soul as a "shiver" is to borrow the vocabulary of the sensory world in order to refer to the characteristics of a nonsensory quality or essence. In order to say that the soul can be subject to "shivers," it is necessary to suppose the possibility of the "soul's" being compared with and eventually represented by something like a leaf being blown about in the wind.[14]

The text discloses a problem with this conception of poetic language: the world of immediacy seems to have collapsed all too quickly here under the weight of a subjectivity that threatens to disappear into solipsism. Far from sharing the ideology of such a solipsism, Gide's text (as well as other so-called symbolist texts) actually performs a critical analysis of it. That is, Gide's text demonstrates how and why this metaphorical conception of correspondences can find no stable ground outside itself against which to project and therefore to support its own reflection. Narcissus requires a subject-object polarity in order to develop his self-consciousness, but without a third term against which to project both interior and exterior in order to determine their respective shapes and limits, he can never be sure he is looking at anything but an empty image of himself. At this point in the text, Narcissus becomes impotent because he is all powerful: "Flowers on the shore, trunks of trees, patches of reflected blue sky, an entire flight of rapid images that waited only for him in order to be, and that under his gaze take on color and substance" (4). Such a state of indetermination is characterized by an "ennui" that is also associated with (and analyzed by) Baudelaire. The subject is reduced to asking whether the objects are real or merely projections of his own interiority: "[Narcissus] does not understand if it is his soul that guides the waves, or if it is the waves that guide him" (4). And so the text progresses by trying to provide another view of symbolic language, one that might rectify the "lethargic canal, the almost horizontal mirror" of false antitheses between the inside/outside metaphors.

This move is prepared in the narrative by way of a metonymic play on the French signifier *élan*. This word, which refers to the level or intensity of some form of energy, is at first applied quite casually to the varying crests in the watery mirror onto which Narcissus projects his images. It reappears two sentences later in another guise, however, when it is said that "all forms force themselves and project themselves

---

14. It could be that Narcissus is judging the beauty of the soul by means of *his* shivers rather than *its* shivers, since the French text reads, "s'il en juge par ses frémissements," where "ses" can refer to Narcissus or the soul. This changes nothing, however, since it makes even more evident the fact that the subject has nothing at his disposal but so-called sensory experience by which to signify that he "knows" something in principle devoid of sensory properties.

[*s'élancent*] toward a first, lost and paradisiacal form" (4). The upward thrust of connotations suggested by the sheer proximity of these two words allows the narrative to progress by turning the horizontal mirror of inside/outside metaphor upright, producing a vertical ladder of transcendental values. Insofar as they *are* transcendental, however, it is no longer possible for the subject to communicate directly with this ideal state from which it has been irreparably separated. The figure for this second conception of poetic language is also contained in the key word "s'élancer," which names the "throwing beyond" movement that characterizes rhetorical hyperbole. Although still based on a relationship of analogy, the substitutions have now been temporalized, and rather than the inside/outside exchanges of metaphor, they are composed of a steady process of wearing away or moving away from an origin. The hyperbolic division of the "here below" and "up above" in this section is a form of the "sublime," in both the religious sense of lost paradise and the psychoanalytical "sublimation," or filtered recollection of a partially erased past.

In the symbolist genealogy at issue here, the model for this conception is undoubtedly the Mallarmé of early poems like "Les fenêtres."[15] As we know, however, hyperbole runs a constant risk of falling from its sublime height into ridiculousness, as when, in this section of Gide's text, Adam modulates the psalmlike seriousness of the opening transcendental language into the colloquial tones of everyday street life. This is the language of parody, and it is clear that the predecessor is not only being represented here; he is also being challenged and even mocked by the one who comes after.[16] Gide's Adam subverts the tradition in which he finds himself by refusing to accept the place allotted him by an all-powerful God. The "acte gratuit" that occurs when Adam decides to break a limb from the sacred tree results in tearing the sacred book in which the "truth" is to be read; it is an act of literary blasphemy. Gide is a good enough reader of Mallarmé to know that, like Mallarmé himself, he too must commit blasphemy by putting

15. "Je me mire et me vois ange! et je meurs, et j'aime / —Que la vitre soit l'art, soit la mysticité— / A renaître, portant mon rêve en diadème, / Au ciel antérieur où fleurit la Beauté! / Mais, hélas! Ici-bas est maître."

16. Once again the "trajectory" of Gide's development may not be at all linear: if *Le traité du Narcisse* already includes the parodic elements of *Paludes* and the "acte gratuit" of *Les caves du Vatican*, then it may be that rather than breaking through to some new literary form or genre, these "later" works merely repeat and formalize what was so radically enacted in the "early" works.

into "doubt" the "Jeu suprême" of whatever he inherits. Such is the impatience of a young writer who, instead of accepting a derived status passively and whatever the actual merits of the text being challenged, decides to compete with God the father. In this context, God merely becomes a figure for the entire weight of a long literary heritage, which can also include the Mallarmé from whom one cannot help inheriting even the futile gesture of refusal itself. But just as there is a Mallarmean version of Baudelaire's "ennui," so too, in Gide's text the initial pleasures of pure parody eventually turn sour and must be rejuvenated by being put into contact with a deeper poetic source. Mere participation in poetic play, although it forms one stage in coming to terms with poetry's very possibility, does not suffice to reveal and account for its underlying principles.

The poet, then, the definition of whose essential character is reserved for the third part of the text, is less like the Narcissus figure of Baudelairian metaphor in the first part than like the Adam figure of Mallarmé's playfulness sketched in the second part. But whereas the parodic intertextuality of Adam, in order to be recognized *as* parody, still depends at least in a minimal way on the opening hyperbole that is constructed on a metaphorical wearing away of an original and now inaccessible paradise, the poet in the last part asks about a wholly delocalized but nonetheless material paradise that would be beyond the reach of any individual to control or to elude. The affirmation "For paradise is all around us" (9) states the virtual rather than the determinate aspect of paradise and clears the way for a figural pattern that would no longer be based exclusively on the mimetic analogies of metaphor and hyperbole/parody. The crucial step in this regard is the comparison of the "scientist" and the poet. The "scientist" is representative of all modes of knowledge that proceed by way of finite "examples" through a gradual process of induction. No matter how complex, no matter how long the chain of substitutions engaged by the scientific method, the fact that each of its steps is incremental and based on some logical tie with a determinate precedent ensures the (analogical) continuity between origin and end required by scientific truth.

For the genuine poet, though, there can be no question of such a continuity between the analogical steps of a supposedly homogeneous process. The theoretical poetics of this last section operates a radical disjunction between appearance and essence. No longer a horizontal relationship of inside to outside or a vertical reflection of paradise in paradise lost, the relationship between the world and its truth turns out to be wholly empty and arbitrary here, as is always the case when the poetic figure must ultimately affirm its analogy to a cloak or clothing: "[the poet] knows that the appearance is nothing but the pretext for each thing, a *garment* (*vêtement*) that hides it and keeps the profane eye away from it" (9, emphasis added). By calling the phenomenon a mere article of "clothing," the poet seems to acquire a great measure of freedom by being able to discard and go beyond its empty externality at the whim of his subjective will. If the tropological models of the first two sections are both grounded to a certain degree in mimesis—metaphor and hyperbole—then the last model proposed would be a nonmimetic figure that holds all the world and the heavens at its own disposal. "For paradise is all around us," in fact, names the capacity of the intellect to *use* the perceived world rather than simply to imitate it as an original model. The heady freedom of the poet who senses this power suggests a figure something like the romantic "irony" Gide was familiar with from his reading of Novalis, but the concomitant risk involved with such feedom, as Hegel well knew, is a wild and aberrant creativity that threatens to escape the limits of any reasonable control whatsoever. And it is true that once the mimetic models have been dispensed with by making the ideal *infinitely* available, the text can give no indication of *how* the poet is to know what he is doing when he moves beyond the metaphorical link of inside/outside or up/down. All the text can say is that the poet is able to produce paradise at whim by means of the unfettered caprice of "guesswork" (*deviner*).

The implications of this risk are inscribed in the text in an unavoidable though particularly complicated way at the very moment that the poet exercises this masterful freedom. Only when the poet has moved beyond the phenomenal garments and descended into the "abyss" of the "Idea," does it become possible to reassign the idea a poetic shape that is no longer subject to the vagaries of time or appearances. This is the truly linguistic and therefore critical moment of the treatise, for the one poetic *acte gratuit* that could actually fulfill such conditions is the originary act of linguistic denomination. As this early text by Gide suggests, there could be no subjective or existential *acte gratuit* without presupposing the positing moment of a nonphenomenal, nontemporal system of signification in which every subject must first appear as a mere name, though without yet being certain of understanding that name as anything or anyone in particular. What the treatise refers to as the "crystalline" work of art will eventually be composed of "words, transparent and revelatory." As such, the work of art will finally function for the poetic subject as the perfect mirror: it is absolutely transparent because it reveals the perfect nullity of whoever knows how to look through it. But despite this rather hyperbolic claim in the last, nonhyperbolic section, Gide reminds us that the traces of the originally wild act of denomination are still present in the persistent danger also posed to the truth of this mirror by the nontransparent, nonrevelatory "pride of the word" (*l'orgueil du mot*).

It is in fact the tension between the word's "transparency" and its potential fall into "pride" that has given so much trouble to Gide's commentators when they try to unravel the seemingly gratuitous relation between the famous "aesthetico-moral note" found in the second section of the treatise (8–9) and the rest of the body of the text. For it is in the appended note that the magic mirror of the poetic Narcissus becomes the place where, against all expectation, "the artist must have sacrificed himself *in advance*" (9, emphasis added). How is it possible to conceive a sacrifice of the self along with a perfect transparency of language? That is, how can the text that should produce the self propose as its own aesthetic model the creation of a crystalline paradise that would lie beyond the reach of all subjects? These questions point back to the poetic act of denomination itself, but when it actually happens within the text it occurs in a mode that is far removed from crystalline transparency, since it wipes out once and for all the possibility of determining with certainty whether the poet is being revealed or sacrificed by the poetic forms that are the only signs of his (or its?) production. The French is indispensable here, for the actual crystal of the poet's own idiom cannot be translated without at the same time shattering the illusion of transparency contained in it: "Le Poète pieux contemple; il se penche sur les symboles, et silencieux descend profondément au coeur des choses,—et quand il a perçu, visionnaire, l'Idée, l'intime Nombre harmonieux de son Etre, qui soutient la forme imparfaite, il la saisit, puis, insoucieux de cette forme transitoire qui la revêtait dans le temps, il sait lui redonner une forme éternelle, *sa* Forme véritable enfin, et fatale,—paradisiaque et cristalline" (9–10).[17]

17. "The pious Poet contemplates; he bends over the symbols, and silently descends deeply to the very heart of things,—and when he has perceived, visionary, the Idea, the intimate and harmonious Number of its Being, which sustains the imperfect form, he

In the italicized possession of the French adjective "sa," it becomes impossible to determine the all-important destination of the poetic "giving" that is being qualified here. "Whose" *form* is being given to what? What is the genre of a given form in which it is possible to read both "he knows how to give it *his* true form" and "he knows how to give it *its* true form," the difference between self and other, or "his" and "its," being the only thing that finally matters in this text? The freedom of the poet is thus neither wholly subjective nor simply impersonal and transcendental, since all it can do is endlessly return to and interrogate the signifying movement that is frozen in this "sa," the one truly poetic act that could promise to take us with any certainty either to the poet himself or to some ideal paradise beyond him.[18] The form of this self-modifying "Form" is therefore the least transparent thing in the whole text, and its "fatal truth" never makes it to the transparency of the sentence because all it finally reveals is the insuperable "pride" of this one French word, *sa,* which *echoes* back and forth between "his" (the poet's own) and "its" (the Idea's) without ever being able to decide between them. Or rather, by finally giving the work of art the *sa as* word, as gratuitous *signifiant,* as a mode of signification prior to the achievement of a completed meaning, this text actually does help to "reveal" the illusion of the aesthetic "transparency" it was meant to maintain. The one place in the text where the moment of linguistic figuration—that is, a category that is nonsubjective, nonempirical, nontranscendental—is being theorized is also a kind of labyrinth in which nothing can be revealed with clarity other than the abyssal pose of mutually exclusive "selves": subjective, objective, transcendental, linguistic.

---

seizes it, then, heedless of this transitory form that clothed it in time, he knows how to give it back an eternal form, *its* [or *his*?] true form at last, and fatal,—paradisiacal and crystalline."

18. It is in this context that the commonplace observations about Gide's early reading of and debt to German romanticism—especially Novalis, whom he translated, and Schopenhauer, whom he commented upon abundantly—could be most fruitfully pursued. What is most often referred to as Gide's "irony" could thus be shown not to be a simple matter of an aloof character or writing style, but rather the outcome of (more or less) philosophical considerations on the relation between (self-)consciousness, language, and the kind of absolute freedom often associated with them both. In this context, too, it would be useful to compare in a more extended way the filiation between Gide and Blanchot—especially Blanchot's reworking of Narcissus's dilemma in "Le regard d'Orphée" *L'espace littéraire* (Paris: Gallimard, 1955), and the pages on Narcissus in *L'écriture du désastre* (Paris: Gallimard, 1980).

What this means, in an overly schematic way, is that the theoretical question of the self *as* symbolic language, at least the way that it has been dramatized in the *mise en abyme* of this text by Gide, is not the product of an existential or psychological predicament but rather the result of a necessary linguistic confusion. It is because the experience of the self had to be written in the first place that the "pride" of the word will always threaten to "prefer itself" and thus block the transparency of the meaningful sentence, or of incipient thought. This also means that the dissemination of genres that can now be read as Gide's truly literary signature can also be reintroduced in a helpful way to characterize the two "Gides" of this text and potentially of *all* of Gide's texts. First of all, there is the mythological, subjective, and self-conscious Narcissus who evolves into the historical, objective, and spontaneous Theseus by means of willfully misreading the duplicitous nature of the word's possessive *sa* as the clear mirror of his own development. Such would be the Gide literary history has adopted in order to make his language function as though it were composed of the "rhythmical and sure sentences" that narrate the reassuring history of French literature that leads from Gide to Sartre and ties them both together in a coherent picture of "twentieth-century" letters. The absolute "experience" of literature Blanchot refers to is never undergone by this Gide, or by this concept of history, since the self-sacrifice they speak of always belongs to the selfsame identity that masters it again and again by rising up from it fundamentally unaltered in a series of sequentially related palingeneses.

And then there is a darker, more theoretically "aware" Gide whose textual *mise en abyme* is more like the experience of literature that would break the thread of this illusory history by tying him rather to Mallarmé and to Blanchot: a Narcissus that recounts the same old story of the self at the same time that it actively metamorphoses the self into something totally different, that is to say, an unheard-of narcissus, or flower of language. For this Gide, the "pride of the word" would perform a linguistic sacrifice that would be more difficult to reassimilate to the genetic concept of aesthetics and ethics, or of subjectivity and objectivity: "I no longer have any other personality than the one that is appropriate to this work—objective, subjective? These words lose all meaning at this point" (*Journal 1889–1939*, 737). Not to repeat these words that have through the writing of the work lost all meaning as a mere formula of self-fulfillment—such would be the task of reading the *mise en abyme* of Gide. To go into the abyss and experience it as an event rather than an empty illusion, according to Blanchot, would be the point at which Gide's work begins to speak of something essential, something like a historical event. And at this point also, according to Gide, words like "subjective" and "objective" lose all meaning by their having delivered themselves over to the radically gratuitous experience of the "book." The experience of the book would only be the discovery that there has never been a reliable subjective or objective perspective from which to decide, once and for all, whether the gregarious objectivity of Theseus is itself merely an illusion, or whether the solitary subjectivity of Narcissus is the means for undergoing the ultimate self-test.

Theseus is not a future and further development that could ever be reached simply by moving temporally or cognitively beyond Narcissus; he names in fact the always-illusory potential of self-reflecting and self-revealing textual figures. The genetic line that attaches the gaze of Narcissus to the hand of Theseus is thus also always the possibility of refusing history by not reading what is ultimately revealed in it as a merely fictional transparency. And this possibility will have been haunting Gide's signature from the beginning, even in the figure of Narcissus.[19] Learning to read that signature in its own *mise en abyme* is the only thing Gide would have known how to give to history. But, as Blanchot reminds us, since this contract with history can only occur as an event, and not as a mere figure, or empty formula, history can only be experienced again and again as an absolute disjunction between these two figures of the mirror and the thread, or the eye that watches and the hand that acts. Or better, history could only be experienced in the disjunction between the transparency promised by any figure or combination of figures and the reading and writing that echoes and undoes such promises by way of a critical analysis. The *mise en abyme* Gide leaves to history thus always remains to happen anew when critical analysis collides with empty formulae. It is therefore given to a future that can only occur when the illusory victory of a self and its world—which the *mise en abyme* describes, embellishes, teaches, and reflects in all its transparency—is pushed into the abyss of writing that it actually performs.

19. At the very beginning, in fact, since it is with a version of this propensity of writing and history to become mere cliché that Gide's first signed text, *Le traité du Narcisse*, begins: "You know the story [*l'histoire*]. However we will tell it again. All things have already been said; but since no one listens, it is always necessary to begin over again" (3).

6 Resisting, Responding: Maurice Blanchot and the Promise of Writing

> I could not tell whether it was a question or just a command, an encouragement. Because I had the impression that these words were not addressed exactly to me, I felt a certain freedom in regard to them: that I, too, should need be, would be able to respond to them lightly. . . . It is a frightful way to be tried or put to the test . . . of whoever has nothing, it requests; the one who responds to its request does not know it, and because of that, does not respond. . . . The appeal is constantly taking place, it does not need to be responded to, it never really takes place, that's why it is not possible to respond to it. But the one who does not respond, more than any other, is imprisoned in that response.
> —Maurice Blanchot, *Celui qui ne m'accompagnait pas*

To include Maurice Blanchot in a discussion of "symbolism" is already to risk stretching the limits of the question to the point of their dissolution. The coherence of the system to which period terms like "symbolism" belong, of course, rests ultimately on the possibility of bringing together into a synthesis a given fact of language with the dates and places of empirical historical observation. But it is not because Blanchot would thus occupy at best a "marginal" and belated position with respect to some hypothetical "symbolist" genre and period—lasting roughly from 1885 to 1916 in France and focused mostly on poetry—that his work most radically threatens such a system of coordination. For by its very marginality, its anachronistic character of being a holdover, whatever "symbolist" component is, in fact, evidenced in the ethereal language of Blanchot's texts could still be said to reflect back on a more "properly" symbolist epoch. One could thus easily say that Blanchot is a symbolist to the extent that his critical writing is concerned with and sometimes even *resembles* the poetic production of Mallarmé, for instance. To say that Blanchot is a symbolist in this way, as long as it is still said only "metaphorically," does not therefore disrupt the historical and metaphorical understanding of literature that it merely repeats. Rather, Blanchot's work unsettles an understanding of symbolism provided by traditional concepts of literary history because it locates *in* the linguistic symbol itself the power to *dislocate* the metaphorical histories that would coordinate without rupture a given poetic act with any properly temporal, spatial, or generic specifications whatsoever.

If Blanchot's work is symbolist, then, it would also have to be so in a wholly nonmetaphorical sense large enough to comprehend Nerval, Mallarmé, Proust, and all those whose texts interrogate the way symbols occur as actual linguistic events in history. As Blanchot's writing demonstrates beyond question, one way the symbol occurs historically is as a collision with and disruption of formalist-empirical models that would narrate a coherent succession of literary periods and genres leading from "symbolist poetry" to "poststructuralist criticism" and beyond.

The word *symbol* comes from the Greek *sumballein,* "to throw together," and this metaphor of correspondence that "symbolism" names is operative whenever literature and history combine to tell the meaningful story of their respective adventures. As long as historical models base their understanding of symbolism (or any other textual event for that matter) on the unquestioned capacity of their own discourse to bring together, or "symbolize," into one system of meaning and knowledge linguistic structures and chronological (or geographical) determinations of empirical events, no matter how wide or flexible the boundaries, they restrict themselves at the same time to being nothing but "symbolist." Moreover, by leaving unquestioned the ultimate capacity of ordinary historical discourse to combine with or correspond to literary structures in an adequate manner, such literary histories remain symbolist in a merely naive and prereflected—ideological—mode. And it is precisely the prevalence of such unacknowledged "symbolist" conceptions of history that Blanchot's rewriting of the symbol can be seen to address.

Or respond to. Blanchot's work responds to the mistaken idea, the historicist ideology, that the truth of history can be modeled on a symbolic structure in which an idea or meaning would be able to correspond fully to the bodily images or empirical events it necessarily appears in. "The symbol does not signify anything," Blanchot states flatly, "it isn't even an image whose meaning would be that of an otherwise inaccessible truth, it always exceeds [*dépasse*] every truth and every meaning, and what it puts before us is this very excess [*et ce qu'il nous présente, c'est ce dépassement même*]."[1] If the symbol does indeed *exceed* every truth and every meaning, it exceeds by the same token every model of history that would seek to contain this truth of the symbol within a unified and meaningful discourse. There can be no such history of symbolism, since the very occurrence of symbols is what resists the necessarily inadequate "symbolic" principles that might otherwise be capable of reducing any occurrence to a stable form of truth and meaning within history.

More philosophically informed than the work of any of the symbolists "properly speaking," moreover, the writing of Blanchot thus challenges uncritical histories of symbolism in yet another way. For it is precisely in order *not* to take seriously the symbolists' potentially disruptive theories of literature (and of history) that virtually all historians of the "symbolist" movement eagerly point out that even the most erudite French symbolists had at best a fuzzy notion of the philosophical foundations underwriting their poetic principles. Blanchot, however, is fully acquainted with the predominantly German tradition of philosophical thought that lies behind the theory and practice of symbolism, and so his own theoretical reflections on the symbol would be less easily dismissed out of hand. Thus, in this same essay devoted to the literary language of fiction, Blanchot is able to enlist, at least in part, the authority of none other than Hegel himself for his theory of the symbol: "Hegel says [in the *Aesthetics*] that the principal weakness of symbolic art is its *Unangemessenheit:* the exteriority of the image and the spiritual content do not coincide fully, so the symbol remains inadequate" (86). Blanchot makes note, nonetheless and in passing, that within Hegel's own dialectical narrative of historical periodization this momentary inadequacy of "symbolic" art is just the beginning of a process of increasing "adequation" that should be able eventually to overcome it philosophically. Despite this, though, Blanchot insists that the originary noncorrespondence in the linguistic symbol must take priority over the symbol's subsequent placement within a developmental scheme of history and of philosophy. For Blanchot, then, and based

---

1. See "Le langage de la fiction," *La part du feu* (Paris: Gallimard, 1949), 84–85. Further references appear in the text.

on an unusual but informed reading of Hegel, history would not finally be the reassuring ground in which the inadequation of the symbol could ever be overcome. Rather, history would be itself the *result* of the symbol's infinitely recurring inability to correspond with and exhaust itself once and for all in the fullness of any definitive truth or meaning.

On the other hand, if, as Blanchot also claims here, the symbol truly puts before us or presents us with the very excess of which it is the vehicle—"ce qu'il nous présente, c'est ce dépassement même"—is it not already in the process of becoming a perfectly adequate symbol of such an excess? By revealing itself as the site of its own "inadequation," does the symbol not ultimately acquiesce to precisely that ideal correspondence with truth and meaning it was supposed to resist? Would not the symbol that manages finally to express the truth of this inadequation be just as false and misleading as the mistaken and inadequate expression of perfectly adequate correspondence it responds to and contests? Such is the enigma posed by the breaking, the rupture of the symbol's supposed correspondence with its meaning into heterogeneous fragments that cannot themselves avoid promising a mirror image of the inadequate and fragmented truth they would present us with.

For the "fragmentary exigence," which could legitimately be said to be one aspect of the rearticulation in Blanchot's own writing of the ruptured unity of the symbol it constantly interrogates, can also be a lure or a trap: "The temptation: the propitious fragment, as if, in its nonunity, it could be alone, the last, the last, without brevity, without place, an obstinateness in reverse; its word, finally cleansed of infinity, taken up again for its own charm."[2] How can Blanchot respond to the ideological obfuscations of the symbol without at last corresponding with them, even if it would be in the inverted image of the symbol-as-fragment that the symbol at last coincided with its own inability to achieve the fullness of meaning? How can the fragment resist the presumed unity of the symbol without responding to, going along with, or finally accompanying it in its own mistaken pretension to be adequate to a fragmented truth? This is the terrible trial and responsibility the narrator of *Celui qui ne m'accompagnait pas* speaks of. It is a call or summons to respond in writing to what always turns out to be "an

---

2. Maurice Blanchot, *Le pas au-delà* (Paris: Gallimard, 1973), 92.

evasive certainty": "Yes, I had to respond to a role that I did not know, but that I was not allowed to mistake. . . . And can it be called a responsibility if it dissipates into the absence of response? A task, but beyond reach, an exigence, but empty . . . and nonetheless a task, a responsibility."[3] What is the role to which one is called, and what does this role, which is also a task and a responsibility, have to do with history and with the symbol? How can one respond to this responsibility toward the evasive certainties of history and the symbol when one can never know how to respond (in)adequately enough to what has actually occurred there as evasions of responsibility?

Ordinarily, that is, under so-called normal circumstances, we understand the role of the respondent to be one of informing and interpreting. Because of a privilege that is often temporal but also, perhaps, one of perspective or point of view, the respondent occupies a place of mediation between an event and the potential meaning or truth of such an event. The respondent's job is first to bring to light and then to reflect on those elements of an event that can most effectively be used to initiate the process of its future interpretation and understanding. To respond in this sense requires certain skills and a certain amount of instruction or learning so that the process by which the event actually takes place can then be communicated in an accurate and intelligible way to those for whom the respondent is speaking or writing. But it can also happen that somewhere along the way, due to unforeseen circumstances, things change, and that therefore the respondent is no longer to be understood in this way as a mere reporter or interpreter. It can happen that the respondent has not so much been invited to speak or write before a neutral and disinterested audience of fellow hermeneuts as summoned or even subpoenaed to answer or testify in a court of law composed of a judge and jury. Let us not forget that only a slight change of context is needed to turn a respondent into a defendant. And this can happen even when your name is not literally printed on the docket.

3. Maurice Blanchot, *Celui qui ne m'accompagnait pas* (Paris: Gallimard, 1953), 56–57. Further references appear in the text. At this moment in the *récit*, the responsibility in question is engaged by a genuine solitude: "I took on the burden, giving it for the time being this name: responsibility with respect to the solitude." For a less narrative example of the difficulty involved here, see "La solitude essentielle," as well as "La solitude essentielle et la solitude dans le monde," *L'espace littéraire* (Paris: Gallimard, 1955).

This, of course, is the strange story—which is also, at least to some extent and in a certain way, the impossibility or collapse of all storytelling—that befalls the anonymous narrator in Blanchot's *La folie du jour*.[4] Written in 1948, the text deals with someone who discovers to his surprise that he is not, or is no longer, dealing directly with the light, the light of day, *le jour,* conceived at once as daylight and the light of the understanding. The narrator, responding to a solicitation that remains unspecified in the first pages of the text, begins to tell a kind of autobiographical story whose possibility is predicated on the light of day: "I am not blind, I see the world and that is my extraordinary good fortune. I see it, this day outside of which there is nothing. Who can take that away from me?" (10). This day, outside of which we are at first told there is nothing, is as capable of illuminating the formative "paths of youth" as it is of descending and penetrating at a different stage the depths of library books and the "somber spirit" of their meanings. And whatever the initiative to which he is responding, the narrator seems at first perfectly capable of using the day retrospectively to bring these facts to light in his own text and then to reflect on them meaningfully: "Those I have loved, I have also lost. . . . I was, however, and almost all the time, extremely happy. That gave me something to reflect on" (11, 12). The surprise in this text is that this pattern of informing and interpreting, of bringing to light and reflecting on, is radically interrupted when the story comes to an episode in which the light itself becomes eclipsed by the question of the day, and when the text consequently slips from being a simple autobiography to becoming the official transcript of a police interrogation.

But what can it mean to refer to the "question of the day" in this way? In this text it seems to suggest both the fundamental question posed *by* the light as such, the principle and source of all luminosity, whether it is conceived as physical or intelligible, *as well as* the purely idiomatic, topical question that finds itself at this particular moment in the light, or in the air. The "light," which allows the story to be told, is itself put into question in the course of the story. Though we should not assume too quickly that we already know whether this occurs because the text's principle of articulation has become for the first time a genuine source of critical reflection (questioning "the day"), or be-

---

4. Maurice Blanchot, *La folie du jour,* édition définitive (Paris: Fata Morgana, 1973). Further references appear in the text.

cause the possibility of such reflection has merely been blotted out in the precritical confusion of immediacy and ideology (the question everyone happens to be discussing, however thoughtlessly, "today").

In any case, it should already be apparent that in Blanchot's question about responding to the "madness of the day" there is as well the necessary question of responding to history and to the symbol. By the time the narrator admits that his illness consists in having lost the thread, the direction, the meaning of the (hi)story he must recount, "le sens de *l'histoire*" (37), we can be fairly certain that, whatever else he means, something in the meaningful functioning of this one word, *histoire,* which ties together and separates history and literature, has also been afflicted. For the aesthetic question of the symbol, which can be posed to the narration as story, or self-reflexive "histoire," has shaded into and contaminated the referential question of the event, which must be posed to the narration as history, or medico-judicial "histoire." This shift is marked in the text's narratological situation when we become aware that the subject is surrounded not merely by disinterested listeners, who are competent to judge a good story, but also or rather by the representatives of medical and/or political authority, whose obligation is to test how things stand with respect to referential and historical matters.

It can also be shown that the way this text uses the "day," or "le jour," is at bottom a narrative and historical displacement of the same theoretical questions Blanchot is examining when he speaks of the "symbol" in the critical essay "Le langage de la fiction." For the light of day also stands behind the Hegelian conception of the symbol, to which Blanchot explicitly refers in that essay. In Hegel, the day is always the metaphysical possibility of the sun's light turning in one smooth motion to embrace both the formal and the historical categories of language's symbolic potential for meaning. As is well known, Hegel's definition in the *Aesthetics* of the beautiful, of which the symbol interrogated by Blanchot is itself an immediate corollary, is "the sensory appearance of the Idea" (*das sinnliche Scheinen der Idee*). Now since the Greek word for "Idea," *eide,* also means light, we end up with a definition in which the correspondence within the symbol between the phenomenal (*sinnliche*) and the intelligible (*Idee*) can be guaranteed only by a daylight that *shines* (*Scheinen*) simultaneously as an outer sun and an inner idea. This means that, for Hegel, the symbolic light of inner reason that joins the intelligible to the empirical "day" can do so only by again turning itself *out* toward a referential and historical process of sequential development.⁵ Within the philosophical and aesthetic tradition that Blanchot places all of his texts, though not without producing certain tensions in it, the "question of the day" is therefore bound to implicate both the linguistic functioning of the symbol as well as a developmental model of empirical history. That Blanchot should respond to the metaphysical tradition of historical and symbolic light by writing a text called "the *madness* of the day" is a none-too-reassuring way to question its foundational authority as well as anyone's capacity to control or resist it.

How, then, is the light of day put into question in this text? On the thematic level, it seems to happen as the result of an unsettling collision. The light, the day, the truth of the day, and the symbol of which the day is also a symbol, having stumbled against a *true event*, was rushing toward its end ("le jour, ayant buté sur un *événement vrai*, allait se hâter vers sa fin," 19-20, emphasis added). Something takes place here, an actual event, an event so cataclysmic and threatening that the light of day itself can no longer support itself against this event. This, according to the narrator, is the beginning of the end, the end of the light, *la folie du jour*. Blanchot seems thus to have substituted for Hegel's collusion between the symbol and its history a *collision* in which their presumed correspondence falls apart into fragments. The story of the day, about the day, and about the symbol that is the day, seems to be interrupted by a historical event, by something that cannot be assimilated to the specular structure of the empirical/intelligible daylight without blotting it out. It should also be noted at this point, though without presuming to exhaust its significance, that this collision also coincides in the story with the "institutionalization" of the narrator. That is, the historical event coincides with the narrator's confine-

---

5. For Blanchot's reference to Hegel's symbol, see "Le langage de la fiction," (86). Hegel's treatment can be found in *Aesthetics, Werke in zwanzig Bänden* (Frankfurt am Main: Suhrkamp, 1979), vol. 13: "The beautiful is therefore determined as the sensory appearance of the Idea . . . but the self-comprehending spirit of the beautiful is only completed in world history's unfolding across thousands of years" (151, 124). Since the symbol is defined later as the "concrete interpenetration of meaning and form," it would be legitimate to understand the unfolding of the beautiful here as the historical development of the symbolic nature of all art (393, 395). For the complications produced in Hegel's own text by the coordination of a developmental history with a theory of the symbol, see Paul de Man's "Sign and Symbol in Hegel's *Aesthetics*," *Critical Inquiry* 8 (Summer 1982), 761-75.

ment within a medico-penal institution as well as his subjection to the linguistic prescriptions proper to it. For the representatives of the law prescribe not only that he be incarcerated: "they gave me a small position in the establishment" (24). They also insist that he tell with clarity the story of how it came to be that he has now been deprived of his light and freedom: "they had asked me: tell us how things happened, 'just' how they happened" (36). What kind of "true event" could possibly be responsible for such a situation, in which an entire tradition of thinking the symbol together with its developmental history collapses and shatters in madness? Can the narrator eventually respond to the demand that he tell *this* (hi)story, and can he do it in such a way that it would then be possible to identify and understand "just" (*au juste*) how such an event could have happened?

In an essay on Blanchot that claims merely to be following the suggestive commentary of Emmanuel Levinas, Jeffrey Mehlman answers these questions forcefully, one might even say brutally. He does so by describing *La folie du jour* as "Blanchot's own liquidation of an antisemitic past," and then goes on to point out: "The originality of Blanchot's *récit* lies in its articulation of an (anti)metaphysical figure with a political and historical meditation."[6] According to Mehlman, then, the metaphysical figure here would be that of the (Platonic-Hegelian) sun, whose "madness" consists in the subversion, from within its own system, of its symbolic potential to unite the phenomenal to the intelligible. The historico-political reality that in turn reflects or articulates this philosophical madness would consist primarily, though not exclusively, of the representation in the text of a Nazi concentration camp. The antimetaphysical figure of a sun gone mad coincides with a political and historical meditation on anti-Semitism and the Holocaust. On a purely formal, thematic level, the identification of the Holocaust as the historically "true event" that would somehow correspond to and be articulated with the disruption of the metaphysical turning of the sun in the light of aesthetic cognition is provocative and certainly deserving of reflection. However, part of the difficulty connected with any reading of Blanchot's text is that it is precisely these *formal,* or symbolic, links between the categories of the

6. See Emmanuel Levinas, "Exercices sur *La folie du jour,*" *Sur Maurice Blanchot* (Paris: Fata Morgana, 1975); and Jeffrey Mehlman, "Blanchot at *Combat:* Of Literature and Terror," *Legacies: Of Anti-Semitism in France* (Minneapolis: University of Minnesota Press, 1983), 16. Further references appear in the text.

"metaphysical" and the "historico-political" that are being put into question and subjected to reformulation and fragmentation by the allegorical narrative.

By suggesting that *La folie du jour* provides what he calls an "*articulation*" of the (anti)metaphysical ("the knell of philosophy") and the empirical ("the glass in the eye"), Mehlman's own narrative history—as well as the paronomastic play (knell/*glas*) he uses to support it—falls sadly short of where Blanchot's text makes its beginning. Mehlman, that is, rearticulates a theoretical delirium and a social insanity back into an unquestioned and unified symbol in which each half (blindly) mirrors the other. The essential question raised in Blanchot's text by the "collision" and eventual undoing of the specular relationship between the metaphysical (light, clarity, reason, theory) and the empirical (a true event) is itself erased without a trace in Mehlman's attempt to reattach them in an inverted aesthetic interpretation that would masquerade at the same time as intellectual history. The final chapter in Mehlman's metaphorical genealogy would even account for a certain form of "French literary modernity"—read deconstruction, Derrida, de Man . . .—by turning it, along with Blanchot's later writings, into the indirectly coded but easily recognizable offspring of "French fascism in the 1930's" (13).[7] But such a genealogy can be maintained only at the price of refusing to take into account what actually takes place in all these texts. In this case, the recourse to a formalistic history that refuses to take the shattered symbol of Blanchot seriously is surely the best way to prevent anything genuinely historical from happening at all.

The question of the holocaust, precisely because of its seriousness, because it has not yet been sufficiently responded to or even articulated, is not simply assumed in Blanchot's text.[8] *La folie du jour*

---

7. Mehlman is perhaps excessively modest in subsuming his commentary on *La folie du jour* under Levinas's. Not only does Levinas nowhere claim a straightforward correspondence in Blanchot between the aesthetico-metaphysical and the empirical, but he goes out of his way to caution against such a simplistic collapse of categories: "*La folie du jour* could therefore be said to be free of all temporal determinations in the current sense of the term, if non-freedom—but the non-freedom less free than every determinism and every tragedy—an infernal non-freedom—were not precisely what this text is about" (59). The question of the "nonfree freedom" of Blanchot's writing from referential determinations based on metaphorical models is treated at length by Levinas in the first section of the essay, "De poésie à prose."

8. Because this particular "true event" has not yet been sufficiently responded to, the typographical convention often used to distinguish between "holocausts" in general

neither liquidates the holocaust nor, and this would be nearly the same thing, monumentalizes it thanks to a simple narrative articulation of symbolic correspondences between particular past experiences and a generalized mode of consciousness and knowledge. It would be more accurate to say that this text attempts to deal with the "true event" of the holocaust in such a way that it would not simply disappear—and for this same reason be capable of reappearing all the more easily—under a specular, metaphorical, and ultimately fictional logic of denial and affirmation. This, at any rate, is what Blanchot actually does say about the "holocaust" in a series of fragments to be found in another text, *L'écriture du désastre*. The first question to be asked seems to approach the event of the holocaust as obliquely and problematically as *La folie du jour,* addressing itself at the same time to the insufficiency of Mehlman's reading of the earlier text:

> *Why is it that all misfortunes, finite, infinite, personal, impersonal, those of right now as well as of all times, have had as substratum [pour sous-entendu], recalling it incessantly, the historically dated, yet undatable misfortune of a country already so reduced that it seemed almost effaced from the map, and whose history extended beyond world history [dont l'histoire cependant débordait l'histoire du monde]? Why?*[9]

Without yet responding, "the holocaust," this fragment already points to the system, the constellation of terms, in which such a name by

---

and a (or the) "Holocaust" properly speaking will not be adopted here. For Blanchot the holocaust is the historical event that ruins, once and for all, all propriety, including that of speaking properly about this event. The lower case is therefore not to be read here as a reduction of the holocaust to a level of generalization or banality that would be wholly improper; rather it is a reminder that the specificity of the holocaust is precisely what deprives us of thinking we already have a proper language in which to speak of it.

9. *L'écriture du désastre* (Paris: NRF/Gallimard, 1980), 64, Blanchot's emphasis. Further references appear in the text. Blanchot's aporetic qualification, "the historically dated, yet undatable misfortune," recalls Levinas's reference to the text's "nonfree freedom" from any "temporal limitation in the current sense of the term." For Blanchot, as well as for Levinas, what is at stake is thinking history in a different way, thinking the historical element that would "extend beyond" the history we now have, and that may not (yet) be available "in the current sense of terms" like "history" and "world." This also means that what is to be understood by a term like "the holocaust" can never be simply taken for granted as being either purely referential ("historically dated") or purely nonreferential ("undatable"). Rather, the task for "history" would be to respond to the "holocaust" as "the historically dated, *yet* undatable misfortune." As we shall soon see, Blanchot also denies to "the holocaust" the possibility of being adequately and meaningfully named as such.

necessity functions, though perhaps not without disrupting the internal coherence of this system.

The system that is composed by these terms is of course history, and it is conceived in this fragment as an intelligible discourse of persons, events, dates, and maps, whose ultimate principle of articulation would be the possibility of asking the question: Why? This question asks about the meaning, the "whys and wherefores," of what is not, or not yet, (fully) *understood*. But it also asks about an event that underlies and participates in the possible meaning of all else, and which itself *can* only be *sous-entendu,* incompletely registered or understood. The question questions the status in history of this one event that seems to exceed the dates, the maps, and even the history of asking why meaningfully that it also makes possible. And in so doing, the question of this event finally questions the question itself, questions history as a meaningful system of correspondences between questions and responses: *Why why?*[10]

The question, then, asks about the one event that is presupposed, implied, and recalled by every other event in history without in turn being explainable or understandable by any of them. By responding, "the holocaust," to this question, however, nothing has been explained or understood, and the question returns elsewhere:

> *The unknown name, outside nameability: The holocaust, history's* absolute *event, historically dated, this all-burn in which all history was set ablaze, in which the movement of Sense was engulfed [s'est abîmé], in which the gift, without pardon, without consent, [où le don, sans pardon, sans consentement], was ruined without giving way to anything that could be affirmed, or denied, gift of passivity itself, gift of that which cannot give itself. How to watch over it [comment le garder], even in thought, how to make of thought that which would watch over the holocaust in which all was lost, including watchful thought [y compris la pensée gardienne]?* (80)

It would be more than just a mere error to understand this to mean that because all the events of history somehow presuppose the unnameable

---

10. The questions of "history," "event," "meaning," and "the question" are all questions of Heidegger to which Blanchot is also always responding, sometimes implicitly, sometimes explicitly. For another exemplary "response" to the questions of Heidegger, see Jacques Derrida's *De l'esprit: Heidegger et la question* (Paris: Galilée, 1987), esp. note 1, pp. 147–54.

"holocaust," because it is history's "absolute" event, the holocaust itself, dated and mapped out with all possible historical precision, was inevitable and therefore in some sense excusable. The holocaust was neither inevitable nor excusable; nor was anything that contributed to it in any way inevitable or excusable. Such an event, in Blanchot's terms, is quite clearly *sans pardon, sans consentement.*

And yet, and yet, to read Blanchot more closely is to be made unavoidably aware that the discourse that refuses to grant pardon or consent is itself only a partial response to the question, a response that, no matter how necessary, no matter how urgent, is still necessarily preliminary and incomplete. That is, such a refusal still does not refuse enough. For if the "excuse" would sidestep the grievousness of the event by means of a retrospective logic of "inevitability," then the "*sans pardon*" would be required by the same token to mediate the "absoluteness" of the event in a retrospective logic of "freedom." In order to affirm or deny the participation of any individual or any act in the event, it is necessary and urgent to reestablish a temporality *prior to* this event itself, one which could be understood, according to individual circumstances and choices, to lead up to or resist it. But it is precisely the oppositional logic of affirmation and denial ruling such distinctions between "inevitability" and "freedom" that is not left intact *by* the absolute event of "the holocaust": *The holocaust, history's* absolute *event in which the movement of Sense was engulfed, in which the gift was ruined without* giving *way to anything that could be affirmed or denied.* What is irretrievably engulfed or undermined (*abîmé*) is the unequivocal movement of Sense or meaning that would allow for absolute determinations of sense and non-sense, as well as affirmation and denial. Which means that, even if we must continue to refuse consent and pardon to whatever contributed to this "absolute event, historically dated," we are still not given the option of restricting our responsibility toward the "undatable" aspect of the event to such determinations. For what is ruined (*ruiné*) in this absolute event, says Blanchot, is the *don,* or the "gift."

Now the "gift" is an extremely complicated and dense word in *L'écriture du désastre,* because it is the place where Blanchot's writing of the "holocaust" intersects with his reading and rewriting in a different idiom of Heidegger's thought. The intersection of Blanchot and Heidegger in this word, moreover, is itself more like a stumbling block, an offense, or a scandal, an *Anstoss* in the Kierkegaardian sense, then, than a place of coordination or symbolic correspondence.[11] For if Heidegger's text is, on the one hand, one that makes it possible to begin to think history and the event in the wake of "history's absolute event," it is at the same time, for Blanchot, a text that is still open to the suspicion of a certain number of tensions or gestures that would necessarily fall short of thinking the "holocaust." This reserve on Blanchot's part toward Heidegger is evident, for instance, in the fragments of *L'écriture du désastre* that meditate on the connection between Heidegger's thinking of the "gift," *es gibt,* and the "event," *das Ereignis*. The event here, *das Ereignis,* is not simply an occurrence, or not an occurrence in the way that we usually, simplistically, think of it as anything whatsoever that "happens." Rather, Heidegger's *Ereignis* would be an event in a genuinely historical sense, since only within the specificity named by this word, according to Heidegger, would the conditions of history's occurring as an event of Being for thought be fully satisfied. For this reason, it is what lies at the ground of any understanding (*sous-entendu*) of what is given us to think by any of history's individual events.

Heidegger calls this structure of historicity the *Ereignis,* then, and Blanchot glosses its relation to the gift as follows: "The word 'gift' is *given* by the German formula of 'there is': *Es gibt:* it gives, it, the 'there,' being 'subject' of the *Ereignis,* the coming about of what is most proper [*Le mot 'donation' est* donné *par la formule allemande de l' 'il y a': Es gibt: cela donne, cela, le 'il,' étant 'sujet' de l'*Ereignis, l'avènement du plus propre]" (169, Blanchot's emphasis). But it is this reference to *propriety* within the act of appropriating what actually comes about historically—the "gift" of the *eigen* (proper) that Heidegger's language is still able to find at the heart of the *Ereignis*—that is ruined by the absolute event, the *Ereignis,* of the holocaust. This complication within the *Ereignis* results, for Blanchot, in a new responsibility with respect to what Heidegger's text can be saying about

---

11. It is always necessary to be reminded that what is at stake in the "holocaust" is precisely the (necessary) impossibility of "thinking" an unthinkable "absolute event" of "history." To the extent that Kierkegaard also "reflects" on history's "dated yet undatable event," his text will be just as much (or as little) about the "holocaust" as Blanchot's. This goes for *L'écriture du désastre* as well as for *La folie du jour,* where, it will be remembered, this reading stumbled upon the collision of the "day" with a "true event." See *Philosophical Fragments,* trans. David Swenson (Princeton: Princeton University Press, 1936, 1962), esp. the appendix to chapter 3, "The Paradox and the Offended Consciousness."

both the "gift" and the "propriety" of whatever can be affirmed or denied on the subject of the historical event:

> *Ereignis* is thus analyzed [by Heidegger] in such a way that the word *eigen*, 'proper,' is brought out, 'the event' becoming in this way that which brings to our being 'the most proper.' . . . It is not the arbitrary aspect that is so surprising here, but on the contrary, the work of mimesis, the semblance of analogy, the recourse to questionable scholarship which makes us victims of a kind of transhistorical necessity. It is true that the requirement for a 'justification' can, in its turn, be taken up and rejected. For there is nothing to justify, here it does not depend on what is just or not just, but rather *gives itself* as an incitement to think and to question [*Il n'y a rien à justifier, cela ne relève pas du juste ou du non-juste, mais se donne comme une incitation à penser et à interroger*]. (152–53, emphasis added)

What is given in Heidegger's text as an incitement to thought and to questioning, according to Blanchot's reading of it, is therefore not simply the propriety (*eigen*) of the event (*Ereignis*), which in this case would be grotesquely unjust, would rather be a regression on Heidegger's part, a recourse to the wholly arbitrary, and for the sake of the most questionable "philosophical" motives. But on the other hand, this also means that there can be no question here of *our* simply conflating, of bringing together into the analogical totality and propriety of one symbol, the improprieties of what is known of Heidegger's actual political engagements in the 1930s with a reading of his texts. That Heidegger himself was capable of regressing from the rigor of his texts for the most questionable philosophical and political motives is more than obvious to any observer and has been amply commented on. But the condemnation of a certain Heidegger along with his silence after the war should not be allowed to become our condemning to silence all that a patient reading of his texts still has to give us to think. And one of the things that is given us is the onerous *thought* of this surprising burden Heidegger puts on his own text when he gives to the arbitrary relation between *eigen* and *Ereignis* the semblance of a meaningful analogy *despite* the recourse to questionable scholarship this makes it necessary for him to have. Precisely this (philosophical) requirement to justify the illusory correspondence between *eigen* (what is proper) and *Ereignis* (the event)—because it threatens to make us dupes of a transhistorical necessity that would be absolutely unjust—is what must be said to be least *proper* to the actual event, or historical *Ereignis*, at stake in this text.

And so, Blanchot reminds us in the fragment immediately following the one we have been reading, it is also necessary to read how in Heidegger the propriety of the event is *also* marked by a process of *enteignen:* the *Ereignis* must become an *Enteignis,* the dispossession or withdrawal of the event. Such a withdrawal of the event's propriety—*das Enteignen des Eignens des Ereignens*—is the "gift" of Heidegger, then, as it is read and transcribed by Blanchot. Blanchot's transcription of Heidegger is also the "gift of passivity itself, gift of that which cannot give itself," a gift that can therefore be a genuinely historical event only on condition that it not give itself over to us as such, in all its illusory propriety (or impropriety).[12] To come back to the philosophical question of "sense" and the "event," but by way of the disastrous idiom of the holocaust, would require, in addition to the logic of affirmation and denial, and beyond determinations of justice and injustice, a different kind of "thought." Only the passivity of a thought that is capable of registering the gift given it in the repetitive withdrawal of the event's propriety would be one that, according to Blanchot, "would be able to watch over the holocaust in which all was lost, including watchful thought." To be "passive" in this sense would be somehow to go beyond "the movement of Sense" engulfed by the absolute event of history. Blanchot will himself make this passive move by rewriting the philosophical movement of sense and propriety that still remains legible in Heidegger's *Ereignis*. He does so by transcribing *Ereignis* into the "vain errance" of his own idiom: "cette dépense qui dérange tout événement. . . . Ainsi l'errance court-elle vainement sur son erre" (153–54). Carried away by the absolute event

---

12. Blanchot does not make reference here to a particular text by Heidegger, but he is more than likely thinking of the essay, "Der Weg zur Sprache," in the collection entitled, *Unterwegs zur Sprache,* as well as *Das Ding,* where it is written: "Dieses enteignende Vereignen ist das Spiegelspiel des Gevierts." For an analysis of how this peculiarity of the "event" in Heidegger is also related to the question of the symbol (metaphor), see Jacques Derrida, "Le retrait de la métaphore," *Psyche: Inventions de l'autre* (Paris: Galilée, 1987). See also Blanchot's fragment in *L'écriture du désastre:* "The disaster is the gift, it gives the disaster: it is as though it went beyond being and nonbeing. It is not the coming to be (the proper of that which happens)—that does not happen, so that I do not happen even to have this thought, except without knowing it, without the appropriation of a knowledge. Or else, is it the coming to be of that which does not happen, of that which would come without happening, outside of being, and as though through drifting? The posthumous disaster?" (13).

of the holocaust, then, the *er* of the Heideggerian *Ereignis* becomes the improper movement, or *erre,* in Blanchot's writing. Such writing disturbs the philosophical propriety of every "événement," making of history's absolute event the task of reading an infinite *"erre-vainement."*

Which also means that such writing and reading will go beyond the movement of sense that is built into the concept of the symbol as it appears in the aesthetico-philosophical tradition. For Blanchot's fragments on the "gift" and the "event" are also the broken fragments of this traditional conception of the symbol, fragments that do not allow themselves to be rearticulated into any totality, or fullness of aesthetic or philosophical meaning. After analyzing how the presumed correspondence between *eigen* and *Ereignis* is to be thought through a necessary "play of the idiom," Blanchot returns to the question of the "gift." If it is now necessary to think what happens to the *Ereignen* as the expropriation of *Enteignen* rather than as the propriety of the *Eignen,* Blanchot goes on to ask, then how can the event of the "gift" ever be made to coincide with what is given: "Who gives? What gives? Inappropriate questions [*questions sans convenance*] that reverberate in the language without accommodating any response but language itself, the gift of language" (170). But it is precisely the inadequation, the *sans convenance,* of these questions to these answers that risks once again making the "gift" of language into a kind of symbol, or "coming together" (*convenance*). When language names itself as inadequation it also gives itself as what it is not, for it remains inadequate to give the radical withdrawal of language it names and therefore betrays. The gift of language is therefore also a poison: "To write is to distrust writing absolutely, while entrusting oneself absolutely to it. Whatever foundation one gives to this double movement, which is not as contradictory as its overly dense formulation makes it sound, it remains the rule of every writing practice: the 'give itself withdrawing itself' " (170–71).

This fragment on the gift of language also warns about the dangerous tendency to worship (or demystify) language as though, being the withdrawn source of its own giving, it were a sacred object, or *Deus absconditus*. Such is the danger of a certain kind of thinking of the symbol as well, according to Blanchot, since it tends to freeze the relation between symbol and symbolized without taking into account the symbol's *historical* potential to "exceed" even its own powers of synthesis and dissolution. The references Blanchot makes in this context include the concept of the "symbol" as it is articulated in Hegel, Humboldt, and, closer to home, though in a different mode, Gérard Genette: "by means of the symbol the unrepresentable becomes sayable or showable" (167–68). For whether they are "believers or nonbelievers" in the symbol makes no essential difference; the symbol remains a sacred object whether it is worshiped for its adequacy to represent (Humboldt) or systematically demystified of this pretension (Genette). In neither case has the symbol's "double movement"—to be necessarily inadequate to express its own inadequate power to represent—been accounted for. The consequences of this duplicitous structure within the symbol become radicalized when the particular "symbol" in question is the name for the absolute event of history, the all-burn of the holocaust that is named in "Auschwitz." For Blanchot, only a passivity that would itself exceed the sacred oppositions of belief/nonbelief, giving/withdrawing, appearance/meaning, visible/invisible, affirmation/negation can begin to approach the invisible symbol of "Auschwitz" itself: "Concentration camps, annihilation camps, *figures* where the invisible has been made forever visible" (129, emphasis added). If the rule of meaningful analogy is truly inadequate, can never be justified, what is the rule of excess or inadequate meaning that rules and justifies the use of a name like "Auschwitz"? How can such a "figure" be fully given in its withdrawal of meaning? What would be proper to the eye that could see the invisible that is made visible in the event of annihilation called "Auschwitz"?[13]

With the name of Auschwitz, we approach once again the question

---

13. A recent example of *la folie du jour,* in which the historicity of "Auschwitz" collides with its rhetoricity, is readable in the dispute that developed between Jews and Catholics over the Carmelite convent that was established in 1984 in a building used to store Zyklon-B during the war. Stories in the *New York Times* of August 29, 1989, help to measure the distance that still separates us from knowing what we are saying when we say "Auschwitz": "Jewish groups began to question the presence of a convent at a place that they felt *symbolized* Jewish suffering . . . culminating last month when a group from New York scaled the walls of the convent, only to be ejected by Polish workers on the site. . . . On August 10, the Archbishop of Cracow, Francsizek Cardinal Macharski, said he was abandoning plans to construct the interfaith center [elsewhere] because of the Jewish demonstrations. 'The Christian faith, as well as *symbols* and piety, were not respected,' he said" (A7). Cardinal Glemp, the primate of Poland, demonstrated beyond any doubt in his statements that it is still possible not even to suspect what is at stake in the name "Auschwitz": "[Cardinal Glemp] also said that the Birkenau part of the Auschwitz-Birkenau complex held the gas chambers where most of the Jews were put to death. He seemed to imply that by placing the convent in the Auschwitz part of the complex, the church had indeed been sensitive to Jewish feelings and had found an *appropriate site*" (A7).

of the question, the response, and the kind of responsibility engaged by all these questions. For if the question is always a question of meaning (*Why?*), then, as we have seen, the responsibility to the holocaust would also require, in part, questioning this question—*why why?*—by *not* responding to it within the same logic in which for each question there would be a corresponding and meaningful response. This logic is no longer wholly legitimate, since it is always predicated, at least in part, on a movement of sense which is itself no longer to be left unquestioned. "Can the disaster be interrogated? Where to find the language in which response, question, affirmation, negation, intervene perhaps, but are without effect?" (43-44)[14] How to respond to the absolute disaster of the holocaust, then, without merely responding, and without therefore confirming the system of sense that was to be questioned, that was in fact questioned by the absolute event of the holocaust? Such a response would be what Blanchot also refers to, "abusively, impossibly," as the "other" responsibility, or as the responsibility to the "other" (45-46):

> Not to respond or to accept a response, such is the rule: which is not enough to prevent the questions. But when the response is the absence of response, the question in its turn becomes the absence of question (the question mortified), the word passes, comes back to a past that has never spoken, past of every word. (54)

"When the response is the absence of response, the question becomes in its turn the absence of question." But Blanchot also insists that this absence of question and response "is not enough to prevent the ques-

---

14. What is relevant is not that Blanchot continues to make use of the question here, since, obviously "can the disaster be interrogated?" or "why, why?" are themselves asked as questions. What is decisive is rather that Blanchot's text makes the question depend for its effectiveness on a different mode of language, which is also one that necessarily exceeds the very questions it continues to ask. In addition to Blanchot's work, two of the most effective contemporary interrogations of the hermeneutic structure in which "response, question, affirmation, and negation" could correspond with each other without remainder are provided by the work of Jacques Derrida and Paul de Man. To a large extent, they are "responses" to what is given, or left to us to think, by the text of Heidegger as well as by the holocaust. The most economical formulation of where these responses are to be situated is undoubtedly provided by Derrida in *De l'esprit: Heidegger et la question* (21-30), under the heading "open questions." The four questions constantly reopened in Heidegger's text by Derrida (and de Man) are the status of the question, the status of technology, the status of the human, and the status of the epoch and its teleology; all four are questions of language, meaning, and history.

tions," which also means that it is not a call to some form of facile irrationality (47); nor is it an abdication of any relationship to meaning whatsoever (86); nor is it the passivity of quietism (31). Rather, it is the formula for a thought and a responsibility: for that alone which watches over, *garde* or *veille,* the passivity of a past that has never spoken the language of question and response in any present. Such would be the past that passes incessantly into every word, but as its absent sense, its ruined sense, its asemic sense, its disaster.

The absent response that comes back to a disastrous past is another of the ways Blanchot rewrites the gift—"gift of passivity itself, gift of that which cannot give itself"—that has no place outside of writing, for such a gift can take place only "in the lack of place and of truth without which the gift of writing, the gift of Saying, giving life as well as death, being as well as nonbeing, would no longer be that expenditure that disturbs every event" (153). The other responsibility, says Blanchot, because its occurrence exceeds the ordinary categories of experience and ethics, would be toward "the word of writing" (47). But to say, as Blanchot never tires of saying, that the gift of *passivité* (passivity) that watches over this *passé* (past) is *writing*[15] is to say something infinitely more and infinitely less than what we usually understand by an absence of response. One cannot even begin to measure this infinity of difference until one has taken the trouble to respond to it—as Blanchot himself has suggested with respect to what is given to think in Heidegger's *Ereignis*—by reading its writing. "Reading writing,"—how is that to be thought? A first and indispensable thought of what is given in such a proposition is simple and straightforward: *One cannot respond until one has read that which has been written.* Or: *Only by reading what has been written does it first become possible to respond.* To respond is reading writing. Such a thought is indispensable, for without it, without connecting the predi-

---

15. This holds as well for the specificity of the responsibility that cannot be turned away from in *Celui qui ne m'accompagnait pas;* the terrible trial the narrator must respond to is the (impossible) question, "Are you writing at this very moment?" As in *L'écriture du désastre,* such a trial requires the gift of passivity—of a past, that is, that has no determinate anteriority. The "other" responsibility to such an event, such a history, is a future of uncertainty that passes incessantly into the word without ever having been or being able to be a present: "At any rate, I could not assign a precise moment to the response that I would make to him [the one who was not accompanying me], if ever I succeeded in saying to him: 'Yes, *at this moment,* exactly *at this moment*'" (130).

cate "reading" to both the subject "to respond" and the objective complement "writing" in order to produce a grammatically correct and coherent proposition, the most aberrant and willful misunderstandings can take place, and in any number of directions.[16]

But even when such preliminary reading has taken place, it is still not enough. For in its very project of forming a meaningful statement, it does not take sufficiently into account the unformed or absent sense of the disaster that Blanchot situates *in* writing: "To write, to 'form' in what refuses form an absent sense [*'former' dans l'informel un sens absent*].... To write is perhaps to bring to the surface something like absent sense, to make way for the passive push [*accueillir la poussé passive*] that is not yet thought, being the disaster of thought" (71). A reading that would not take account of such a "disaster," or "absent sense," in writing always stops short of the question of the holocaust, even when it seems to be writing about nothing else. So it is necessary to read writing differently, necessary to allow the absent sense to come to the surface, necessary to leave a space in reading writing for the abyss that is the disaster of thought and meaning. Such a space unsettles the connections and coherency of grammatical units and produces a reading that could no longer be conceived in passive opposition to writing, as though we knew already what kind of activities both "reading" and "writing" were, as though we knew what the "abyss" were in which the movement of sense was ruined.

"Reading writing for the abyss," then, can no longer name a reading that is able, actively or passively, and on the basis of a simple *desire* or

---

16. One of the very first misunderstandings comes about with respect to the question of the holocaust and language. "Reading, writing the holocaust": is it not derisively irresponsible to link the holocaust in this way with the question of language? "After all, it is all a question of language." Is such a thoughtless cliché not the height of arrogance and lunacy? But is there an alternative to the necessity of making such a cliché into a thought and a responsibility? If there is any access to the experience of the holocaust, can it be conceivable independently of the question of language? As communication, as memory? "But the danger (here) of words in their theoretical insignificance is perhaps to presume to evoke the annihilation in which everything always goes under, without heeding the 'be quiet' addressed to those who have known only *from afar and partially* the interruption of history. However, *to watch over* the disproportionate absence, it has to be done, has to be done incessantly, because that which begins again out of this end (Israel, all of us), is *marked* by this end with which we can never be done *waking ourselves up*" (134, emphasis added). Whose acquaintance with the holocaust—here, now—would not be, from afar, partial? Coming to terms with the "marks" of this distance—and the specificity of *all* the ways such "marks" can occur, can be registered—such would be the responsibility of a watchfulness and a waking.

understanding, to jump over the asemic abyss of the disaster that is now inscribed in writing. It would begin instead to name a kind of reading whose own passivity is not opposed or reducible to any other activity. Such a reading responds to the abyss of writing by not (just) responding to it. In other words, it responds to the "other" passivity of writing with an "other" passivity of its own. What would such a reading writing be?

> There is an active reading, productive—producing text and reader, it carries us beyond [*elle nous transporte*]. Then the passive reading that betrays the text, by appearing to submit to it, by giving the illusion that the text exists objectively, fully, supremely: wholly. Finally, the reading no longer passive, but of passivity, without pleasure or joy, would elude both comprehension and desire: it is like nocturnal watchfulness, 'inspiring' insomnia in which the 'Saying' beyond the all has been said [*le 'Dire' au-delà du tout est dit*] would be heard and in which the testimony of the last witness would be pronounced. (157–58)

Reading, then, does not actively produce from scratch a writing that would therefore have no hold on it, nor does it passively submit itself to following a writing that would preexist it fully and objectively.

According to this fragment, reading eludes the temporal determination of both a comprehension directed toward the past and a desire oriented toward the future, and in so doing becomes a kind of witness to an indeterminate past that itself *opens* an unpredictable future. Reading is a "saying" that begins to "inspire" only when all seems to be said and done. Reading is a passive "saying" that extends a writing that is not yet fully and objectively there into a future that would be beyond all that has ever been said. Reading allows writing to be heard again and again by allowing the abyss that opens up beyond all that is said in comprehension and desire to be pronounced for the first time. It is, therefore, says Blanchot, the testimony of the last witness to this absent sense, and this is a very grave thing to say in a text that is called *l'écriture du désastre* and that speaks of the holocaust. It may mean that late in the night, after all the other witnesses have spoken or written, then something like reading will also have to be heard and that reading is last in terms of importance and urgency. But it may also mean that it is already very late and that there is no longer any witnessing whatsoever outside of reading, that all other witnessing—

saying, writing—must now go by way of reading if they are ever to happen at all.

"Reading writing," then, is a witnessing of the abyss, but how precisely does it testify to this? For Blanchot—and for all those who come after the holocaust, that is, for us—reading writing cannot simply disclose this abyss as a "something" (sense) or a "nothing" (absence, non-sense) that could ever be read passively in order at some later time to respond to it (actively and perhaps by writing). Reading writing is itself the *passivité* that witnesses or watches over the "absent sense" that incessantly passes into every written word now read as *l'écriture du désastre*, the writing that is given us to think by the disaster. And the way that reading writing witnesses or watches over the words' absent sense, says Blanchot, is in a *cry* of silence: *"How to watch over [the holocaust] . . . how to make of thought that which would watch over the holocaust in which all was lost, including watchful thought? In the mortal intensity, the elusive silence of the limitless cry"* (80). How to read: A writing and a crying whose absent sense is excessive with respect to all language: "The cry, like writing, tends to exceed all language . . . the patience of the cry, that which does not stop with non-sense, while remaining nonetheless outside of sense, a sense infinitely suspended" (86).

For those who read writing after the holocaust, the ruin of infinitely suspended meaning can only pass into the silence of writing's limitless cry: *le sens absent passe dans le silence du cri innombrable de l'écriture.* Such is the risk of our responsibility. It is a risk because the suspended sense it speaks of necessarily threatens in a very real way to make the most serious of questions the most frivolous and perversely meaningless. It is not the limited threat posed to sense by non-sense, which can always be recovered retrospectively by a calculated return to sense. The risk here would be the far more threatening possibility that there would no longer be a secure vantage point from which to tell sense and non-sense apart, that their suspension as an opposition would be excessive, infinite. And this is *our* responsibility because it is only on the condition of such a risk that it is possible to watch over the absolute suspension of sense that is always threatened *by* the holocaust. For it follows that a kind of discourse that (mistakenly) believes itself to be once and for all sheltered from such a risk of meaning's perversion, rather than its mere destruction, believes itself by the same token (and just as mistakenly) to be absolutely sheltered from the perversion of meaning that is forever named by the holocaust. Such infinite protection, were it attainable, would preclude the possibility of witnessing and watching over that from which it would be sheltered.

L'écriture du désastre/le silence du cri: the silence of the cry in which, Blanchot tells us, the holocaust can be watched over, becomes readable in the writing of the disaster. And this absent or suspended sense of the holocaust becomes readable there beyond any calculable logic of affirmation or denial, beyond any calculable procedure of comprehension or desire. It becomes readable in the undermining and perversion of sense and in the ruin of the gift, of the radical withdrawal of the gift of language in its very excess. It becomes readable in the *cri* that lies silently at the heart of *écri*ture. Such is the risk of reading writing, and such is the risk of history. For how would it ever be possible to calculate with certainty the overdetermining effect of the seemingly random and gratuitous letters *c-r-i* within the deadly and intensely serious logic of Blanchot's text? To respond adequately to this question it would be necessary, in this one text which names and discusses the holocaust, to decide and reflect on: 1) whether the crucial relationship that links *écriture* and *cri* to the watching over of the holocaust is freely motivated by a privileging of the concept "wailing" over the concept "writing," or vice versa; 2) whether the play of the letter, which is discussed in this text with respect to the configuration "passivité/passion/pas," is purely idiosyncratic and senseless in this particular case, and thus is not intended to play a semantic role here. It would be necessary to decide, in short, whether *c-r-i* are mere letters that have not yet begun to function as meaningful language, or whether they are already the words of a kind of language that always and everywhere signifies a "wailing" over the thought of its disaster.[17]

---

17. These considerations and questions are aggravated rather than resolved by referring them to a text called, significantly enough, *Was Heisst Denken?*, in which Heidegger interrogates the relation in Nietzsche's text between writing, crying, and thinking: "Im Geschriebenen erstickt der *Schrei* leicht, vollends dann, wenn das *Schrei*ben sich nur im Be*schrei*ben ergeht und es darauf absieht, das Vorstellen zu beschäftigen und ihm ausreichend immer neuen Stoff zu liefern. In Geschriebenen verschwindet das Gedachte, wenn das *Schrei*ben es nicht vermag, im Geschriebenen selbst noch ein Gehen des Denkens, ein Weg zu bleiben. . . . Aber Nietzsche musste *schrei*en. Und ihm blieb keine andere Weise dafür, als zu *schrei*ben [The cry is easily stifled in what is written, especially when the writing only ends up in a descriptive account or narration and aims merely to engage the imagination and keep it occupied by continually providing enough new matter for it. Thought disappears in what is written when the writing is not able to remain after all, even in what is itself written, a means for thinking, a path. . . . But Nietzsche had to cry. And there was no other way for him to do it than in writing" (*Was Heisst Denken?* [Tübingen: Max Niemeyer, 1984], 20).

Such a decision is not simply possible; we have no language in which to speak of the conditions of language, to speak meaningfully of the moment in which meaningless letters become meaningful words, in which inarticulate cries become meaningful writing: "The cry, like writing [*le* cri, *comme l'écriture:* the cry which is like writing, but also, perhaps, the cry conceived *as* writing], tends to exceed all language, even if it can be recovered as an effect of language" (86). For a mere "effect" of language could never be used to account for that language's very possibility. Blanchot's concept of the symbol, to the extent that it too exceeds all meaningful language, is, like the cry, not just an effect of writing but the irrecoverable condition of writing "itself."

And yet, whatever we think of it, however we try to dispose of it, or recover from it, this scandalous "collision" in Blanchot's text between a "reflection" on the holocaust and the absolutely random "event" of the letters *c-r-i* is *true;* it actually does take place. It is a true event, *un événement vrai* or *ein Ereignis,* that occurs *at the risk* of turning the absolutely essential question of the holocaust into an abyss of word play, into the most improper degradation of the absolute event it would watch over. But contrary to a facile kind of thinking and an outmoded kind of logic, the questions of history and responsibility cannot even be broached in connection with the holocaust short of facing up to the occurrence of such an absolute threat to meaning. Or rather, short of this threat, that the most essential and proper question become the most perversely meaningless and futile of exercises, the concept of responsibility can represent only a purely formal and therefore deluded return to a thinking and a logic made historically inadequate by the holocaust. To take the risk of an actual responsibility by reading writing, though, is not to decide its outcome in advance by refusing to take it seriously. To begin to read is not to respond by pretending that it is possible to know in advance whether *l'écriture du désastre*—the writing about the holocaust as well as the writing the holocaust will always have become for us—will be able to recall anything at all, will itself turn out to be a meaningful question or a futile exercise of forgetting.

To raise the question of reading writing, of the *cri* in *é*criture, for instance, is not the same as celebrating it as a sacred gift or denouncing it as frivolous play. It is to respond to this event by not resisting it, or to resist responding to it by merely answering for it, as though all were actually said and done and could as a consequence be duly celebrated or denounced. For this reason, reading writing is a witnessing, or a responsibility toward a certain past, but a past that necessarily opens the question of an uncertain *future*. History would be this responsibility to remember for the future a past that is constantly in danger of passing away, that is constantly being forgotten in the word of writing that is necessary to preserve it. History would therefore be the requirement to remember what it means to forget:

> If forgetting precedes memory or perhaps founds it or has nothing to do with it, to forget is not only a lack, a fault, an absence, an emptiness . . . forgetting, neither negative nor positive, would be the *passive exigence* that neither accommodates nor removes the past, but, designating in it that which has never taken place (as in the "to come" of the future [*comme dans l' à venir*] that which could never find its place in a present), refers to nonhistorical forms of time, to the other of all times, to their eternal indecision, or their eternally provisional indecision, without destiny, without presence. (134–35, emphasis added)

This kind of "other" history remembers what it means to forget by suspending ordinary historical forms of time and space in a provisional, indecisive, nonteleological *text:* a passive writing whose "infinitely suspended sense" resists anticipation, predictability, or calculation in the present and therefore always remains "to come." Such a passive exigency—the past—that always refers to a textual history "to come" is therefore also a kind of promise.

It is not a promise, though, in the sense that it promises *something;* such promises belong to the outdated logic of programmability and totalization that makes any "future" theoretically superfluous because it is already knowable in advance. The claim to symbolic mastery between the promise and what is promised—between the visible and invisible of the figure or between the past/present and future of history—implicit in such systems of thought is also potentially totalitarian. For it pretends to saturate and account for all unpredictable factors, and it thereby refuses to tolerate the openness and actual future of a promise that would not yet know how to correspond fully with what it is promising. We already know the outcome of such totalizing promises, and they do indeed deliver exactly what they promise: they make the future superfluous in principle by making it in fact intolerable. The responsibility of reading writing, on the other hand, is promising only to the extent that, and as long as, it makes no promises whatsoever about its own future as promise. In Blanchot's terms, the promise is a form of writing that eludes both comprehension and desire, and for this reason it remains unpredictably open to the historical openness of its future.

To take a risk, to give one's word, to speak of responsibility, to point toward the future, to promise: what kind of response to the question is that? Especially when one has been asked only to recount and reflect on the written facts of the past, to tell a story that would correspond to the facts of this textual history "just" as they happened (*au juste*). But is it possible to make a meaningful story out of such historical "events" as the ones at issue here? Is it possible not to? These are some of the questions asked during the abyssal course of *La folie du jour*, or rather, some of the questions of the day to which Blanchot's text, *La folie du jour*, responds abyssally. The narrator of the text gives two versions or two incompatible fragments of response to the demand to reattach literature and history into a symbolic whole, or historico-aesthetic meaning. One version seems to be the story of his life as a writer and the events he has been party to, and this version tries to include within it an account of how the writer watched as the day went mad, of how he watched as the light of day was interrupted and was on the verge of going out. The other fragmented response, which collides with and is more or less disruptive of the response provided by the first, speaks of a different kind of accounting, of a language that speaks by resisting responding to the questions that have always been asked of it. In this kind of language a silence enters the words in such a way that they begin to speak, or cry, all by themselves, beyond any past knowledge or future expectation, that is, beyond the comprehension and desire of the authorities already in place. This other response, this response that is the absence of response, will also be when the words begin to be responsible for, to watch over and to promise a different kind of story and a different kind of history, though without knowing just what it is they are promising precisely because they are promising only to remember that which has not yet ever been heard or seen: "no . . . never again."

7 Beyond Movement: Paul de Man's History

The Triumph of Life warns us that nothing, whether deed, word, thought, or text, ever happens in relation, positive or negative, to anything that precedes, follows, or exists elsewhere, but only as a random event whose power, like the power of death, is due to the randomness of its occurrence. It also warns us why and how these events then have to be reintegrated in a historical and aesthetic system of recuperation that repeats itself regardless of the exposure of its fallacy.... Reading as disfiguration, to the very extent that it resists historicism, turns out to be more historically reliable than the products of historical archeology.

—Paul de Man, "Shelley Disfigured"

There is a curious little anecdote that Paul de Man stops to tell in the middle of one of his essays. It is an anecdote that interrupts a particularly dense argument about how history happens, an argument in which de Man must juggle questions about formalism, referentiality, pedagogical and political authority, dialectical development, and the practice of deconstruction. What is staged there as he turns aside from the argument at hand is the imperturbable insistence, in the face of all these more or less precarious and pressing "historical" matters, on maintaining the importance of a certain piece of paper on which something has been written. What makes the anecdote so funny, or distressing—or both—is the reaction de Man imagines taking place as a result of such an insistence, which is also a warning: "but who cares for this darned piece of paper, the last thing in the world we want to hear about and ... the only thing we actually get. As we would say, in colloquial exasperation with an obtuse bore: forget it!"[1] The piece of

1. See "Hypogram and Inscription," *The Resistance to Theory* (Minneapolis: University of Minnesota Press, 1986), 42.

paper this staged interruption is written on is worth reflecting on, though not for its anecdotal value, whose relevance to de Man himself is obvious enough, but because what it says about history is so difficult to read. And it is so difficult to read precisely because, unlike so many of the pseudotheories, -accounts, and -interpretations of history that promise to tell us whatever we want to hear, it actually says something about the only kind of history we're ever liable to get. But how is history written in Paul de Man?

Paul de Man? History? *Sauve qui peut!* The words are no sooner uttered than the general alert is sounded and there is a mad scramble for the door. Of course, it doesn't seem to matter much just how you get there, provided you get out in time. Time was, one managed to avoid the question by swearing up and down there just wasn't any history to be found in de Man, or anything like what was supposed to resemble history. These days, though, the quickest route of escape from the problem seems to follow the opposite path, the question being most economically disposed of by presuming there is nothing but history in de Man, and a most shamefully recognizable one at that. In the end, though, both responses to the place history occupies in de Man's writings would be the same. The lack (or excess) of empirical historical reference that is commonly (and mistakenly) associated with de Man's practice of rhetorical reading can always be reassimilated to an ongoing and more comprehensive picture of continuity and change genre in a familiar system of literary studies and politics that would thus be left unchanged by it. Both reactions, insofar as they have no effect whatsoever on the way we actually think about and deal with history, are therefore self-interested attempts to reduce de Man's wriings once and for all to the status of a nonevent. As such, they also serve to reappropriate de Man's work for our own purposes by not reading it, thereby leaving us free to pursue all-too predictable interests and ends without bothering ourselves with him and the more troubling aspects of his textual "obtuseness." What is forgotten in either case, as we are reminded and admonished by de Man, is that little piece of paper on which may be written the only kind of history that is worthy of the name. For a history that cannot account critically for the acts of both remembering and forgetting that comprise it can be nothing but a sorry illusion. But what would a genuinely critical and textual history look like, and would it still leave us enough time afterwards to look for and recognize ourselves in it?

To some extent, it must be granted that the writings of de Man suggest that he is merely an opponent of history and historical modes of discourse. A gesture that returns in many of his essays is the summary dismissal of the usual terms of literary history. For de Man, the structures of ordinary historical discourse often conform to temporal and genetic patterns of filiation that cannot be confirmed by the texts such patterns are being used to read, and de Man doesn't hesitate to criticize them for this. Conceptions of history that are based ultimately on *organic,* that is, natural and nonlinguistic, referential models turn out to be singularly inconclusive and inappropriate with respect to linguistic structures of meaning whose temporal and historical status is not given a priori. In "Sign and Symbol in Hegel's *Aesthetics,"* for instance, there is a very strong sense of a rejection of just such history. At the end of the essay, de Man identifies the specific disjunction in Hegel's work between the subject and its predicates as being one between philosophy and history, which de Man says is also a disjunction between literature and history. And he concludes with a grammatical disjunction of his own, which almost seems to exemplify the one he has just been describing: "The reasons for this disjunction . . . are not themselves historical or recoverable by ways of history. To the extent that they are inherent in language . . . the disjunction [*sic*] will always . . . manifest itself as soon as experience shades into thought, history into theory."[2] We get the impression here that there is something like a mutual exclusion operating between history and theory, and that they cannot be easily connected in the critical language they both must use to appear. Eventually, it seems, linguistic considerations will make history yield to theory, just as, in de Man's own formulation, "experience shades into thought."

But at the same time there are other references in de Man's writings, and not just in the last essays, that take us in a somewhat different direction and that cannot be construed as a simple rejection or negation of history. Alongside what de Man himself would in his later work call the *ideological* mystifications of literary history, which are to be criticized and resisted, there is the possibility of another history. Such a history would be neither simply empirical nor yet modeled on mythogenealogical laws but rather would be one that begins to acknowledge

---

2. See "Sign and Symbol in Hegel's *Aesthetics," Critical Inquiry* 8 (Summer 1982), 775.

and account for the complexities of the very language in which it must be written.³ If we are ever to understand anything like de Man's true place *in* history, then, we must first uncover and analyze this "other" concept of history that actually takes place in his texts. This other kind of history is sketched out in its broadest strokes in his unfinished project for a critique of aesthetic ideology, that is to say, of a "symbolic" conception of language and thought whose critique is made necessary and carried out by writers like Kant, Hegel, Benjamin, Kleist, and Baudelaire. The inclusion of Baudelaire in this list, moreover, is of no little significance. For by examining the "symbol" and its dysfunctionment in the work of Hegel *and* Baudelaire, de Man clears the way for remarking that it may be precisely those writers we like to distance ourselves from by calling them "symbolists" who go furthest in unmasking and disrupting our own uncritically "symbolic" notion of the symbol and the kind of ideological histories that inevitably go along with this notion.⁴

But if it is in fact the "symbolists" themselves who can be said to unmask the symbolic ideology at the root of traditional schemes of literary and historical movement, then this also means that, if they are to be read at all, such texts must always be read against the grain of the prevailing conceptions of what constitutes a "movement," a "school," or a "generation" of writers. This could be done only by

---

3. A remarkable example that is by no means atypical is this conclusion to a 1969 essay: "Clearly, such a conception [of literary history] would imply a revision of the notion of history and, beyond that, of the notion of time on which our idea of history is based . . . literary history could in fact be paradigmatic for history in general. . . . If we extend this notion . . . it merely confirms that the bases for historical knowledge are not empirical facts but written texts, even if these texts masquerade in the guise of wars or revolutions" ("Literary History and Literary Modernity," *Blindness and Insight* (Minneapolis: University of Minnesota Press, 1983), 164–65. When de Man starts writing again after the war, the question of history recurs with systematic regularity, though always as a task to be reconceived rather than as a familiar topic of experience or of knowledge. Literature is a privileged form of discourse for de Man to the extent that, unlike ordinary historical discourse, it cannot bracket the question of its necessarily linguistic dimension, and therefore does not so easily escape the self-reflexive moment required of any genuinely historical consciousness.

4. Jacques Derrida, whose use of quotation marks in this regard is always exemplary, puts it well in a recent essay that returns to the question of de Man, the symbol, and history: "One may also follow . . . a certain itinerary of de Man as that of a progressively acute thinking of disjunction, that is, a progressively coherent critique of the 'symbolist' and organicist totalization" ("Biodegradables," *Critical Inquiry* 15 [Summer 1989], 816).

simultaneously taking into account the so-called historical symbolists and those who cannot be said to belong to the same system of chronological, formal, or thematic classification without shattering its unity. In other words, there can be no genuine reading of symbolism until it begins to include writings that could exceed the limits of the system necessarily referred to and contained by any such label of classification as "the symbolists *properly speaking.*" To appreciate the full extent of the disruption to the "symbolic" conception of history and literature performed by these writers, it would not be enough merely to modify or reverse our image of the family resemblances that are still traceable among members such as Nerval, Baudelaire, Mallarmé, and Proust. Rather, it would also be necessary to read Nerval along with Saussure for instance, or Baudelaire in relation to de Man, or Mallarmé alongside Blanchot, or even Proust in light of the uncertain textual status of Roe v. Wade.

On the other hand, de Man's texts—for that matter, all texts—are not only readings that are able to analyze and undo the symbol and its ideology. That is, *as* texts, and unlike so-called empirical events, they could never be assumed to occur once and for all in the fullness of a single, univocal experience or meaning. Such readings, therefore, are themselves writings that, as such and at every moment, are in turn potential victims of such a concept of the symbol and its ideology of figural correspondence and totalization between event and meaning. Only by responding to the complications actually written into these texts about historical complications can one allow them to *happen* historically themselves as anything other than the kind of merely formal description or narration they warn against. Only in this way is it possible to preserve them from a historicist reassimilation and reduction to a belief in the same kind of symmetrical patterns of temporal development and understanding that their readings help to dispel. And this is one of the things it means for a text to be, in the terms of Paul de Man, an "allegory of reading."[5] If allegories are always allegories of

5. See "Allegory (*Julie*)," *Allegories of Reading* (New Haven: Yale University Press, 1979), 205: "The rhetorical mode of such structures can no longer be summarized by the single term of metaphor or of any substitutive trope or figure in general, although the deconstruction of metaphorical figures remains a necessary moment in their production. They take into account the fact that the resulting narratives can be folded back upon themselves and become self-referential. By *refusing*, for reasons of epistemological rigor, to confirm the authority, though not the necessity, of this juxtaposition, Rousseau unsettles the metaphor of reading as deconstructive narrative and

the impossibility of reading, it is not because reading cannot happen; it is because they necessitate that reading, like history, become a textual occurrence that could never be absolutely exhausted but only always again undertaken anew at the very point of its incompletion.

In this respect, one of the most reliable, and therefore difficult if not outright impossible, modes of access to the question of history in de Man's work would be by way of the "event" that will be able to take place in his texts only after we reread the increasingly necessary critique of "symbolic" aesthetic ideology and history that has always been there. In order to have access to this critical event, moreover, we would in addition have to be able to measure how something else that had always already been in the texts de Man wrote since the war could, after it became known in 1987 that he had written other texts during the war, begin to become a new textual effect of all his writings. Such an effect is in fact historical, for it actually happens; but since it is a textual occurrence it is also absolutely undatable and unlocatable by means of purely empirical observation. The only historical "now" that could legitimately be said to make a difference here would be the one that would be able to make these same writings into something neither wholly different from nor simply identical to what they once were thought to be. And such a historical moment also cannot take place unless our understanding of the "event" that occurred long ago itself becomes subject to further alteration through its necessary reinscription in what remains irreducibly specific to all the texts in question. The complex temporality of this kind of textual occurrence, which we also call "reading," could never be adequately conceived in terms of a simple historical line or circle or any other geometrical figure or representation, and therefore could never be used simply to erase the specificity of one text (or event) by assimilating it to the supposed priority of another event (or text). For the same reasons, the temporality of this textual now could also not *not* disturb the figural concepts of "past, present, and future" from which our ordinary models of understanding history and its events are derived in an unquestioned manner. To begin to measure the effects of such an event on de Man's own text, it would therefore be necessary to face up to a

---

replaces it by a more complex structure." "More complex," here, especially in juxtaposition to the word "unsettles" can only be taken to mean less secure, more fragile, that is, open to change and therefore more *historical*.

kind of historical past that, because it is now textual, always lies ahead of us in the future task of its reading.[6]

One of the places that just such a past remains to be read is in de Man's 1983 essay on Baudelaire's poem "Correspondances."[7] If ever there were an adequate "symbol" for what symbolism in French literature is supposed to look, sound, and even smell like, it would have to be this sonnet, itself constructed out of poetic "symbols" in order to talk about and explain how "symbols" should work in poetry. On the other hand, de Man's treatment of the theme and functioning of the symbol in "Correspondances" cannot be understood independently of his suspicion in the same essay that a reading of this poem is bound to encounter questions and problems of a distinctly *historical* nature. For if it is true, as de Man remarks, that "Correspondances" can only be read as a companion piece to another text, "Obsession" for instance, and that this produces a figural relation between the texts that "is itself structured like a symbol: the two sonnets complement each other like the two halves of a *symbolon*," it is equally true that this

---

6. Again, in relation to a reading of de Man, Derrida has best articulated the strain this kind of event puts on the temporality of ordinary narrative histories: "The future will not have been indifferent, not for long, just barely a half century, to what de Man wrote one day in the 'newspapers and journals of today.' . . . But in the several months to come, the very young journalist that he will have been during less than two years will be read more intensely than the theoretician, the thinker, the writer, the professor, the author of great books that he was during forty years. . . . But what about later?" ("Like the Sound of the Sea Deep within a Shell: Paul de Man's War," *Critical Inquiry* 14 (Spring 1988), 591). De Man's own formulation of this structure of textual history is most concisely articulated in his reading of Shelley's *The Triumph of Life:* "At this point, figuration and cognition are actually interrupted by an event which shapes the text but which is not present in its represented or articulated meaning . . . the task of thus reinscribing the disfiguration now devolves entirely on the reader. The final test of reading . . . depends on how one reads the textuality of this event, how one disposes of Shelley's body" ("Shelley Disfigured," *The Rhetoric of Romanticism* [New York: Columbia University Press, 1984], 120–21). One should note the implication in de Man's essay that in order to dispose of the body—or the skeleton in the closet for that matter—*historically* rather than ideologically, it is necessary to treat it as a specifically *textual* event. This sort of "event" is a "task that devolves" on reading and its future, much as Derrida's question, "But what about later?"

7. See "Anthropomorphism and Trope in the Lyric," *The Rhetoric of Romanticism*. Further references appear in the text. For a pertinent discussion of the place of Baudelaire's "Correspondances" within a canonical literary history of French poetry, see Jonathan Culler, "Intertextuality and Interpretation: Baudelaire's 'Correspondances,' " *Nineteenth-Century French Poetry*, ed. Christopher Prendergast (Cambridge: Cambridge University Press, 1990).

figural necessity also produces the familiar gesture of "*historicizing* them into a diachrony or into a valorized hierarchy [that] is more convenient than it is legitimate" (253–54, emphasis added). It is not simply the case that by ultimately situating the two sonnets with respect to each other by means of historical or generic categories that one tends, more or less contingently, to shift the emphasis away from the particularities of the poems in order to broaden the scope of their analysis and relevance. It is de Man's contention that such schemes of historical and generic classification *must* avoid or forget what the texts are actually saying. No historical or genetic model of understanding can be adequate to the reading of a text, for the simple reason that such models are themselves the *result* of textual effects rather than a reliable means of determining them. Hence de Man's implacable conclusion, which is also the moment he insists on another model for history: "Generic terms such as 'lyric' . . . as well as pseudo-historical period terms such as 'romanticism' or 'classicism' are always terms of resistance and nostalgia, at the furthest remove from the materiality of *actual history*" (262, emphasis added).

The question remains, though, as to the status of "actual" history in de Man, as well as what it would mean for this history to occur in its "materiality" rather than as a mere form of "resistance and nostalgia." What can be learned about history from Baudelaire's theory and practice of the poetic symbol? Earlier in his essay, de Man makes reference to what could be considered a necessary first step in reading what he considers "the materiality of actual history." Noting the reversed symmetries between "Correspondances" and "Obsession," he suggests that the symbolic relationship between the two poems can be approached from a so-called literary-historical point of view only at the risk of disrupting the coherence of such a terminology. Putting texts side by side in order to describe and interpret chronological relationships of before and after, says de Man, one is bound to notice and react to rhetorical patterns of difference and complementarity. But these patterns of part and whole (where "Correspondances" comes out and names nature in its totality, "Obsession" compiles a list of scattered forests, seas, and sky), of reversals (the serenity of "Correspondances" turns into a torment in "Obsession") and of complementarities (the Greek temple of "Correspondances" is balanced and completed by the Christian cathedral of "Obsession") are not themselves reducible to chronologically determinable phenomena or experiences. They not only cut across the limits of one proper name; they can also occur indiscriminately within one and the same text. Rather than presenting us with empirically observable data, they are *tropological* relationships of similitude and difference that are produced independently of the particular empirical figures that are used to constitute them. As such, these patterns are a result of rhetorical figures like synecdoche, chiasmus, and metaphor that can be revealed as such only through a process of reading logically *prior* to any determination of them in a meaningful historical scheme. Using the empirical five-year temporal difference between the two poems to describe (or reconfirm) a developmental history of nineteenth-century French poetry is a subsidiary gesture that can only be added to or superimposed upon the linguistic structures that not only exist independently of such a history but actually condition our knowledge of it. Thus, "the terminology of traditional literary history, as a succession of periods or literary movements, remains useful only if the terms are seen for what they are: rather crude metaphors for figural patterns rather than historical events or acts" (254).

In the kind of move that seems to have become habitual with de Man, ordinary historical terms, then, turn out to be not so historical after all. Rather, they are metaphors, and crude ones at that, for the *figural* relationships they try to cover up and forget. But if pseudohistorical terms of literary classification, because they are merely disguised metaphors imposed upon the texts from without, cannot themselves teach us anything about the actual history of literature, then perhaps reading the metaphors that are in fact written into these texts will turn out to be our only reliable means of learning what the texts actually say and do about history. And what, after all, is de Man's reading of "Correspondances" if not a sustained reading of metaphor—and not such a crude one this time? In fact, the metaphor that de Man identifies and reads in "Correspondances"—*les transports de l'esprit et des sens*—is not only the metaphor of metaphor, and thus the symbol of "symbolic" and aesthetic ideology. It is also the metaphor or symbol of history considered as a means of motion and development through time and the kind of understanding that would be proper to it. The poem, as read by de Man, is therefore itself the miniature but infinite expansion of the aesthetico-historical concept of temporal and cognitive expansion. The symbol is a kind of poetic "transport" that serves to link the sensory and intellectual orders or experience and finally appears in the last verse of the poem:

> *l'expansion des choses infinies . . .*
> *Qui chantent les* transports *de l'esprit et des sens.*
>
> *the expansiveness of infinite things . . .*
> *Which sing the* transports *of the mind and the senses.*

What this means is that in order to read what symbolism tells us about history we should exercise all possible restraint in first talking about romanticism, classicism, or symbolism, much less deconstructionism, as though such terms could have any meaning independent of what occurs in the texts that are assumed to partake of and conform to them. Instead, we should turn our attention to reading what takes place in the text as the metaphors eventually move from the materiality of their rhetorical structure (*les transports*) to constitute figures of cognitive and historical reference (*de l'esprit et des sens*).

First of all, according to de Man, and like any text, moreover, "Cor*respond*ances" can be read as an answer, a hermeneutical process of question and *response* that in the case of this poem is even spelled out in the letters of its title. The implied question takes the following form: "What is nature, and what is man's place there?" The first lines of the poem seem to reply by affirming that nature is a temple in which man is as at home as he is among his own kind. The fact that the glances bestowed on man in line 4 are "familiers" rather than, say, *méfiants* or *menaçants* reinforces the idea that the relationship between man and nature is not only *not* antithetical but that there is indeed a kind of *family* bond or resemblance at work here. The culmination of the poem, then, in the mutual *transports* or exchanges between the mind and the senses, between man and nature as it were, is already prefigured in the first lines of the text. What de Man is careful to show here is that the link that will work to create this impression of a family resemblance between man and nature is a self-consciously *verbal* one that cannot be taken for granted as being first given by either man or nature. This primordial aspect of language is made explicit, according to de Man, by the fact that man's relation to nature is itself established in the poem by way of "confuses *paroles*," and then further mediated in the following verse through the "forêts de *symboles.*" Man may be related to nature as in a family, but this relation can itself take place only as a result of specifically linguistic structures like *paroles* and *symboles.*[8]

It is thanks to the mediations of these symbols, thanks to the verbal relays that progressively link man and nature, that the text is finally able to assert the possibility of amalgamating varying orders of difference and raising them ever higher into an ultimate synthesis of mutual transports.[9] And it is easy enough for de Man to identify the symbolic or tropological principle that propels the poem toward this climax as *metaphor,* or simile, since the number and importance of substitutive comparisons based on a linking *comme* in the text can hardly escape any reader's notice. Thus, and in spite of any logical difficulty involved, the poem moves through its ascending stages with the utmost assurance, suggesting along the way that sounds are "like" smells, that the vastness of light is "like" the vastness of night, or that the expansive activity of such an intangible thing as the mind can be "like" the ascending movement of burning incense. The architectural emblem for this process of establishing analogical links appears in the construction of the temple in the first line, a construction built on the borders of finite and infinite space, between the heavens and the earth. Made up by piling stone upon stone, the temple eventually encloses an airy

---

8. See "Correspondances": "La Nature est un temple où de vivants piliers / Laissent parfois sortir de confuses paroles; / L'homme y passe à travers des forêts de symboles / Qui l'observent avec des regards familiers."

9. While it is certainly more rhetorically precise, de Man's analysis is anything but new up to this point. Marcel Raymond's remarks about Baudelaire and the role of modern poetry, while not derived explicitly from a reading of "Correspondances," can be seen to proceed from an unacknowledged assumption that this text is emblematic of the symbolic status of *all* poetry: "On the basis of this confused mass of material . . . the poet will go on to create an order that turns out to be . . . the infallible expression of his soul. And this expression—although the elements from which it is composed seem to refer to purely *natural* things—will be nonetheless essentially *supernatural.* For the soul . . . can find its true home only in a spiritual beyond toward which nature strives. The poet's task is to open a window on this other world . . . to allow the self to escape its limits and to *swell* to *infinity.* In this movement of *expansion* the mind's return to unity is pointed out and accomplished" (*De Baudelaire au surréalisme* [Paris: Corti, 1940], 22–23, emphasis added). What de Man does do, by actually examining the operation of these *idées reçues* within the poem, is to show that such a "symbolist ideology" of poetry is much more a fiction foisted upon the text by historians of literature than an actual event written into the texts themselves.

space that seems limitless in its power to suggest the transcendence of a meaning that could fully respond to the initial confusion produced by the poem's most fundamental questions. And within the ecclesiastical space of a temple it does indeed seem perfectly natural to bring together the different orders of sound and smell in a kind of liturgical service where expanding layers of incense can borrow the voices of what would otherwise have to remain in the entirely foreign register of song or chant, as when it is stated in the last stanza that, "le benjoin et l'encens / . . . *chantent* les transports de l'esprit et des sens [benjamin and incense / . . . *sing* the transports of the mind and the senses]."

However, complications on the level of the rhetoric of the poem, though not necessarily apparent on the level of its theme, are seen by de Man to contaminate the key word *comme* near the end of the text. One of the most memorable moments of this noncanonical reading of "Correspondances," which itself runs the risk of being canonized into an anti- or countercanon of interpretation, occurs when de Man is able to identify a syntactical ambiguity that leaves open the possibility that the text's so-called symbolist pretensions to totalizing expansion may fizzle out in an aimless stutter of enumeration. After demonstrating how the initial *comme* that links the various senses of sound, color, and scent is able to achieve a figure of speech by allowing the poem to call their relationship to one another a form of "echo" or "response," de Man comes to the following verses:

> *Il est des parfums frais* comme *des chairs d'enfants,*
> *Doux* comme *les hautbois, verts* comme *les prairies,*
> —Et d'autres, corrompus, riches et triomphants,
>
> *Ayant l'expansion des choses infinies,*
> Comme *l'ambre, le musc, le benjoin et l'encens . . .*
>
> There are scents *fresh* like *the skin of children,*
> *soft* like *the oboe, green* like *the prairies,*
> —*And others, corrupt, rich, and triumphant,*
>
> *Having the expansiveness of infinite things,*
> Like *amber, musk, benjamin, and incense . . .*

Just before the expanding tropes of comparison allow the incense to turn into a song of hosannah, the *comme* in line 13 seems to hit a false note. For while it is clear that *frais* can be used here to link both scent and touch, that *doux* can cross from scent to sound, and that *verts* is meant to mediate between scent and color, how are we to read the final *comme* in the poem?

In other words, by asking *how* to read we are also asking about the place of articulation of this particular "like" or "as": what is its actual *syntax* prior to the resulting statement of the poem's symbolist project and meaning? Does the line that contains these scents relate to the *expansion des choses infinies* of the preceding line, thus preparing the final synthesis of mind and matter by suggesting that the experience of infinity can be understood *by analogy to* the seemingly infinite expansiveness of finite things like amber, musk, and incense? In this case, the syntax would produce an understanding that at least implicitly would proceed something like, "l'ambre, le musc, le benjoin et l'encens sont [*comme*] des choses infinies." And while it is clear that these scents are not actually infinite substances—like the mind or soul of man is supposed to be—the property of expansion that is common to both and that grounds the figure of metaphor here can certainly be used to help us *represent* the activity of such nonsensory phenomena.[10] On the other hand, the text simultaneously contains another possibility. We can and should ask whether the figure of comparison comes apart here in a lifeless enumeration of smells. These verses can also be read in such a way that the quality of infinite expansion, which should occupy the central position, becomes purely appositive, making the final *comme* depend exclusively on the species noun *parfums* in line 9. Thus, we would be reading: "Il est des parfums frais . . . / —Et d'autres . . . / Comme l'ambre, le musc, le benjoin et l'encens." In this case, there would be no comparison established and therefore no symbolic correspondence achieved by the poem's key word, *comme*. Rather than functioning as a prepositive conjunction of comparison that is able to link two different orders of experience, as would be dictated by the "symbolic" ideology of the text, the *comme* here would be merely the adverbial preposition of exemplification. It would be a kind of "such

---

10. Since this is the syntax that is most compatible with an unquestioned thematic understanding of the "transports de l'esprit et des sens" in the final verse, it is not surprising that it turns out to be the reading of choice, as is readily apparent in the English translation of the poem by Richard Howard (*Charles Baudelaire,* Les Fleurs du Mal, newly trans. Richard Howard [Boston: Godine, 1982], 15): "There are odors succulent as young flesh . . . / while others . . . / possess the power of such infinite things / as incense, amber, benjamin and musk."

as" serving only to introduce a tautological list of perfume names, and it would only link what follows in a purely mechanical way through the intervening commas, which are themselves potentially endless but without inherent significance.

Reading the poem becomes in this way a question of deciding between the conjunctive and adverbial value of this one key word, but nothing in the text read can allow us to make this choice with certainty.[11] And what hangs in the balance of this decision is nothing less than a coherent understanding of the poem as a symbol for symbolism. For it is one thing if the experience of infinity is being likened to familiar physical substances such as amber and musk, since then we would have the metaphorical linking of two distinct regions that can eventually come together (*sumballein*) in what the text refers to in its sixth line as a deep and dark *unity,* "une ténébreuse et profonde unité." But it is quite another if, in addition, or between the lines as it were, this supposedly monumental text finally tells us that there are perfumes and then there are perfumes. Such a possibility, which is introduced by the adverbial *comme* of enumeration and which remains irreducible with respect to the actual syntax of the poem, would hardly permit the kind of unilaterally transcendental meaning that is usually claimed for this text. Nonetheless, it is not a question of erasing one of the possibilities in favor of the other, of claiming that Baudelaire "meant" this or that, or stating univocally that the *comme* of exemplification could ever do away entirely with the *comme* of analogy. The fact that these two incompatible readings must continue to exist side by side without the possibility of ultimate resolution is what makes "Correspondances" into a genuinely textual event in the first place.

At any rate, it is at this point that de Man turns his attention to those all-important *transports* of the final line, and he does so by claiming that the unexpected possibility of reading a tautological list of smells in line 13 allows in turn for the concluding transports to become liter-

---

11. There also seems to be a good deal of uncertainty as to the exact grammatical status of a term like "like." In English, a distinction is made between the conjunctive and all other uses in order to condemn it, but a trace of conjunction is often present anyway. Whether the distinction is between conjunction and preposition or extends to the level of adjective and adverb, the syntax of "Correspondances" will still be ambivalent in a radical way since, whatever the grammatical appellation, one reading allows for a comparison ("infinite things are *more* like musk than they are like benjamin") while the other reading does not ("there are other perfumes *like* benjamin, musk, etc.").

alized in a most curious way. What is of interest for the question of symbolism and history is that it is also at this point that de Man once again makes reference to a vocabulary heavily invested with historical implications. He does so by first playing on the fact that the word *transports* can legitimately be read as a translation from the Greek *metaphorein*, a word that today designates the mundane transfers or *correspondances* within an urban system of public transportation as well as the more aesthetic metaphorical substitutions that are supposed to occur in this poem between the mind and the senses. De Man then asks whether the interruption of the transcendental ascension of "Correspondances" by the enumerative adverb *comme* in line 13 should be understood at the end of the poem as a prosaic, that is, *empirical*, transposition of the ecstatic transports of lyrical poetry into the economic code of transports that must take place in the daily life of any city. If the *comme* of line 13 cannot guarantee the vertical and hierarchical substitutions that promise an ascension from the earth to the heavens by way of lyrical temples, perhaps the horizontal churning of enumeration, like the stops along the Paris *métro*, can be used to take us along a more solidly earthly path. Such a reading would be a form of classical ideology critique and would itself move along the lines of debunking the ideology of symbolism or aestheticism in favor of a more historically aware discourse of political economy.[12] What de Man is again hinting at here, of course, is that whereas the naively historical terms of traditional literary criticism turn out to be crude metaphors for underlying figural patterns, the possibility remains that rhetorical terms, like metaphor, might prove to be a reliable tool in the

---

12. De Man's implicit reference here and elsewhere in this essay is to Walter Benjamin. See Benjamin's *Charles Baudelaire: A Lyric Poet in the Era of High Capitalism,* trans. Harry Zohn (London: Verso, 1983). The "spatial displacement" de Man mentions with respect to the verbal ending of meta-*phorein*, as well as the reference to a colder form of "analytic self-consciousness," recall Benjamin's discussions of the Baudelairian *flâneur*, himself a kind of peripatetic philosopher. Similarly, de Man's description of the prosaic transposition of ecstasy into economic codes sounds very much like Benjamin's account of how Lamartine's "heaven" collapsed once and for all into the "marketplace" of Baudelaire. However, rather than simply borrowing the terms of his reading of Baudelaire from Benjamin, it is much more likely that de Man is also reading Baudelaire at least in part in order to set up the possibility of later reading Benjamin, in particular the uneasy relationship between historical and allegorical discourse, which was first analyzed by Adorno in his letters to Benjamin. For the first part of such a reading, see de Man's " 'Conclusions': Walter Benjamin's 'The Task of the Translator,' " *The Resistance to Theory.*

uncovering and diagnosing of ideological tensions that erupt between aesthetics and politics, or between literature and history. An interpretation of the text that could in this way disclose the subway system lurking beneath the lyrical transports of symbolist poetry would be a first and important step in such a direction.

But de Man goes on to point out that at this stage of the game such ideological demystification may occur here in appearance only, for the vertical transcendence of metaphysics or mystical symbolism and the horizontal connections implied by an economically based sociopolitical critique can actually share the same philosophical presuppositions, which are not themselves necessarily shared by the poem. Of these, undoubtedly the most important would be the unquestioned assumption of and reliance on semantically determined substitutive transfers that can take place without undue difficulty between different orders of experience. Whether we transfer from finite to infinite, or from base to superstructure, it is still possible to consider each displacement as an incremental relay that is not in itself disruptive with respect to the unified system of cognitive motion and circulation in which it would occur. And since *this* sort of prosaically economic interpretation is no less dependent for its understanding on figural relationships and intersections produced by rhetorical exchanges—or metaphorical *transports*—than is the lyrical reading of "Correspondances," it cannot be considered a priori any more "historical," or less "aesthetic," than the pseudohistorical terms of canonical literary history it would displace. In slightly different terms, then, we could say that all particularities notwithstanding, the *transports de l'esprit* and the *transports des sens* are both essentially "transports" that seek to *merge* symbolically two distinct regions, whether they be heaven and earth or the shopping arcades and political barricades of Paris. Hence, de Man further implies that a straightforward application of ideology critique "is not by itself disruptive with regard to the claim for transcendental unity." By subscribing uncritically to tropological patterns of movement by transfer, this kind of pseudohistorical reading will end up establishing only its own negatively specular "correspondence" with the metaphysico-aesthetic ideology of the poem that it claims to demystify.

The "sobering literalization" de Man refers to here—which should be read not only in conjunction with the syntactic indecision of "comme" he has just documented and analyzed, but also with the further reference he will make at the end of the essay to "the *mate-*

riality of actual history"—cannot therefore be reduced to a simple turn or inversion leading directly from metaphysics to economics, or from aesthetics to political thought. This literalization of the word *transports* is historical through and through because, unlike any of the previous "moments" of the poem's metaphorical project, it actually manages to have or, better, to *achieve* materiality. The tropological exchanges (*transports*) described and valorized throughout the text may forever be stymied by the repetitive list of disarticulated substantives in line 13, but it is beyond doubt that the word *transports* is actually written into the final line of the poem. Not only does this particular literalization of Baudelaire's transports take place in the poem, but it is also the one material historical occurrence that threatens to prevent all else from ever happening there as anything but a self-deluding dream of historical escape and transcendence.[13]

In other words, for de Man, the events and disruptions of what he calls material history are truly sobering because they are *literal;* they could never be a simple matter of figural substitutions *between* the opposing but fully complementary categories of *l'esprit* and *les sens*. The "symbolic" potential of language to join and hold together in a profound unity radically different orders of experience and thought is therefore not itself merely transferred historically from a transcendental aesthetics to an economics of prose and politics, leaving intact the unquestioned possibility of continuous historical "movement" and understanding between all these realms. Either the actual disarticulations that occur materially in history occur in such a way as to disarticulate once and for all any pretense to reduce them to a symbolic coherence between thought and being, "l'esprit et les sens," or we have no business talking about "history" in the first place. To be more precise: at issue in de Man's reading of Baudelaire is not an illusory disruption that would move only between a figural and a literal *meaning,* or between one *kind* (or moment) of meaning and another—aesthetic and political, lyrical and economic, preindustrial and postindustrial, and the list could of course be extended. Rather, the literalization de Man analyzes would be the shattering literalization of meaning into its inarticulate particles, a radical fall from the meaning of the

13. For a reading of "materiality" in de Man, as well as its relation to Marx's text, especially *The German Ideology,* see Andrzej Warminski's essay, "Ending Up/Taking Back," which serves as a preface to Paul de Man's *Aesthetic Ideology* (Minneapolis: University of Minnesota Press, forthcoming).

word to the materiality of the *letter*. As such, the literalization of symbolic *transports* should be "sobering" indeed, for it would be an actual event that befalls the organization of meaning (and of history) itself, including the epochal possibility of making distinctions (as well as syntheses) among the figural ("l'esprit") and the literal ("les sens") upon which any such organization has to be based. What thus befalls the metaphorical transports of thought and being in the literal materiality of the word "transports" cannot as a consequence be conceived as any kind of ordinary "movement" at all, since it is much sooner the falling apart of the word's symbolic meaning into the potentially endless dispersal of its insensate and insignificant letters.

That such a "fall" is indeed what de Man has in mind here can be confirmed by way of a remark he makes earlier in the essay concerning the three orders of language that must function side by side in "Correspondances." After pointing out that the dialectical process and progression of the poem is self-consciously verbal, de Man goes on to add: "Language can be the chain of *metaphors* in a synesthesia, as well as the oxymoronic *polysemy* of a single word, such as 'se confondent' (or 'transports' in 1.14) or even, on the level of the signifier, the play of the syllable or the *letter*" (245, emphasis added). The "play" referred to here—which has little or nothing to do with aesthetic or subjective self-indulgence—is the play that belongs constitutively *to* language; it is language's own potential to dissolve out of semantic unity (or its most common variant, semantic plurality) into the subsemantic particles of its letters. Considered in themselves, of course, letters always allow for unheard-of substitutions and reversals—or *slips*—of meaning that could never occur as such on the level of the ensuing signifieds, either synesthetically between the different orders of sense perception or polysemantically between the various meanings covered by any given signifier.[14] And de Man himself offers as a most remarkable

14. It is worth noting in this context that in his lecture on Walter Benjamin, de Man will return to this notion of the symbol that is broken down beyond the possibility of meaning into something like its letters: "The problem is best compared to the relationship between the letter and the word . . . namely, the letter is without meaning in relation to the word, it is *a-sēmos*, it is without meaning. When you spell a word you say a certain number of meaningless letters, which then come together in the word, but in each of the letters the word is not present . . . the symbol and what it symbolizes, the trope and what it seems to represent, do not correspond. . . . Therefore the distinction between symbol and symbolized, the nonadequation of symbol to a shattered symbolized, the nonsymbolic character of this adequation, is a version of the others" ("The

example of this necessary play in language the poem's very title, "Correspondances," which, he says, "is like the anagrammatic condensation of the text's entire program: 'corps' and 'esprit' brought together and harmonized by the *ance* of assonance that pervades the concluding tercets: from *ayant, ambre, chantent* to *expansion, sens, transport,* finally redoubled and re-echoed in *enc-ens/sens*" (245).

The assertion that the poem's entire aesthetic program can be found embedded in its title is a striking one indeed, and the test of de Man's own rhetorical powers is to some extent to be gauged from how far one is willing to assent to the interpretative demonstration that follows. Whatever else, though, "the anagrammatic condensation" in question, which now occurs in Baudelaire's as well as in de Man's text, should also give us pause. For it is as reliable from a strictly philological or epistemological point of view as the commonest pun or word play; that is to say, like the play of the syllable or letter it is an example of, it has no epistemological authority whatsoever. In adducing a purely poetic effect (paronomasia) to further his exegetical argument, de Man is following, if not parodying, a long tradition, whose most important modern philosophical representatives would have to include Hegel as well as Heidegger.[15] The fact that the French word for "correspondences" can be said already to contain both the "body" and "soul"— whose harmonious union the poem of the same name will eventually

---

Task of the Translator," *The Resistance to Theory,* pp. 88, 89, 90, 91). De Man will go on in the conclusion of the essay to give a very precise formulation of how this shattering, disintegration, fragmentation of the symbol, which never was an original unity, is also the basis for how history is to be understood in Benjamin.

15. Hegel's recourse to the idiomatic "genius" inherent in German is well known. One interesting example in this context would be how, in the crucial argument about the essence of being and its necessarily mediated development through time, Hegel makes the proof depend at least in part on the fact that in German, essence, or *Wesen,* is already legible in the past participle of *being (sein)*—which just happens to be *gewesen.* See the section "Doctrine of Essence" in both the *Encyclopedia* and the *Logic.* Heidegger is usually much more meticulous in elaborating his "etymologies"; however, there remains the famous example in the *Introduction to Metaphysics,* where he insists on the privilege of German with respect to thinking, and the even more curious interview with the *Spiegel,* where he seems happy to confirm that the French, when they begin to think, must do it in German if they are to do it at all! Such gestures in the writings of Hegel and Heidegger are neither simply "legitimate" nor "illegitimate"; one cannot even presume to have access to them without carefully relating them back to the textual arguments from which they are derived. In de Man's case, it would certainly not do simply to assert that his discovery of a near-anagram in Baudelaire's title impugns his argument, since his "discovery" is much sooner a rhetorical example (or *mise en abyme*) of this very argument than a logical explanation for it.

claim to sing—is nothing more than an accident; and this can be proved quite easily by translating the same title from the French into English or German. But more pertinent to the reading of the poem than denouncing or reveling in such idiomatic "accidents" is taking into account in one's own reading and writing the "necessity" of their being able to happen in any language and the "actuality" of their occurrence and effects in the specific text being read. Whatever else de Man is doing, by tracing what he has been calling all along the poem's tropological "program" of analogical substitutions to the absolutely random but literal event produced in the subsemantic syllables *cor, espr,* and *ance,* he also draws our attention to an essential question about the intelligibility of the text. Is it now possible to decide whether the poem that celebrates and exemplifies the "seamless articulation" of the mind and the senses thanks to analogical symbols is itself determined by the cognitive principles of a mind or by the purely chance encounters occurring between subsymbolic fragments of written signs?

At any rate, like the seemingly more playful discovery of "mind," "body," and "assonance" in the (French) title, "Correspondances," the "sobering" literalization of material "transports" underscored by de Man near the end of his analysis must be considered in the light of this understanding of the shattered symbol. For this "sobering" moment is itself brought on in the wake of the dysfunctioning of the poem's most powerful means of analogical symbolization; that is to say, it occurs when the founding preposition of resemblance, *comme,* can no longer do its job without exceeding the stability of its syntax. De Man couldn't be clearer about the necessity of this accidental coming apart of the symbol in line 13: "That the very word on which these substitutions depend would just then lose its syntactical and semantic univocity is too striking a coincidence not to be, like pure chance, beyond the control of author and reader" (250). What is historically and textually necessary, according to de Man, are precisely those events whose accidental occurrence lies beyond the reach of anyone to control.

And like the necessary occurrence of pure chance on which any genuine history or text depends, the enumerative *comme* that cannot now be erased from this poem does not even depend for its power on this particular word's being there in the first place. For—all appearances to the contrary notwithstanding—it is the word that depends on the accident and not the other way around. This accident is therefore not due merely to the oxymoronic polysemy of metaphysical and economical "transports," or metaphors. In other words, it is not like the juxtaposition of incompatible *meanings* that become legible in the poem when the long and distant echoes of various sense perceptions *se confondent*, a juxtaposition of meanings that is contingently accidental and which, as de Man points out, "can designate the bad infinity of confusion as well as the fusion of opposites into synthetic judgments" (245). When de Man finally declares that the trouble with "metaphor" in this text does not reside, first and foremost, in the particularity of its individual displacements (*phorein:* to carry) but rather in accounting for the general law of directionality that must ground them all (*meta:* beyond), he has left questions of semantically determined accidents, or analogical and oxymoronic polysemies, far behind: "The problem is not so much centered on *phorein* as on *meta* . . . for does 'beyond' here mean a movement beyond some particular place or does it mean a state that is beyond movement entirely?" (251). A look at the dictionary, of course, will tell us that the word *metaphorein* can easily *mean* both an ecstatic movement beyond thought and sensation into a common transcendental realm and a spatial movement beyond some particular place to another in a postindustrial city. But what makes the accidental literalization of this particular word so sobering is the fact that its actual occurrence in the poem necessitates asking another, more radical because more generalized, version of the same question: how could the symbolic concept of "metaphor," or Baudelaire's translation of it in the word *transport*, ever *mean,* in the words of de Man, "a state that is beyond movement entirely"?

Although the very question of such an attentive reading of the word "metaphor" may at first seem willful or of rather limited exegetical interest in this context, we should recall that, in differing guises, the potential of the human mind to "move beyond" the senses as well as its own limits is a familiar topos in philosophical as well as aesthetic and even historical discourse. In an overly schematic way, we could even say that it is precisely this potential that determines the possibility of any form of dialectical thought and history, including such landmark though problematic versions as Pascal's "man infinitely passes beyond man," Rousseau's concept of man's perfectibility, or Hegel's concept of spirit's *Aufhebung*. Nietzsche and Heidegger, of course, continue to reflect on this question of the mind's infinite potential for moving beyond itself while distancing themselves from it in varying ways and degrees. Within this particular "tradition" of texts, moreover, any reading of the *transports* in Baudelaire will inevitably intersect with linguistic and philosophical questions pertaining to the relation of metaphor to a transcendental theory of historical development and understanding. To this extent, then, the title of de Man's essay ("Anthropomorphism and Trope in the Lyric") is itself somewhat misleading, since the real thrust of his reading does not help in elucidating the generic status of the lyric, or in determining what is lyrical by defining and delimiting within it the relation between trope and anthropomorphism. The terms *anthropomorphism* and *trope* are of interest here only insofar as, taken together, they point toward the necessity of postulating a poetics as well as an anthropology, a science of language as well as a science of man. Together, that is, they designate the possibility of distinguishing between and eventually coordinating literary criticism and social history by founding both of them on a concept of analogically determined meaning whose own future understanding—as becomes clear in the truly privileged example of the subject of all possible knowledge or science, "mankind"—is projected into a series of continuous and ever more self-conscious "movements beyond." What is of genuine theoretical import in the lyric, then, and what is condensed in Baudelaire's linguistic *transports,* is the lyric's fundamental relationship to what de Man himself calls this temporal and subjective "*motion* of understanding" (261).

So when de Man asks the question about how the "beyond" inscribed in the word *transport,* which by definition posits and names movement, could ever take us away from what it posits, he is himself taking the question beyond a classical understanding of aesthetic (and philosophical) meaning by literalizing the poem's own word for "metaphor" into the play of its syllables. He is literally taking the word for symbolic synthesis, *transport,* apart, breaking it loose of any prior semantic determination, and asking about the relationship of the letters, or syllables, among themselves. *Transport,* of course, comes from the Latin roots *trans* and *portare,* and it is the etymological reference here that can take us back to and ensure the order of its meaning. For etymology is still a semantically determined category based on observable substitutions and reversals that always occur within an unreflected, that is to say, ideological, concept of temporal movement. Such a concept of language's process and development finally ensures that the word, even when it is broken into its constitutive parts, will still be able to *mean* a kind of meaningful carrying from one place to another, or a *logical* movement beyond any given place of origin, or *root*. The etymology of the word can therefore be used to ask whether and to what extent the "transports" of the mind are linked to the "transports" of the senses. That is, it can be used to ask about whether the "transports" in this poem designate a metaphysical or empirical·category of motion. But in neither case is the word's capacity to signify a "movement beyond" radically disrupted. This capacity to signify is not left unaffected by the actual *order* of the word as it is reinflected by de Man's reading, however. For the literal syntax of the syllables of the written word, before they have been organized according to semantic principles of etymology, can just as easily be read in such a way that they are made to ask about a beyond of movement, about an event that takes us beyond metaphorical movement once and for all. What befalls the analogical understanding of symbols in reading "Correspondances" in this way is therefore an accident that, because its occurrence lies entirely beyond the control of a *logic*—either as analogy or etymology—makes it necessary by the same token to put into question any model relating historical occurrences to their future meaning by way of a teleological movement capable of taking us from a source and/or toward an endpoint. This would be equally true whether the metaphysical model underlying such teleological transports is understood as a principle of metaphysical transcendence or of immediate empirical political change.

Now in order to appreciate the theoretical and historical implications of de Man's reading, we should recall that what allows for this bizarre ordering of the word "transport" in the first place, what allows for its literalization into the play of the syllable, is itself a linguistic principle of ordering. It is the indeterminable *syntax* of the word *comme* in line 13: "Comme l'ambre, le musc, le benjoin et l'encens." De Man says that this *comme* "relates to the subject 'parfums' in two different ways or, rather, it has two distinct subjects" (249). By making us aware of the syntax of *comme* in line 13, de Man reminds us of the syntax, or the disposition of the letters and syllables, of the word *transports* in line 14. And by pointing out the fact that the word *comme* in line 13 actually does have two subjects, de Man reminds us that on the level of the letter, on the level of syntax prior to any semantically overdetermined decisions, it is always possible to read of two incompatible subjects in any text.

For what syntax in fact names is the material disposition of letters that is the condition of *carrying* meaning (a kind of *portare* or *phorein*, then, as in the words *transports* or *metaphor*) without itself originally *having* any meaning. This carrying property of syntax can be seen to relate to the meaning produced beyond it in the two radically different but equally necessary ways that the *portare* of metaphor relates to its qualification *trans*. Or, as de Man says, "it has two different subjects." It all depends on what kind of reading any text as such receives and whether the focus, or subject, is the meaning intended (*logos*) or the actual production of intentional meaning (*lexis*). If the carrying of *portare* is already presupposed semantically as an insufficient though preliminary form of meaning, then the focus will be on the ultimate accomplishment of this movement; "carrying" will be its own subject and "beyond" will merely be its somewhat redundant attribute. Such a movement would be truly dialectical. That is, it would progress by a series of discrete negations—beginning with a negation of its own syntax—in order to be able simultaneously to have itself as subject and to move continually beyond itself. In this way it would have always already entered the semantic field of tropes that alone would be capable of completing the motion of expansion implied in the achievement of any meaning. In this case, the syntax would read, "movement beyond," and would in fact be designating the traditional concept of "metaphor" that is at the foundation of aesthetics as well as the familiar concepts of history tributary to it. By way of the dialectical reading required by the stated meaning of the poem, the surface order of its syntax merges with or turns into the semantic depth of the symbolic correspondences implied in all metaphorical models of understanding.

But if the carrying capacity of *portare* has its material condition of possibility elsewhere, if its own movement is truly based on something that is itself not yet meaningful *as* dialectical movement, then the *trans* here has to be taken more seriously, or, as de Man says, more "soberly." Read now with *trans* as its subject, that is, as a purely lexical element whose relation to a movement of meaning cannot yet have been established with certainty, the text prevents this carrying from completing the trajectory it assigns itself *as* metaphor. It prevents the carrying from ever becoming a homogeneous movement and thus cuts itself off from its own meaning as movement in the very moment it comes into being. And it does this by restricting the status of the carrying to an objective predicate of "beyond," which then simply marks itself as the place that actually is "beyond"—or, more precisely, "other than"—movement. In this case, the text would have to read, "beyond movement," and it would inscribe in an ironic way the text's most meaningful word for "metaphor," *transports,* as the place, or the site, of its other—that is, mere syntax. But the fact that, in the one case, "syntax" turns into "metaphor" and, in the other, "metaphor" turns into "syntax" cannot be taken as evidence of any kind of symmetrical or "symbolic" reversal. This is because, in the first instance, the "turning" is already the tropological turning *of* metaphor—itself capable of merging the two opposed categories into the meaningful unity of a symbol—while, in the second case, the aimless turning of a purely syntagmatic "metaphor" drains the symbol of all determinable meaning despite its continued materiality as text.

For these two radically heterogeneous readings of "metaphor," the whole question comes down to how we can determine the "subject" of its syntax: how can we determine the meaning of that which allows for meaning to be determined only "beyond" its own occurrence? Is the subject of syntax a symbolic movement that is already meaningful in itself, or is its subject just another syntactical component that is "beyond" the movement of meaning altogether? By allowing the syntactical aberration of *comme* in line 13 to literalize the *transports* of line 14 into a linguistic state that is beyond figural movement entirely, de Man opens the way for what we might call a "syntactic"—as opposed to "symbolic"—reading of the "transports" linking thought and being. *Syntax (suntassein),* like *symbol (sumballein),* of course, designates the fundamental potential in language to "gather together," or, more technically, to *articulate* different parts of speech together. But in the case of syntax, as we have seen, this principle of articulation functions prior to, or independently of, the presence in the system of meaningful entities. Such entities are always based ultimately on the special ontological status of the noun and its attributes, and therefore they can be brought together and related in the symbol only after the founding principles of a more general syntax have been established. Syntax, then, as this principle of instituting and codifying any formal relations as such, is the material condition of possibility, the *ground* as it were, of the symbol, which refers merely to a subordinate principle of relating predetermined meanings among themselves according to a universal logic. De Man's reading of Baudelaire's "Correspondances," to the extent that it can account for the traces of this syntactic ground in the poem's metaphorical, that is to say, *failed,* project to move completely beyond it, is therefore more historically reliable than readings that take the possibility of such movement for granted by ignoring its material conditions altogether.

But can the inaugural institution of a principle of formal order, which is named by syntax "itself," ever be disclosed *as* the irreducible historical ground of all symbolic meaning without immediately becoming aberrantly meaningful in its turn? Just what kind of "history" would result from a process of reading that, in retracing the contours of this syntactic ground, could never prevent itself once and for all from turning into a flight from its own (negative) knowledge about meaning and the elusive laws of its own production?

Because of the very nature of his reading, de Man must confront such questions as these when he turns his attention back from the "transports" at the end of the sonnet to the "temple" at the beginning. "If nature is truly a temple," he remarks after interrogating the problematic status of the poem's tropological movement, "it is not a means of transportation" (251). And he goes on to add: "In this realm, transfer tickets are of no avail. Within the confines of a system of transportation—or of language as a system of communication—one can transfer from one vehicle to another, but one cannot transfer from being like a vehicle to being like a temple, or a ground" (252). The stony temple of "Correspondances," which opens the way for the aborted "transports" of the rest of the sonnet but seems itself to lie beyond tension and beyond motion, becomes an emblem for the syntactic ground of the poem's stated investment in the principle of *metaphorein,* since it does in fact stand alone and therefore can function as a concrete figure for that which would indeed remain "beyond movement."

What surprises here, of course, is not so much the reference to a familiar Baudelairian "temple," but rather de Man's odd recourse to the tropological term par excellence, "like" (*comme*), at the very moment he reinscribes this temple in his own unconventional analysis of the poem's "ground," or syntax: "one cannot transfer from being like a vehicle to being *like* a temple, or a ground." But how can syntax—which names the stationary ground of all tropological meaning and is first disclosed in the reading of Baudelaire's poem through the loss of symbolic movement suffered by the *comme* in line 13—then be said itself to be *like* a temple? At the very moment the metaphorical transports of understanding seem to be interrupted and immobilized beyond hope, de Man's reinscription, or echo, of the word *like* requires that a new movement of reading take place to account for the occurrence of this anomaly in his own text. We cannot now understand the "like" of this temple simply by reference to a tropological movement of analogical adequation and meaning that has just been demonstrated to be impossibly problematic, and yet we are offered no straightforward alternative for understanding it any other way. Because this residue of the temple in the reading process, which requires but blocks an understanding of de Man's text, can no longer be considered simply metaphorical—since it occurs textually only after the figural movements of tropes have been subjected to critical analysis and disclosed as highly unstable—it can be said to be *historical*. A textual event like this becomes historical precisely by occurring in a mode that necessitates *and* leaves open a future determination concerning its own status.[16]

For the temple that stands apart in the first line of "Correspondances," and which de Man finally says is "like" a ground, is an exceedingly curious and potentially misleading structure. It does not appear exclusively, in "Anthropomorphism and Trope in the Lyric," in the form of a textual principle of syntactic disposition that would condition and disrupt all the tropological movements of meaning in the poem. When de Man first makes reference to this temple, he calls it an "architectural construct" as well as a "verbal building" (247). It is already an *icon,* then, or metaphorical trope, and what it represents from the very beginning is language's ineradicable figural potential to build semantic structures that rise higher and higher in their claim to transcend representation in an act of pure knowledge. By later asserting that the ground of syntax that conditions Baudelaire's version of this "symbolist ideology" is also "like" the temple in line 1 of the

16. One of de Man's better known terms for the complexity of this mode of occurrence is "allegory": "[Such structures] take into account the fact that the resulting narratives can be folded back upon themselves and become self-referential. . . . since this model cannot be closed off by a final reading, it engenders, in its turn, a supplementary figural superposition which narrates the unreadability of the prior narration. . . . . Allegorical narratives tell the story of the failure to read" (*Allegories of Reading,* 205). It is because the textual disclosure, or allegory, of the historical failure to read and understand *can* be folded back upon itself that it *must* engender a future act of reading to assess the limits and effects of its own knowledge. Or, as de Man puts it in a different but related essay, "language itself dissociates the cognition from the act . . . This is also why textual allegories on this level of rhetorical complexity generate history" (*Allegories,* 277).

poem, de Man's text is thus not simply contradicting itself; it is issuing an implicit warning about the inevitability of the tendency to monumentalize even this nonsymbolic ground into a metaphorical structure of transcendental claims and meaning. If, as is suggested by de Man's use of the temple to represent both the metaphorical vehicles and the syntactic ground of the text, we have no meaningful access to anything—including the material foundations of language and history—except through a potentially delusive language of figures (of *like* or *comme*), then it might appear as though even the most rigorous analysis of ahistorical and symbolic ideologies were bound to fail. By calling the material conditions of history a stationary "temple" (or ground, syntax, inscription, writing, or anything else for that matter), one also immediately returns history to the system of analogical circulation and transcendental worship its disclosure served originally to demarcate itself from. If there truly is no escape from the circularity of such metaphorical temple-building—whether in the methodological guise of aestheticism, materialism, or deconstructionism—then we may as well resign ourselves to living as comfortably as possible with all those "pseudo-historical terms of resistance and nostalgia" that are, as de Man relentlessly reminds us, "at the furthest remove from the materiality of actual history" (262).

But there is another way to read the historical status of this temple which is also a "verbal building," and this time the reading would no longer have to consist in a simple return to a figural or symbolic structure of thought strictly speaking. The kind of verbality de Man associates with the temple in line 1 is not just based on straightforward substitutive tropes of resemblance such as: metaphorical meaning is a temple that stretches upwards toward the sky; or, the immobile laws of syntax are the stationary stones of a transcendental temple of meaning. The role played by the temple in the text is not restricted to providing a sensory *representation* of the figurative/semantic (or non- or even disfigurative/syntactic) structure of language, though the reference to such structures is a constitutive aspect of this role. A temple is like the material grounds of history in yet another way as well: it can *occur* only as a written text that allows for and requires reading. For unlike all the sensory sounds, smells, tastes, textures, and colors that make up the poem's metaphorical "correspondences" properly speaking, a temple is something that could never become immediately present as such to perception or consciousness. Unless it consists in a series of codified inscriptions that must first of all be *read,* a temple cannot be recognized as anything other than the empty *building* it would otherwise have to remain. A temple is a *verbal* building because it necessarily has its beginning in the word. This is the word that in the beginning must carve out the grounds of all eventual meaning by marking itself as and consecrating itself to the future of understanding: *this* is such and such a temple and it is dedicated to. . . . This founding verbal act is not itself based on a resemblance or an exchange, it is not originally a figure, a vehicle, an icon, or a symbol, but it is what necessarily engenders the future possibility of all of these devices of meaning.[17]

A temple, then, is not just "like" one or another of the constitutive aspects of language, a temple *is* language and nothing else because it can *be* only through the verbal inscriptions that alone have the power to make it what it is. A rose may be said to be as fair by any other name, but a temple can be considered a temple—that is, a place made holy through its dedication to being and its meaning ("les transports de l'esprit et des sens")—only so long as the inaugural act of language responsible for making it into such a temple remains legible in its traces. To go on to say, as the poem actually does at its own inception, "La Nature est un temple," is also to insist on the only direction a genuine understanding of history and the temporality appropriate to it could possibly take. All the world can at every moment be turned into a

---

17. A most pertinent reference in this context is Heidegger's essay, "The Origin of the Work of Art," where the temple is analyzed in terms that, in an uncanny way, recall Baudelaire's sonnet as well as announce de Man's reading of it. However, de Man's thinking, even at its closest proximity to Heidegger, still does not correspond to it entirely. Where Heidegger seems to emphasize the potential of the symbolic temple to "gather together," de Man will focus on its inherent disjunction. This difference in emphasis, or in accent, would have significant effects on their respective thinking of the poetic temple in its relation to the figure and the event, as well as to subjectivity and historicity. A brief but representative citation from Heidegger's essay will have to suffice: "A building, a Greek temple, *represents* nothing. It simply stands there in the middle of the rock-cleft valley. The building encloses the *figure* of the god, and in this concealment lets it stand out into the holy precinct through the open portico. By means of the temple, the god is *present* in the temple. . . . It is the templework that first *fits together* and at the same time *gathers around itself* the *unity* of those paths and relations in which birth, death, disaster and blessing, victory and disgrace, endurance and decline acquire the *figure* of destiny for human being. The all-governing expanse of this open relational context is the world of this historical people. . . . Standing there, the building rests on the rocky *ground*" ("The Origin of the Work of Art," *Poetry, Language, Thought,* trans. Albert Hofstadter [New York: Harper and Row, 1971], 41–42, emphasis added, translation modified).

temple, or text—that is, a linguistic process of meaning production that requires reading for its future understanding—but no temple could ever simply be natural or be fully understood according to natural laws, except through a new linguistic act of deceit and forgetfulness. History, as it is disclosed by the temple of "Correspondances"—for de Man as well as for Baudelaire—is therefore a *textual* process governed by laws that would be proper to the acts of inscription and reading rather than a natural process patterned on the chronological continuity and change of empirical entities. That is, truly historical activity and movement must not only be calculated in terms of the occurrence and meaning of so-called natural events. Beyond that, it must take into account how and why such formal calculations can themselves occur historically only by means of a linguistic act whose own specificity may remain wholly foreign to all else.

And so the temple in "Correspondances," at least the way it is read by de Man, marks neither a simple return to a tropological system of symmetrical reversals and cognitions on the one hand nor the unquestioned replacement of that system by a completely new model of language and history on the other. As de Man himself once described the complexity of the structure in which such a term of reading is necessarily caught, "it is equally balanced between both, and equally poised between both."[18] Proceeding by way of a critical analysis of the text's constitution of a tropological, or symbolic, program of meaning and knowledge, de Man's reading finally discloses the material ground, or temple, that actually conditions that program of complementary mediations between being and thought (*les transports de l'esprit et des sens*). But this disclosure of what de Man calls in his essay on Shelley "an event that is no longer simply imaginary or symbolic" (121) must itself occur in a language whose potential for symbolic totalizations, or ideological temple-building, is all the more redoubtable for its capacity to state the dilemma with increasing clarity and precision. De Man's recourse to a language of analogical tropes, of *like* or *comme,* precisely when the reliability of such a language can no longer be taken for granted, is therefore a historical necessity. Its occurrence, like that of all events, becomes truly historical only by respecting *both* the orig-

---

18. In the as-yet-unpublished lecture entitled "Kant and Schiller," to appear in *Aesthetic Ideology,* ed. Andrzej Warminski (Minneapolis: University of Minnesota Press, forthcoming).

inally random inscription that alone can prevent any occurrence from disappearing without a trace *and* the movement of logical consistency such decisive acts engender without themselves ever matching up to. The word *temple,* insofar as it now functions textually as both a trope of analogical resemblance and an inaugural act of inscription and codification, is therefore one of the places where de Man's reading of Baudelaire occurs materially. It leaves a trace in de Man's text that is itself *like* the ground, or temple, he has been describing as the necessary condition of the poem's own historical occurrence. Because it is thus poised equally between a language of cognition and a language of inscription, such a temple also acquires the status of history by demanding reading in its own right.

Understanding history in this way as the unpredictable and ever-provisional outcome of charting the necessary but noncomplementary relations or, better, interferences, between tropological structures of cognition and the material forces of inscription could therefore never result in a chronological pattern of sequential and continuous movements. Rather, the rhythms of this understanding would have to be punctuated at every moment by the possibility of innumerable interruptions and reprises. In the case of de Man's "Anthropomorphism and Trope in the Lyric," for instance, the analysis that ends by emphasizing the radical break between the first line of "Correspondances" and the rest of the sonnet becomes immediately reinscribed in a further process of interpretation that eventually discloses a "similar" break between the syntactic incomprehensibility of "Correspondances" taken as a whole and the tropological intelligibility achieved with such relative ease in "Obsession." Certainly one of the more legitimate ways to prevent the historicity of de Man's own reading movements from coming to a grinding halt by being put into a temple (or behind bars, for that matter) would be to subject this final understanding of "Obsession," as "a text of recollection and elegiac mourning" (262), to a new critical analysis in its turn. For if, as de Man points out, "there are always at least two texts, regardless of whether they are written out or not" (260), then the two texts in "Obsession"—just as the two texts in the sonnet "Correspondances" or in the word *temple* or in the signature "Baudelaire," and this list could be infinitely extended—remain to be written out and accounted for.

At any rate, the temporality of textual history, this process of subjecting to critical analysis the operative conditions, claims, and effects of various discourses and institutions—canonical French literature for one, but there are others as well—could itself be considered a somewhat random and repetitive operation in comparison to the complementary sequences of meaning we tend to project onto the continuum of empirical historical time. Noting this repetitive and random aspect of reading, moreover, allows us at last to situate with slightly more precision and relevance the supplementary portion of "Anthropomorphism and Trope," which is consecrated, of course, to Nietzsche. For the "temple," or ground, that supports de Man's reading of Baudelaire and the "symbolist ideology" of aesthetic theory in "Correspondances" is to be found in the enigmatic pages on Nietzsche's critique of the metaphysical complicity between rhetoric and epistemology. This truncated presentation and analysis of Nietzsche does not participate directly in the main body of the essay, but it cannot be fully separated from it, either. De Man's initial gesture, which links epistemological with rhetorical considerations by using a general reflection on truth to introduce an examination of the lyric in nineteenth-century poetry, consists in quoting "Nietzsche's perhaps better known than understood definition of truth as tropological displacement: 'Was ist also Wahrheit? Ein bewegliches Heer von Metaphern, Metonymien, Anthropomorphismen . . . [What then is truth? A mobile army of metaphors, metonymies, anthropomorphisms . . .]' " (239). This citation from Nietzsche, though, is of more interest than for simply providing the terms from which de Man will derive the title of his own essay, "Anthropomorphism and Trope."

The disjunction the analysis of lyric poetry will eventually disclose between the constitution of the symbol and the meaning that it symbolizes—in the case of "Correspondances," between the temple itself and the figural movements of sensory and cognitive expansion it makes possible and houses—is another version of the radical disjunction de Man reads in Nietzsche's definition between truth as trope and truth as power. Nietzsche's text, according to de Man,

> not only asserts that truth (which was already complicated by having to be a proposition as well as a proper name) is also a power, but a power that exists independently of epistemological determinations, although these determinations are far from being non-existent: calling truth an army *of tropes* reaffirms its epistemological *as well as* its strategic power. . . . The sentence that asserts the complicity of epistemology and

rhetoric, of truth and trope, also turns this alliance into a battle made all the more dubious by the fact that the adversaries may not even have the opportunity ever to encounter each other. (242–43)

The particular question of the rhetorical status of the lyric turns out to be a question about the epistemological status of philosophical discourse in general, and this questioning of rhetoric and epistemology cannot stop until it has run its course in a confrontation with the truth of history.

For truth, according to de Man's reading of Nietzsche and Baudelaire, is not just a formal structure of knowledge and, as such, a simple matter for epistemology. Truth is also, and perhaps more fundamentally still, the power required for something to occur, and therefore it belongs primordially to the category of history. Something is true not just when it fulfills certain logical criteria; rather, something is true— including logical truth itself—when it actually happens and leaves a mark on the world. It is true that the material truths governing history do not always conform to the rule of logical coherence that would govern the propositional truths of epistemology. Though it is of course equally true that no such knowledge as this could itself ever come into being without recourse to precisely that logical ideal of intelligibility and consistency it ultimately contests. As the place where both kinds of "truth" struggle to appropriate the specificity of the other—where knowledge struggles to make its understanding happen, and where power struggles to know what it is doing—history becomes a text composed of heterogeneous and thus warring forces. De Man calls this text the formation of an alliance that has turned into a *battle,* and he further says it is "a battle made all the more dubious by the fact that its adversaries may not even have the opportunity ever to encounter each other" (243). What makes this battle *dubious,* de Man points out, is certainly not that one could ever doubt it takes place—nothing could be further from the truth. Rather, it is a dubious battle because, despite the intensity of its onslaughts and the number of its casualties, it remains difficult to ascertain for sure whether the true adversaries "even have the opportunity ever to encounter each other." It is therefore the shape and limits of the battlefield itself, the criteria necessary to determine with sufficient epistemological precision the actual identity and position of the combatants involved, that is liable to become the most hotly embattled issue of all. "Whatever truth may be fighting," de Man reminds us, "it is not error but stupidity, the belief that one is right when one is in fact in the wrong" (242). What would be truly stupid in this regard would be the belief that one is already fighting on the side of right when it has not yet been established for certain where exactly the sides are to be drawn.

Be that as it may, to affirm, as de Man does, that truth cannot be enlisted to fight against error can sound rather nihilistic. And it *is* nihilistic provided one takes the trouble to read this word according to the very particular criteria de Man himself has been careful enough to provide us with. "Understand by nihilism," he cautions in a lecture on Benjamin, "a certain kind of critical awareness which will not allow you to make certain affirmative statements when those affirmative statements go against the way things are."[19] The kind of history, textual history, that de Man is after, then, is simply an attempt to document and account for the way things are—rhetorically, epistemologically, historically—no matter how baffling this proves for the drawing of familiar lines of alliance and battle. To take history seriously is to face up to its truths, to the specificity of all its events. De Man's reading of what happens in Baudelaire's lyric poetry discloses how the integrity of truth has been put into error by being irremediably caught and therefore set adrift between an enumerative language of stuttering power and a tropological language of knowledge. Unless and until things can be reasonably demonstrated to be otherwise, this textual plight of truth is simply the way things are *historically*. There is no turning back from the revelation of this plight, and to pretend otherwise would not be an error but sheer stupidity, "the belief that one is right when one is in fact in the wrong."[20]

---

19. The warning is made in reference to Benjamin, during the question-and-answer period, in fact, after de Man's lecture on the "Task of the Translator" (*Resistance to Theory*, 104, further references appear in the text).

20. To be in the wrong in this sense is, first of all, a logical consequence of an impairment suffered by the model of truth to occur as a "symbolic" unity of Parmenides's being and thought ("les transports de l'esprit et des sens"). But the historical *effects* of the undoing of this model—in particular, the effects of refusing to recognize this impairment, or of insisting it is the proper of the "other"—in individual cases and according to infinite and irreducible differentiations, extend well beyond the merely formal categories of logic. De Man spells this out in an essay on Kleist: "More important still is the fact that the original perfection, the exemplary wholeness of the aesthetic model is itself, however slightly yet unquestionably, impaired. Up till now, we have read the young man's blushing ('er errötete . . .') as mere shame, a wound of the ego, but it now appears that the redness may well be the blood of an injured body. The

By the same token, de Man can *also* claim that to call a concept of history "nihilistic" in this sense—meaning only that it takes into account things as they are shown necessarily to be in all their negativity—"would have to be understood as a very *positive* statement about it" ("The Task," 103). To be positive in this sense is not merely to be affirmative about things, it is rather to *resist* affirmative statements that go against the way things are and that therefore cancel themselves out by turning into empty fictions or mere wishful thinking. It is to participate in the truth of history in a critically productive way, even if truth itself has occurred there textually in the mode of error: "the occurrence can be textual, is generally textual, but it is an occurrence, in the sense that it is . . . not the end of an error, but the recognition of the true nature of that error" ("The Task," 104). The true nature of the error that is recognized in reading "Correspondances" has to do with the mutual dependence and disruption in the poem between the truth of tropological knowledge and the truth of blind inscriptional power. The truth of this error also turns out to be the necessity of its historicity: genuine history occurs only as the endless *errancy* of truth between a language of knowledge and a language of power. Being neither fully cognitive nor purely impositional by nature, the language of truth is set forever adrift between both of these unappeasable limits, producing an unforeseeable future out of the impossible task of securing a firm knowledge of its own past.

These two languages of truth, or rather these two dimensions of the only true language we now have, do not therefore correspond with one another, much less with any event as such. They do not come together to constitute with themselves or with anything else the meaningful unity of a "symbol." Between language as movement (trope) and language as ground (inscription), there is no common ground or movement; there is only the collision of a textual impasse, or aporia, in which the events of history must come together in all their interminable

---

white, colorless world of statues is suddenly reddened by a flow of blood, however understated" ("Aesthetic Formalization in Kleist," *The Rhetoric of Romanticism*, 279), as well as in another essay on Baudelaire: "This pale and white text of recollection . . . turns red with a brutality that takes us out of the inwardness of memory . . . into a very threatening literality" ("Reading and History," *The Resistance to Theory*, 66). For a suggestive retracing of the inscription, however understated or silent, of a historical flow of blood into the textual event of de Man's writings, see Shoshana Felman's "Paul de Man's Silence," *Critical Inquiry* 15 (summer 1989), 704–44.

randomness and heterogeneity. But the move that retraces this aporia of cognition and power—which is in fact beyond the power of the symbol and all its pseudomovements to capture once and for all—is precisely what can occur textually in the event of reading "Correspondances," and when it happens it is itself as true and irreversible as any other historical event. History, for de Man, is the move that can occur only as this ever-recurring recognition that historical truth is already caught in the power of a language that lies beyond the movements of its own understanding and knowledge—which is as well a warning about why such a history is so fragile and so easily forgotten. Because it can leave its mark on the world only as a written piece of paper, the errant truth of this history must now be endlessly read if it is not simply, and in all stupidity, to disappear.

Index

Abrams, M. H., 115
Adorno, Theodor, 209
Althusser, Louis, 29
Apollinaire, Guillaume, 97
Aristotle, 101
Attridge, Derek, 11
Austin, J. L., 29

Barthes, Roland, 12, 13, 18
Baudelaire, Charles: "La chevelure," 129; "Correspondances," 7, 96, 159, 201–30; "Le flacon," 129; "Le goût du néant," 129; and irony, 43; "Obsession," 201–3, 225; "Spleen II," 129; as symbolist, 34, 36, 37, 49, 78, 129, 137, 160, 162, 198, 199
Benjamin, Walter, 29, 130, 135, 198, 209, 212–13, 228
Benveniste, Emile, 100–101
Bersani, Leo, 84
Blanchot, Maurice: *Celui qui ne m'accompagnait pas*, 168, 171–72, 187; *L'écriture du désastre*, 165, 178–94; *La folie du jour*, 173–78, 194; "Gide et la littérature de l'expérience," 148–52, 166, 167; "Le langage de la fiction," 169–71, 174–75; "La littérature et le droit à la mort," 149; *Le pas au delà*, 171; "Le regard d'Orphée," 165; "La solitude essentielle," 172; "La solitude essentielle et la solitude dans le monde," 172; as symbolist, 7, 9–10, 29
Brodsky, Claudia, 110

Brun, Bernard, 116
Burt, E. S., 64

Chambers, Ross, 39, 54, 68
Cohn, R. G., 84
Coleridge, Samuel, 37
Culler, Jonathan, 201

Dällenbach, Lucien, 146
Davies, Gardiner, 68
Debray-Genette, Raymonde, 116
Deleuze, Gilles, 108, 125, 135
De Man, Paul: "Aesthetic Formalization: Kleist's *Uber das Marionettentheater*," 228–29; "Allegory (*Julie*)," 134, 199–200, 221; "Anthropomorphism and Trope in the Lyric," 201–30; " 'Conclusions': Walter Benjamin's 'The Task of the Translator,' " 209, 212–13, 228–29; "Criticism and Crisis," 18; "The Epistemology of Metaphor," 134; "Hypogram and Inscription," 195–96; "Literary History and Literary Modernity," 198; "Kant and Schiller," 224; "Promises (*Social Contract*)," 221; "Reading and History," 229; "Reading (Proust)," 113, 119; "Roland Barthes and the Limits of Structuralism," 18; "Shelley Disfigured," 34, 195, 201, 224; "Sign and Symbol in Hegel's *Aesthetics*," 119, 175, 197; as symbolist, 7; and textual history, 8, 29, 186

231

Derrida, Jacques: "Biodegradables," 198; "La double séance," 93; *De l'esprit*, 179, 186; *De la grammatologie*, 11, 16, 18; and irony, 65; "Like the Sound of the Sea Deep within a Shell: Paul de Man's War," 201; *Positions*, 11; "Le retrait de la métaphore," 183; "La structure, le signe et le jeu," 1, 18; "Survivre," 140; and textual history, 8, 29, 31
Descartes, René, 56, 60, 61, 76, 88–91
Diderot, Denis, 76
Doubrovsky, Serge, 115

Eco, Umberto, 35–37, 43

Faye, Jean-Pierre, 69, 71
Felman, Shoshana, 229
Freud, Sigmund, 8, 64
Frey, Hans-Jost, 80

Gasché, Rodolphe, 39, 100
Genette, Gérard, 111–13, 114, 115, 117, 121, 185
Gide, André: *Les caves du vatican*, 161; *Les faux-monnayeurs*, 143, 147; *L'immoraliste*, 147; and irony, 43; *Journal*, 146–47, 153, 155–56, 157–58, 166; *Les nourritures terrestres*, 142, 145, 147, 153–55; *Paludes*, 142, 145, 147, 161; *Si le grain ne meurt*, 145; as symbolist, 7; *La tentative amoureuse*, 147, 149; *Thésée*, 144; *Le traité du narcisse*, 144, 156–67; *Le voyage d'Urien*, 142, 150
Goethe, Johann Wolfgang von, 45
Gossman, Lionel, 10

Hamacher, Werner, 134, 151
Hegel, G. W. F.: and the *Aufhebung* of metaphor, 215; and irony, 163; and organicism, 45; and self-reflexivity, 40; and the symbol, 170–71, 174–75, 185, 197, 198
Heidegger, Martin: and the cry in writing, 191; and the event, 179–87; and the move beyond metaphor, 215; and the temple of metaphor, 223; and textual history, 8–10, 29
Howard, Richard, 207
Humboldt, Wilhelm von, 185

Jakobson, Roman, 12, 13
Jameson, Fredric, 10
Jauss, H. R., 97–98, 102
Jeanneret, Michel, 39
Johnson, Barbara, 68, 138

Kant, Immanuel, 28, 37, 198
Kaufmann, Vincent, 68
Keats, John, 64
Kierkegaard, Søren, 8, 43, 65, 180–81
Kleist, Heinrich von, 198, 228
Kristeva, Julia, 68

LaCapra, Dominick, 10
Laforgue, Jules, 157
Lamartine, Alphonse de, 209
Lejeune, Philippe, 115
Lentricchia, Frank, 10
Levin, Harry, 114–15
Levinas, Emmanuel, 176–77, 178
Lévi-Strauss, Claude, 12, 18
Louÿs, Pierre, 34

MacIntyre, C. F., 83–84
Mallarmé, Stéphane: "L'après-midi d'un faune," 70; "Un coup de dés," 90; "Crayonné au théâtre," 91; "Crise de vers," 70; "Le démon de l'analogie," 102; "Une dentelle," 77–105; "La dernière mode," 68, 69; "Les fenêtres," 161: *Igitur*, 88; and irony, 43; "La musique et les lettres," 81–82, 94, 102; "Notes sur le théâtre," 99–100; "Le pitre châtié," 64; and poetic flowers, 110–11; "Richard Wagner," 94; "Sauvegarde," 71–77, 78, 79, 81, 86, 99, 101, 102; "Le sonnet en yx," 102; as symbolist, passim; "Tout orgueil," 78, 80; "Le vierge, le vivace et le bel aujourd'hui," 32–33
Marx, Karl, 8, 211
Mehlman, Jeffrey, 176–78
Merrill, Stuart, 34
Mockel, Albert, 34
Montaigne, Michel de, 56, 60, 61, 152
Morrissette, Bruce, 146

Nerval, Gérard de: "Artémis," 67; *Aurélia*, 39; "El desdichado," 106; *Sylvie*, 34–67, 91; as symbolist, 107,

Nerval, Gérard de (*cont.*)
  169, 199; and textual history, 7, 80,
  123, 128, 137
Nietzsche, Friedrich, 8, 42, 65, 97,
  191, 215, 226–30
Noulet, Emilie, 84, 96
Novalis, 163, 165

Parmenides, 228
Pascal, Blaise, 54, 76, 215
Paulhan, Jean, 142, 147
Pavel, Thomas, 29
Peirce, C. S., 29
Plato, 108
Poe, E. A., 37
Poulet, Georges, 62, 88, 109–10, 111,
  112
Prendergast, Christopher, 39, 41, 43,
  45
Proust, Marcel: and irony, 43; *A la recherche du temps perdu*, 106–41; as symbolist, 34, 35, 46, 169; and textual history, 7, 199

Raymond, Marcel, 205
Régnier, Henri de, 34
Ricoeur, Paul, 10
Riffaterre, Michael, 10, 98
Rimbaud, Arthur, 144
Rivière, Jacques, 142–43

Rousseau, Jean-Jacques, 56, 60, 61,
  76, 215

Said, Edward, 10
Sartre, Jean-Paul, 144–45, 149, 166
Saussure, Ferdinand de: *Cours de linguistique générale*, 10–31; and textual history, 8, 33, 199
Schlegel, Friedrich, 43
Scott-Moncrieff, C. K., 139
Solger, K. W. F., 43
Sollers, Philippe, 69
Schopenhauer, Arthur, 37, 165
Steinmetz, Jean-Luc, 68
Symons, Arthur, 69, 71

Terdiman, Richard, 68
Tieck, Ludwig, 43
Todorov, Tzvetan, 31

Valéry, Paul, ix–xi, 34, 151, 153, 154,
  158
Verhaeren, Emile, 34
Villiers de L'Isle-Adam, 78, 86, 87,
  88, 90

Warminski, Andrzej, 61, 211
Weber, Samuel, 11, 19
Wellek, René, 30–31
White, Hayden, 10
Wilson, Edmund, 30, 43, 79–80, 108,
  143–44

Library of Congress Cataloging-in-Publication Data

Newmark, Kevin, 1951–
 Beyond symbolism : textual history and the future of reading / Kevin Newmark.
  p. cm.
 Includes bibliographical references and index.
 ISBN 0-8014-2577-8 (alk. paper)
  1. French literature—19th century—Criticism, Textual. 2. French literature—20th century—Criticism, Textual. 3. Symbolism (Literary movement)—France. 4. Symbolism in literature. 5. Literature and history. I. Title.
PQ295.S9N49   1991
840.9′15—dc20   91–55056